# THE LEGEND OF LIVING WATERS

*Jack Swanson*

For Jane and Stan,
    Fellow CHS Classmate "1957."
Your creation of the updated
1957 CHATTER was a
marvelous feat! I've shown
it to many friends and family
and their in awe at the
results of your efforts. Thank You.
    The Chatham stories are on
Pg 22-29. There is a European
Vacation saga on page 181.
    My Best Wishes and Prayers,
                        Jack

# Farewell to Fences

## THE LEGEND OF LIVING WATERS

# Jack Swanson

Living Waters Press
Oconomowoc, WI

Illustrated by Linda Brannan

Published by
**Living Waters**
P.O. Box 437
Oconomowoc, Wisconsin 53066


First Printing October 1996


ISBN 0-9654842-0-3

# Dedication...
## To Three Generations of Family

My mother and father, Dwight and Mildred Swanson, for their endless love, affirmation, faith, and provisions.

My wife, Karen, for thirty plus years of love, understanding, companionship, and Christian example. For bounding beyond the call of motherhood in nurturing and cherishing our children.

My children, Krista, David, Jeremy, Jennifer, and Jolie for fulfilling my dreams as a dad. For individual beauty of character that each one brings to the family fold. For being "Badger Boosters" and "Packer Backers" even during the devastating drought.

*"A new commandment I give to you,
that you love one another;
even as I have loved you,
that you also love one another.
By this all men will know that you are my disciples,
if you have love for one another."*

John 13:34-35

*"One of the things God seems to be doing in our day
is breaking down the walls of denominationalism
and racism in our country.
It is our hope and prayer that the walls
between Roman Catholics and Protestants will
crumble at the foot of the cross of JESUS."*

Ashley Nearn — Promise Keepers

*"Christ calls all His disciples to unity.
My earnest desire is to renew this call today...
believers in Christ, united in following in the footsteps
of the martyrs cannot remain divided...
Believers cannot fail to meet this challenge.
Indeed, how could they refuse to do everything possible,
with God's help, to break down
the walls of division and distrust,
to overcome obstacles and prejudices which
thwart the proclamation of the Gospel
of salvation in the cross of JESUS,
the one redeemer of man,
of every individual...
The unity of all divided humanity is the will of God.
For this reason, He sent His son, so that
by dying and rising for us, he might
bestow on us the Spirit of love.*

Pope John Paul, II — Encyclical, "That They May Be One"

# Contents

# Acknowledgments

My deepest gratitude to:

❀ My wife, Karen, who in addition to sharing this story, loaned me the octagon section of her Victorian office for creative inspiration. She also proved to be a proficient proofreader.

❀ My kids, Krista, David, Jeremy, Jennifer and Jolie for showing enough respect to laugh at the readings.

❀ My senior and only editor, Tom Coates, who doubles as my tennis partner. To register any grave grammatical grievances, please call him at 1-800-568-7836.

❀ My tag-team typing Trojans for not cursing at my cursive writing — Kay Steensland-Mendyke, Marilyn Bond, Dallas Goeb, Linda Arkell and Jennifer Swanson

❀ Pat Siok, a local Irish lass, who performed watercolor wonders on the cover in between leading pilgrimages back to her homeland.

❀ Linda Brannan, a true artisan minus the artistic temperament, for her adroit cover design and illustrations.

❀ Krista Swanson, photographer extraordinaire, for her timeless tintype photo on the back cover.

❀ David Swanson, Jeremy Flint and Jeff Hupe for providing professional promotional services, with a smile.

❀ Tim Spransy, nationally known sports and portrait artist, THE GREENBAY PACKERS 75TH ANNIVERSARY PRINT, for cover consultation.

❀ Jim Swanson and George Sargent, the computer connection consortium, who kept our PC's clicking and vanquished all viruses.

❀ The "Great Cloud of Witnesses" who inspired me to live the life and tell the story. May you rest forever in the loving arms of Jesus. You will never be forgotten. Fr. Michael Bransfield • Jay Dalton • Dr. Larry "Ike" Davis • Fr. George

De Prizio • Dr. V. Raymond Edman • Sue Gerstner • Rev. Harry Greenwood • Fr. Joe "Ignatius" Hunt • Mabel Kamp • Mary "Minnie" Main • Bonnie Neumann • Adele Miller O'Shaughnessy • Tony Reno • Loret Miller Ruppe • Clyde Shaw • Eugenia Shaw • Scott Soergel • Bishop Chandler Sterling • Agnes Svenson • J. Harold Svenson • Kenny Thompson • Bill Toll • Rev. Andrew Ulrich

❀ Multitude of living friends whose contagious enthusiasm for this project has set me free from the snare of the fowler— "writers block". I know who you are, you know who you are, and everyone would know who you are if my publisher hadn't run out of paper!

❀ The Living Waters Prayer Fellowship, teachers, preachers, and Pastoral Team for thirty years of encouragement and support in lifting Jesus higher. A special recognition of the Living Waters advisors for walking the walk of the quickened word—"By this shall all men know that you are my disciples, if you have love for one another."—John 13:35 R.S.V. Rev. Ferd Bahr, Ft. Charles Doan, Fr. Dick Korzinek, Fr. Ken Metz, Rev. Edwin Ziemann.

❀ Bernice "Mom" Ziemann and Edwin "Dad" Ziemann, our adopted parents, for faithfulness, fun and a fuller dimension of the Holy Spirit.

❀ My God-parents Disa and Ted Nelson who are resplendent role models in bridging the gap between the "GOOD NEWS" of John 3:16, and "LOVING YOUR NEIGHBOR"—Matthew 25:35-40.

# Foreword

Rarely do we experience people who take Jesus' ideals literally. Oh, people may talk about them and interpret His words literally, but to apply them to life, that is something different. In the delightful little story, "MR. BLUE", by Myles Cormoily, we follow the antics of a simple young man who decides to take Jesus seriously. It is fantasy, but so beautifully whimsical, that you don't want the story to end.

*Farewell To Fences: The Legend of Living Waters*, by Jack Swanson, tells the true-life story of a remarkable husband and wife, Jack and Karen, who decided to take Jesus seriously. After wandering through spiritual deserts and pathless jungles trying to make sense out of life and understand all the contradictory interpretations of Jesus and His message, they finally found their way home and, in the peace and serenity of their next-found haven, charted a life course for themselves that is truly astounding. Reading their story is like a walk through the world of modem evangelism, with all the names so many of the readers will recognize. The personal anecdotes about these pioneers in evangelism and the Charismatic movements in the various churches will provide a warming facet to this very touching account of the journey of these two searching pilgrims.

One of the most moving parts of the book is the section about the fifty-eight troubled young people Jack and Karen took into their home over a fifteen year period and treated them as their own children, sending them to school and some even to college. That is such a powerful testimony to faith and to their love of God. When you read the heartwarming stories about their own children and their individual sagas through the inspiring, yet frightening adventures happening all around them, you will feel a personal kinship to each of these beautiful young people.

I hope this not-so little story will find a far-reaching readership. I am sure it will touch the hearts of everyone who experiences this beautiful family.

Joseph F. Girzone

# Preface

I have been Jack's wife for thirty-three years and am a happy survivor. Thirty-one years ago, we founded Living Waters, an ecumenical Charismatic prayer fellowship. We have also had the privilege of sharing our spiritual beliefs and experiences with an amazing variety of groups, both Christian and secular. My preparation for this challenge includes having grown up in a turbulent family and having received and excellent education in psychiatric social work, as well as in adoptions. Little did I dream where my personal relationship with Jesus Christ and meeting of a handsome smiling North Park College grad on Miami Beach on Christmas vacation would lead me. These years have been quite an adventure!

After Jack and I married, we realized that we had a common love of children, and a concern for the multitude of children who did not have a nurturing home. It all began with a forlorn little four year old who planted himself on our doorstep each evening, waiting for us to come home from work. That began an avalanche of needy young people who we had the privilege of helping parent over the years. Over sixty kids lived with us from seven months to seven years, with many more coming for short stays, when pressures mounted beyond their tolerance. We have had the joy of raising five children of our own. Krista and David are biological, Jennifer and Kathryn Jolie are adopted from South America and Jeremy has been a son to us for most of his life. I treasure being a mother; Jack has been a wise and loving, very involved father. Most of our children have chosen to work in the counseling professions. They all have a heart for Jesus and enjoy a wide variety of people. I wonder why?

Jack and I have had a common heart for Jesus and the bringing together of His people from diverse Christian denominations, cultures and races. "Building Bridges" and helping tear down fences has been part of our shared "calling." Through teaching, prayer for healing and coming together in community to concentrate on what we believe rather than on our differences, we have come to realize more fully what it means to be a part of the Body of Christ.

I am so grateful to God, for bringing Jack and me together to live out life this way. As you will be able to tell upon reading Jack's book, the way has been superbly worthwhile, but at times, it has been painful and certainly stressful. There are moments when we have felt like pioneers and at other times, we realize that we are just a small part of the continuum of the living history of the Church.

Life with Jack is never dull. As you will note, he has an active sense of humor (my book will probably be more serious.) His humor has often been healing, a respite in between the busy demands of our life here on Oconomowoc Lake. Jack is not only my husband, he is my best friend. He is a strong, steady man who has the love and respect of our children and of many friends. He is an athlete, an enthusiastic football fan, a wise investment counselor, a travel guide for our family and now an author. I have watched him grow, develop and mature over the years. He has been able to accomplish many things he never would have thought of doing in the early years. We have helped each other stretch, as we have attempted to follow what we and our fellowship have discerned as God's leading.

Karen Swanson
Oconomowoc,
Wisconsin

# Prologue

Twenty years ago, near the end of the "Jesus People" era, friends urged us to write a book about our diverse experiences. Whenever the subject resurfaced we rapidly deep-sixed the suggestion as premature, presumptuous or both. I never lost my composure over the possibilities because I always assumed any prospective epic would be created by Karen anyway! I was wrong!

In 1986 we flew to France for a six month family sabbatical. For the first time in memory I had time on my hands, so I put them to use — writing. This seemed like a Christian way to deal with mid-life crisis. Little did I know at the outset that the crisis would last for ten years, endless drafts and three hundred plus pages.

Upon my return to the States, I presented a friend the first draft of one of my chapters for his perusal. The next day he handed it back with a firm offer of five-hundred dollars not to be included in the book! Hard up for cash after a six month sojourn - it was an offer I could not refuse.

However, following the example of directors of school plays who conscript casts of thousands to ensure family packed theaters, I have crammed multitudes of friends, relatives, and countrymen between the covers. If everyone mentioned would purchase one copy of *Farewell to Fences*, it would be an instant bestseller.

The stories are true-to-life, but numerous names and places have been changed to give the guilty a second chance.

Jack Swanson
Oconomowoc,
Wisconsin

# Post Prologue

The sale of this book to any speed reader is strictly prohibited. It took me ten years to compose this epic; it would be distasteful for any ravenous raven to devour its contents in an hour!

# 1

# In The Beginning

I was born at an early age in the geographical center of a concrete jungle—Orange, New Jersey. Orange is nose-to-nose with nasty Newark and a hand grenade toss from the haunting hovels of Hoboken. I entered this Garden of Eden called The Garden State eighteen days before the 1930's decade ended, but I remember it well.

My dad, a Certified Public Accountant working on Wall Street, covertly planned my mid-December arrival so he could claim an extra tax exemption. After waiting nine long years for this coveted tax break, he wasn't treating it lightly. The year before he tried to talk my mother into adopting.

I didn't mind being born in 1939—it was a vintage year. The nation was well down the road of recovery from the Great Depression. Prosperity peeked around every corner as the demand for military munitions flooded every far-flung factory. Hitler started picking on the Poles and two days later Great Britain and France declared war on the Third Reich. FDR warmed up at his fireside chats, while his lips spoke neutrality.

Bobby Riggs, a brash upstart, had just rigged Wimbledon while the annihilators from the North, known as the Green Bay Packers, pulverized the New York Giants, who played like city slickers in the NFL championship game.

John Steinbeck's "Grapes of Wrath" held the nation in its grip while the golden age of Hollywood was having its heyday. The studios, having created their own caste system for the stars, cranked out over 400 movies in 1939. Eighty-five million patrons a week paid a quarter apiece to peer at Dr. Kildare, Charlie Chan, Mr. Moto, Andy Hardy, Gunga Din, the Hunchback of Notre Dame and Wuthering Heights. The Wizard of Oz premiered in Oconomowoc, Wisconsin, while Gone With the Wind had to settle for Atlanta, Georgia!

After serving my seven-day sentence in the nursery, the doctor finally sprung me so I could get home for Christmas. There was much rejoicing as my parents showed me off to scores of friends and relatives. My parents had so many friends from their church, it took them months to pick out my godparents. They definitely made the right decision; Disa and Ted Nelson have been outstanding spiritual role models for me all my life. My home was filled with nurturing love and faith as the family framework for growth.

All four of my grandparents were born within fifty miles of each other in a pristine lake, pine-forested, rock-bound region of Sweden called Småland. They emigrated to -America around the turn of the century for religious and economic reasons. After settling in the Humboldt Park area on the North side of Chicago, they became leaders in the Swedish Evangelical Mission Covenant Church of America, which was a pietistic breakoff from the Lutheran State Church of Sweden.

My parents met in the Covenant Church as kids and got married in their early twenties. Dad was financial secretary for Wolcott Blair, a wealthy Chicago businessman. When Mr. Blair moved to New York City in the early 30's, my parents headed east and settled in East Orange, New Jersey. Two years later Dad joined Bayer and Clausen, a Wall Street C.P.A. firm, and eventually became managing partner.

## The Paperless Parson

Continuing in the tradition of his heritage, Dad held every position possible in the East Orange Covenant Church, except Pastor. I noticed that Pastor Carl Peterson, who had been entrenched there for over twenty years, always looked nervous when Dad came to church with a Bible tucked under his arm! Dad's aspirations never stopped at the local level. His numerous denominational positions on a national level included being on the board of North Park College in Chicago, from which both my brother Jim and I graduated.

When I was in third grade we escaped the concrete jungle and settled in the greener pastures of Florham Park, New Jersey. Two months after we moved in, Dad became director of Brooklake

Chapel, a non-denominational Sunday School one block from where we lived. After Sunday School we raced to church to claim space in the third pew, so we could have an up-front view of the preacher's tonsils. Tonsils were rare in those days. Most kids had them extracted at an early age so they could overdose on ice cream!

We alternated attending the Covenant Church, which had relocated in Livingston, and the Presbyterian Church in Florham Park. We were camped in the third pew of the Presbyterian Church the morning the pastor announced a moratorium on marriage ceremonies. The National Presbytery upon reviewing Pastor Cromwell's credentials concluded he didn't possess the proper papers for uniting couples in holy wedlock! Two hundred trusting twosomes he had joined in wedded bliss were living in sin and raising little illegitimates! The equally yoked looked as if they'd been choked as they received the post-nuptial news in their pews. Their paperless parson had put them asunder!

The Pulpit Committee was promptly pulled out of hibernation to search for a more sanctified shepherd before the flock tied the nuptial knot around Pastor Cromwell's neck!

## We Want Willkie

One of Dad's other interests was polarized in the world of politics. As a rabid Republican, he witnessed three white elephants get trampled by the FDR steamroller. The next white elephant was Wendall Willkie, the humble Hoosier from Hicksville. Willkie's supporters billed him as a modern-day David destined to bring the Goliath of the New Deal down to earth.

Dad was President of the "We Want Willkie Club" in East Orange, and attended the Republican National Convention, June, 1940, in Philadelphia. He brought Mom and their diapered darling of six months, who was determined to be Wendell Willkie's youngest supporter.

Willkie emerged as the darkhorse of this deadlocked convention, as the galleries packed with grass-rooted neophytes went delirious. Thunderous shouts of "We Want Willkie, We Want Willkie" echoed off the rumbling rafters. The delegates stampeded to mount their darkhorse by the wee hours of the morning. The barefoot boy from Indiana was crowned to carry the GOP banner into battle, and deliver the New Deal its death blow.

Reporters rallied around anyone wearing a Willkie button. A Life magazine photographer discovered the huge "We Want Willkie" button dangling from my diapers and plastered the picture coast to coast with the caption, "Willkie's Youngest Supporter."

Not even the bambino bit helped the Hoosier hayseed against the noble New Yorker. The slingshot found its target, but the stone ricocheted off FDR's forehead and mortally wounded his attacker. Willkie lost in a landslide that eventually claimed his life. He died a defeated man four years later.

## Those Caissons Keep Rolling Along

When Willkie's youngest supporter became a high school freshman, we moved to Chatham Township, New Jersey, into a rambling ranch style house with a farm behind it.

I was hoping this change of scenery would curtail my piano playing career. After three long years the same crashing sounds kept coming from the keyboard. My teacher, Carl Castor, had resorted to earplugs as his last bastion of self defense. Carl rolled in every week, in his cozy convertible, from Palisades Park high up on the Hudson River. He studied at Julliard Conservatory and was rumored to have the same pedigree as Paderewski! He had excellent students, but I wasn't one of them.

In my case Carl got paid to listen, not teach! I was as clever on the keys as a cat in a hot tub. Every time I hit a nasty note, he would light up another Camel and slide down a couple of octaves in his chair. However, Carl was crafty enough to conceal my keyboard klutziness from my parents. He hated to lose a captive cash-paying customer.

I attempted to display my ineptitude directly to Mom and Dad, but they were mired in the depths of denial. I thought the recitals would force them to face the music! Why was Carl Castor's oldest student still playing "The Caisson Song," while kindergarten kids were parading up and playing prominent pieces like

"Malaguena?" My Dad was a C.P.A., but he couldn't add two and two together in this case!

He even volunteered my brother Jim and me to play "The Caisson Song" as a duet at the Swedish Old People's Home in the Bronx. Being on their Board of Directors he delighted in attending their dinners where he was known as "Double Dessert Swanson." Swedes from the old country were known by their occupations or pre-occupations. Some of Dad's friends from Chicago were called "Curtain Stretcher Carlson," "Outhouse Ohlsson" and "Manhole Magnusson."

Jim looked more like a musician than I did, but that was his only advantage. It didn't help that we were pounding on an uptight upright that sounded as if it had been tuned by Omar the Tent Maker after being dragged across the desert by a thirsty camel. We got the message when the folks started fidgeting with their hearing aids.

Desperate for a diversion I conned Carl Castor into playing ping pong and shooting buckets after each weekly lesson. As he started to get a large charge out of our extracurricular activities, it cut into our keyboard time. Ten minutes was plenty of time to practice "The Caisson Song" anyway.

My parents never suspected why I stopped protesting piano lessons. I'm sure they assumed my next stop was Carnegie Hall.

Mom sold real estate for G. Kimball Coleman and Co. in Chatham and rarely arrived home before 5:00 p.m. One dark day she came home early and blew our cover to blazes! As she passed the abandoned piano she heard a ruckus rising from the basement. We submissively surrendered, but left the paddles on the table so the evidence could not be used against us. After a curt confab, Carl retreated to his convertible and I went to my room.

During dinner Dad was brought in on the basement bust. His lively lecture ended in a reprieve for Carl Castor.

Carl came crawling back in a weakened state of stature. His professional pride had been pricked by the public revelation of the ping pong ploy. Eternally embarrassed, and running low on endorphins to kill the audible pain, Carl cashed in my career. He gave two weeks' notice, which was noble of him considering the covert circumstances, and walked out a free man after serving a seven-year sentence captive to "The Caisson Song."

My parents could not find a replacement for Carl. The word was out and it wasn't good. You can't kid the public in a small town. As the Good Book says, "He who has an ear, will eventually hear." It didn't help that some busybody tipped off the P.T.A. Piano Teachers Anonymous was a potent force in Chatham in the 50's!

## One Flew Into the Septic Tank

Dad was a working warrior most of the year. Some weeks he spent over sixty hours on audits and tax work. This left the taxing yard tasks to his sons. Early every Saturday morning we were greeted with laborious lists of chores. The Old People's Home called him "Double Dessert Swanson," but we called him "Slave Driver Swanson!"

Jim and I dealt with these irritating impositions in different ways. Jim never put up a protest. Why should he? He wasn't planning on doing any of the work! I took issue with the legendary lists to the point that Dad suggested I become a lawyer. However, when the fireworks fizzled, I did the drudgery and made Jim do his part.

One Saturday Dad had a special project. The septic tank had been making strange noises and he summoned the Sixth Scent Sanitary Service to rectify the problem. They caught two squirrels skinny-dipping and arrested them on the spot! A month later the head honcho of Sixth Scent gave us the Good Housekeeping Seal of Approval to cement the slab over the opening.

Dad had a hernia hang-up, so the heavy work was up to me. Straining to lift the slab waist high, I took two steps forward, but the stone sealed off my view of the hole. Discombobulated, I lost my balance and stepped straight down into the tank as the slab crashed to the Earth like a downed discus! Sinking fast past the slimy sides, I grabbed for the top of the tank. Waste deep in the murky mire and lacking the leverage to pull myself up, I searched skyward for hasty heavenly help. Slave Driver Swanson was so limp from laughter, he was only one sway away from joining me in the tank.

Fighting furiously to stay afloat with no scuba diving equipment in sight, my whole life flashed before my eyes. There was no glimpse of Glory down there and it wasn't as hot as I pictured Hades. From an obstructed Protestant's view it appeared more like the purge of Purgatory. What a way to go! I could see the headline of the Chatham Courier, "Sixteen Year Old Succumbs to Septic System."

In my darkest hour I suddenly saw light at the top of the tank. Dad regained his composure and like a pillar of power pulled me free from the dismal abyss.

My shoes felt as soggy as a salamander sandwich smothered in mayonnaise as my mother came to check out the piercing, primitive sounds surrounding the area. Registering seismographic shock on her face as she gazed at my dirty, dripping duds, Mom interrogated us. Dad responded with a candy-coated version of events as I stood as a living witness to the weakness of his recollection.

Mom commanded me to can my clothes immediately before I contracted the infamous impetigo. This dreadful disease turned your skin into a sea of seeping sores faster than you could shuck your shorts. Dad brought out a fresh set of clothes so our nosy neighbors wouldn't think we were running a nudist camp. He buried my soiled clothes so deep they were in danger of winding up in a Chinese laundry.

Dad never gave up. After burying our mistakes, we sealed the slab in five minutes flat. The Lord confirmed in our hearts that as long as we kept looking up He would bail us out of our most blatant blunders.

## Don't Shoot the Dandelion Picker—
## He is Doing the Best He Can

The subterranean session in the septic tank had a sobering effect on me. Everything happening subsequently seemed uneventful. Particularly mundane was mowing and maintaining our lawn. Dad's tasks all went downhill from there. Days of uprooting dandelions with a pronged metal hand tool was unadulterated drudgery. Attempting to avoid this back-breaking eviction game, I praised the aesthetic attributes of these elegant, youthful yellow flowers. However, Dad, having no sentimental attachment to this endangered species, ordered them eradicated before they multiplied.

On the third day of dandelion detail I was working near the rear of the house when suddenly a foreign object struck the side of my neck with a fierce force. The hostile invader ricocheted off me and hit the house. Feeling rejected, I grabbed the right side of my neck and encountered blood. I ran behind the bushes abutting the field to search for my assailant. There was no sign of life.

Not knowing whether the weapon was a sling shot or a submachine gun, I retreated to the siding of our house for my first clue. When I dug the misguided missile out of the wood, I was staring a .22 caliber bullet in the face.

With blood trickling down my back, I headed for the farm to get a more accurate assessment. As I closed in on the barn, a young boy bolted out with a rifle swinging from his right hand. His mother emerged and I showed her my wound. Solving the case with the savvy of a Sherlock Holmes, I startled the woman by shouting, "Your son just shot me in the side of the neck!"

After examining the oozing evidence, she wiped the wound with a tattered towel. I was too shaken to worry about infection.

Meanwhile, the rifleman, looking a shade shy of thirteen, was as nervous as a night crawler about to get the hook. His mother rifled a series of questions at him and his only response was he had been shooting rats around the barn. "Well, you sure got a big one," I interjected. Upon further interrogation, the lad stuck to his story and even offered to produce decomposing evidence of the dearly departed! I passed at a peek at the carnage. His mother offered to call a doctor, but I declined.

Convinced that my wound was the result of a renegade ricochet which veered a half mile off course, I went home and called my mother instead. Bad news travels fast, so I wanted to spare her the shock of hearing about the shooting secondhand. When she answered, I calmly said, "Guess what, Mom? I just got shot." Stone silence ensued so I repeated my proclamation adding, "It isn't serious." She took it seriously as she shouted that she was on her way home to rush me to the doctor.

I waited out front with my prized .22 caliber trophy tucked in my pants pocket.

Mother drove to the doctor's as if I had been shot in a bank robbery and we were in the getaway car. Moving at this speed was more life-threatening than the wound!

Moments later I was sitting in Dr. William Carson's examining room. Appearing puzzled I filled him in on the missing pieces as he examined my neck. Dr. Carson concluded that the wound was limited to an "L" shaped abrasion produced by the glancing bullet. If the lead had landed one inch to the left I would have spent eternity pushing up dandelions! No long-range complications were anticipated but the police would be contacting us as Dr. Carson had to report all gun wounds.

Signs of life returned to Mom's eyes as we stopped at the train depot to pick up Dad. The first thing he asked was, "How is the dandelion project going?" I replied, "Dad, the Lord makes us pay the price if we destroy the beauty of his natural order!" This was the same message I meted out a few days ago, but this time I had more ammunition to back up my argument.

As I pulled the evidence from my pocket and pointed to my wound, Dad's mouth hung open as if he was on a fly-catching expedition. The last time I saw this look was when he tangled with a tough tax auditor and lost his client's case.

Dad expressed great empathy and gave me the next day off. However, the day after, Slave Driver Swanson had me back in the dandelion patch dodging bullets.

The rat killer's insurance man came out of the closet quickly to close the case. His pitch, "Sign on the dotted line and everything will be fine." He neglected to say for whom! As he dangled the reward of two hundred dollars before my eyes, I wondered how much he was offering the rats. At least my faculties remained intact enough to refuse this insult. The man got the message when I reminded him this wasn't a Monopoly game and I had no intention of passing "GO." I was holding out at all costs.

As days passed on, the scar became less visible. Even the metal memento disappeared. It slipped out of my shirt pocket along with a plastic retainer designed to hold my teeth in place. My orthodontist replaced the plastic, but he couldn't bring back the bullet.

## The Class of '57
## Survives the Chem-lab Blast

It wasn't long before I had another brush with being blown into oblivion. The Chatham High School chem-class supplied the setting.

I was such a chemistry klutz, the Lord blessed me with a brilliant lab partner to pull me through. Tom Phipp's original recipes were so clever that every chemical company in Northern, New Jersey had their eyes on him. Unfortunately our teacher Mr. Gomba didn't!

There was always tons of time for Tom to test his talents after we finished our assigned experiments. One day when Mr. Gomba was looking the other way, Tom fired up the Bunsen burner to cook his latest chemical concoction. As he poured an extra portion of hydrochloric and sulfuric acid into the mix, it rocked the entire room with a tornado intensity blast!

Even Mr. Gomba got a good shot of acid fifteen feet away! Reduced to a zombie state, he ditched his glasses and feverishly rubbed a white soap solution on his face to combat the burn. I ran to the restroom to assess my damages before the mirror. Fortunately my face was spared, but my pants were so riddled with holes they appeared as if they had been the target of a shotgun terrorist. I could feel more air get in as the acid ate away!

Knowing Dr. Jeter, the principal, would get the jitters if he was charged with running a nudist camp, I hurried home to trade my Swiss cheese ensemble for more rugged attire.

By the time I returned, Tom was in the office and many friends were in the first aid room. Fortunately no one was seriously hurt, but there was a lot of chem-lab equipment that needed replacement.

Mr. Gomba never lost his good nature, but he stuck closer to us than a shadow for the remainder of the semester.

I didn't know whether Tom went on to bigger and better things, but I heaved a heavy dose of relief when the Una-Bomber turned out to be Ted instead!

My only other close encounter at Chatham High was when I came one slip knot away from being lynched by Mr. Lynch, my no-nonsense Latin teacher.

Looking as grim as a grounded grouper, Mr. Lynch paced up and down the classroom aisles looking for his next "translation victim". When he stopped to swing his stocky frame on your and your buddy's shoulder, you knew you were in serious trouble! Once while performing his Tarzan routine on my turf he spied a chapter heading I had changed from "Winning a Beachhead" to "Winning a Fish Head". Mr. Lynch was not amused. He tore into me like tar paper about to be separated from the shack! I did double-time translations on the blackboard for two weeks after school to atone for my sins.

# 2

# College Capers

The following fall I entered North Park College on the North side of Chicago. I got in by the grace of God and a big boost from my dad's boot-straps. He was a board member.

I played football in my freshman year, but my career was cut short by a nagging knee injury. I started hitting the books instead of the dummy on the field. However, there was still no danger of setting the dorm on fire by burning the midnight oil.

Many of us would nibble on NoDoze all night before a test, and zoom into the exam like zombies suffering from zodiac arrest. A friend, Arnie Olson, devoured so much NoDoze that he zonked out during the test. They removed him from the room on a stretcher. Being a Christian college, they allowed Arnie to retake the test. The second time only his test score suffered.

We exerted most of our energies on the "Freshman Format of Fun and Games." Fred Fredrickson, the dorm counselor for the fourth floor of Burgh Hall, was a main target.

One night after Fred made his final rounds, my roommate Jim Erickson and I, with able assistance from Mark Fohlin and Jeremy Johnson, commandeered enough rope to tie up the door handles of the entire fourth floor. The tightly secured doors couldn't be opened from the inside, as they were directly across the hall from each other. We gave an extra twist to Fred's rope so the saintly seminarian couldn't escape to call the campus cops.

The sounds of silence were broken in the wee hours of the morning by the pulsating pounding of some poor soul suffering from acute kidney pressure! Relief was only a few doors away at the communal commode, but the kid was captive in his room. Bellowing like a bull moose on an all-night bender, the whole North side of Chicago had been alerted. Meanwhile Fred Fredrickson, who had been sprung by a friend from first floor, turned into a knife-wielding wacko as he hacked his charges free.

In the midst of this Mardi Gras atmosphere, Fred looked as if he was about to string up the culprits with their own weapon. Fortunately he didn't have a clue, as we mingled with the masses. Frustrated, Fred finally retreated to his room, dragging a few hundred feet of rope.

## The 100 Yard Flash

Dave Wickstrom, a powerful athlete who played fullback for North Park, was a force on the field but the perennial pounding made him punchy. He would do almost anything on a dare.

A few of Dave's faithful fans offered him fifty dollars to run with a football one lap around Burgh Hall in broad daylight, without pads or pants. To keep his cover, he could wear his helmet!

Dave was decked out for his daring dash in a white terrycloth bathrobe. He looked as if he was about to take on Rocky Marciano in a fifteen rounder. He got rid of his robe and dashed out the door like a back destined to score. The freshmen on fourth, forewarned by Dave's friends, cheered and jeered this ferocious flasher. Peeping Pauls and Paulas peered from porches across the street.

Dave covered the distance in record time, but he wasn't home free yet. His last hurdle to overcome was the locked door at the other end of the dorm. The fifty dollar flasher had been foiled by his friends! Dave delivered a round of karate body chops to the door, but it stood its ground. Dave ran for cover in a clump of bushes by the dorm.

Meanwhile Fred Frederickson was alerted and started to search for the streaker. In no mood for a neighborhood chase, Dave surrendered willingly. There was no welcoming committee to greet this odd couple. All revelers had retreated to their rooms.

After a dressing down by school authorities, Dave was given a light sentence for his first offense. The football coach washed his feet of the affair. He wanted his star fullback back in uniform for the big game. On Saturday, Dave Wickstrom streaked for two touchdowns to the delight of his faithful fans.

After the game, the one hundred-yard flasher finally collected his fifty dollars which he earned the old fashioned way. The promoters even threw in twenty-five more for the betrayal at the back door.

## The Sunday Morning Mystique
## of Maxwell Street

No semester was complete without a trip to Maxwell Street on the near west side of the city.

"Nails" Morton, the White Knight Mobster, was born in this brawling open-air bazaar in 1894. At the turn of the century the Street had a higher crime rate than the worst wards of Brooklyn. "Nails" spent his early years battling the hostile ethnics surrounding the area. Italian, Irish, Russian and Polish gangs waged a war to wipe out the West Side Jews. Peddlers were punched and old men's beards were set on fire!

By prohibition days, "Nails" Morton made Maxwell Street safe for his people. 70,000 bargain hunters descended on this mile-long market every Sunday morning. Every sight, sound and smell known to mankind emanated from stores, stalls and stands. Old world sausages and salamis were competing with wilting wildcat fur wraps. You could have a live turkey killed and carved in front of your eyes.

When the market master blew his whistle at 8:00 a.m., everything was fair game. Every huckster this side of Hades had some kind of offbeat operation in full swing. Hired "pullers" worked the Street like prison wardens after escaped prey. He could guarantee you a zoot suit for $12.00 at Smokey Joe's before you were ever yanked into the store.

On my maiden trip to this Taj Mahal of Merchandising I was accompanied by two friends. Jack Lundbom, a native Chicagoan, was the leader of the pack. He was street savvy and big enough that no "puller" could push him around. Jerry Sandberg was more laid-back.

The first item that drew our attention were women's white fur coats for five dollars. The only glitch to this giveaway was that the furs were glued to the ground, soaking wet in someone's backyard! When Jack tried to lift one of these lovelies he wound up with only half the fur in his hand. We concluded they had been shot on sight.

Our next stop was a small clothing shack named "Johnny B. Goods." After a hard sell, I purchased a pair of wool slacks for six dollars. The trousers being two feet too long required alterations. The salesman gave me a numbered ticket and sent me across the street to a rundown building.

I was greeted harshly by a character whose face looked as if it had fallen into a bowl of cereal and curdled. With a sneering snarl he claimed he never heard of "Johnny B. Goods" and ordered me off the premises. Without any hemming and hawing I grabbed my pants and split.

Meanwhile "Johnny B. Goods" had been given a top-to-bottom transplant. The door was locked, the shades were drawn and there was no sign of the sign. I left before the hunter turned into the hunted. It was open season on North Park College students.

I found my friends a few blocks down the street. They were pondering a pig's knuckle some hawker was passing off as a paperweight. When I told them about my pants purchase, Jack laughed and warned, "Stick with me and you won't be swindled."

Minutes later a swarthy smoothie in a big white Cadillac sidled up to the curb and motioned for us to come over. Jack jumped at the chance, and Jerry and I followed.

Hiram was his name and we pretty well guessed his game. The trunk of his homemade haberdashery was filled to the gills with three-piece gray suits. The dusty duds appeared as if they were swiped from a mortuary in the midst of an earthquake!

Our discernment died the moment Hiram offered the ensemble for fifteen dollars. Jack haggled him down to twelve. Jubilant over our find, we took our trophies back to Burgh Hall to try on.

Jack's large jacket and vest were so tight they affected his breathing and the seams split in his struggle to escape. There was no earthly purpose in trying on the pants. They would have parted faster than the Red Sea!

Jerry encountered the opposite problem. Weighing in at 130 pounds soaking wet, he came off as a baggy comedian from the vaudeville era in his three-piece special. The crotch massaged his knees when he walked. If someone chased him he would break a leg.

My medium fit fairly well but looked as if it was featured in the infamous fashion magazine "Underworld Quarterly." Along with its lack of style, cut and lining, little gray fuzz balls started to form. Not fit to donate to charity, I added this suit to my Halloween arsenal.

Hiram had the last laugh in "The Case of the Lying Labels." What the labels read were immaterial. The suits were all the same size! At least this time, Jack, the Maxwell Street shark, had also been swindled.

Maxwell Street never disappointed. It always lived up to its advanced billing. If you are into paying big bucks, patronize Marshall Fields on State Street. If you are searching for the deal of the decade, head straight for Maxwell Street. You might be beseeched, fleeced and beaten, but you will never be bored!

Despite the Dan Ryan expressway and a battalion of bulldozers, Maxwell Street still stands four blocks long. "Nails" is known as the man who made it safe for swindlers to operate openly. His sacrifices will never be forgotten.

## Rigor Mortis Sets In At Rutgers

By my senior year the campus scene got more serious. It was time to sift through the numerous possibilities that could affect my future. Was I ready for the cruel cold world of work? If pranks were a prerequisite for a successful business career, I had it made.

Uncle Sam cast his dark shadow around my footsteps, while his open door policy created a chilling draft. Enrolling in graduate school would shake Uncle Sam for awhile and earn the credits I needed to make accounting a career.

I chose Rutgers Graduate School of Business in Newark, New Jersey, as my next stop because they have an MBA program specifically for students going into Public Accounting. Only thirty students were accepted into this thirteen-month course.

I graduated from North Park on June 7, 1961 and started at Rutgers two days later. I commuted from my home in Chatham on the Erie Lackawanna Railroad.

Rutgers was a real revelation. If I didn't study here I would disappear faster than when I stumbled into the septic tank. Nineteen of my classmates were Ivy League and the rest were from the upper crust of the East's smaller schools. One pompous patrician from Haverford talked with such a nasal twang he sounded like a woodchuck with oak wedged up his nostrils. I had serious doubts about the chump from Chatham competing with these Wisemen from the East for the required "B" average.

One of the professors was even more of a concern. Dr. Ulrich Von Otto, who taught Business Finance, had a Prussian presence that could put the fear of God in an avowed atheist. His booming voice and brown beady eyes packed enough power to singe the skin of any student ill-prepared!

I needed to smoke the peace pipe with this proud Prussian no matter how sick it made me. The second week under his scrutiny I discovered the secret—feed him the same diet he was dishing out. His lectures were laden with key phrases. I appealed to his pride by putting all his phrases back into my answers on the exams. The highlight of my Rutgers experience was extracting an "A" out of Dr. Von Otto in this four-credit course.

Social life was a lost art at Rutgers. Bebopping and maintaining a "B" average didn't mix. Neither was Newark the Paris of the New World. Moving from Chicago to Newark was like living in Jersey City and winning a week in Hoboken!

My non-academic activity was attending church so I was eligible for their softball team. Two nights before finals I tore a tendon in my left foot sliding into third base. The next morning I added aluminum crutches to my school wardrobe.

Adding insult to injury, my severe slice at Springbrook Country Club two days before got me in a real jam—my skin broke out in an acute case of poison ivy. My blisters were as big as bismarcks with the jelly oozing out.

I paraded to school each day plastered with pink paste and supported by paraplegic crutches. Newark in July was a time to fry. Rutgers rejected air conditioning as too revolutionary!

The "Big Eight" camped at our doorstep. The "Big Eight" was not a football factory or hit squad, but the first string international public accounting firms.

After interviewing with all eight in the friendly confines of the campus, I took a look at three on their own turf. Ernst and Ernst, treating me as if I had won the Heisman Trophy, tried to lure me by lulling me to sleep in their limousine. After weeks of deliberation I decided to accept Arthur Young & Co.'s offer in Chicago. Newark was never in the running and in New York you still had to wear a homburg to work.

## Moonlighting on Miami Beach

Prior to my two-month internship with Arthur Young, I headed for Miami Beach, the Mecca of the modern world, for Christmas vacation.

Packing the car was no picnic. Dad was disturbed when he discovered I was hauling my 110 lb. Charles Atlas barbell set along. When I saw all the luggage, I took pity on him and agreed to drop ten pounds. The Pontiac moved like a submarine on a secret night mission as it scraped out the driveway in early morning darkness. Dad always launched expeditions early to beat the heat, the traffic and anything else worth beating out there.

In spite of the weights, we arrived in Miami Beach in record time. We checked into the Kenilworth Hotel, known as Arthur Godfrey's garrison, because he quartered his TV troops there during the 1950's. His most famous flash-in-the-pan was the silver-voiced heartthrob, Julius La Rosa. Julius aroused Arthur's red-haired dandruff to the point where he was fired by his fiery boss during a live telecast! Arthur created as much controversy in the air as on the air. He got busted for buzzing the Brooklyn Bridge while imitating a kamikaze pilot.

The bellhops weren't covered for hernias, so I left my Charles Atlas entourage in the car.

Miami Beach wasn't much warmer than New Jersey. Sun worshippers stuffed into sweat suits were rolled up in army blankets. It was so cold the man-of-wars were passing up people and performing push ups in the sand to stay warm! From the ninth floor window it looked like the Marines had landed.

Too cold for beach blanket bingo, I donned my North Park sweatshirt and headed for a miniature golf course a half-mile down the beach. Suddenly I heard a sea-siren wail "North Park College." Shell-shocked, I reeled around to follow this celestial sound.

This wasn't a flashback to Greek Mythology. This Charybdis was for real. What nymph on Miami Beach knew about North Park? Even native Windy City whizzes never heard of the place!

Partially blinded by her bright orange slacks, I worked my way through a maze of humanity. Still smiling, she introduced herself as Karen Mulberger from Elm Grove, Wisconsin. She graduated from Wheaton College six months before, which explained the North Park connection. Wheaton College, located west of Chicago, is a Christian arch rival of North Park. They compete in sports and for students. Any kid who transfers automatically loses his sanctification! Wheaton's most famous alumnus was evangelist Billy Graham, until Karen graduated. Now they share the dubious distinction.

My search for the miniature golf course was sidetracked by a sand trap. We talked until sunset. Karen was attending the Graduate School of Social Work at the University of Wisconsin, in Madison. She made it clear that the U.W. scene had no living resemblance to Wheaton's campus. It was like starring in "The Ten Commandments," and making your next movie venture "Animal House!"

Karen arrived at the Kenilworth with her family two days before. She described at great length two gorgeous guys she had already dated. The only hitch was her mother, Lorraine Mulberger, couldn't hack them because they weren't Christians. Apparently Karen already considered me a Christian, even though I attended North Park. That's one sign of the end times! Wheaton is saturated with sanctified saints, whereas North Park is known as the Babylon of the evangelical world.

My initial attraction to Karen was her orange slacks and compelling voice. Now her sweet smile, bubbling personality and physical beauty were taking over. I was sinking fast with no quicksand in sight. The Lord was my only hope. I beseeched Him for the boldness of John the Baptist, the courage of David, the strength of Samson, the wisdom of Solomon, the patience of Job, the perseverance of Paul, and the love of Jesus. A true Wheaton crusader couldn't resist all those attributes.

Dad got suspicious when he realized Charles Atlas was still stashed in the trunk of our car.

The next morning we went shelling. Karen was in command as she searched the shores like a sandpiper opening a scrap yard. My assignment was to lug the loot in a large pail. She even dabbled in decomposing driftwood and beatup bottles. The sea urchins were my undoing. They might be dead, but they still stinketh! If Charles Atlas rubbed noses with one of these beauties Dad would have to trade in his car.

After three hours of toting washed-up relics, we collapsed on the sand to survey our finds. We accumulated enough junk to construct competition for the Kenilworth. A more immediate problem was sneaking the booty past hotel security and into Karen's room.

## The Last of the Red Hot Mamas

That night we ditched the Kenilworth and headed for the Diplomat Hotel in Hollywood, Florida. Playing it safe we triple dated in Dad's car with our brothers, Jim and Mike. Wheaton girls didn't gravitate towards night clubs, but the tender tone of Vic Damone couldn't do much damage.

Mike's girl was a sparkling blonde from Paducah, Kentucky, by the name of Adrienne. The two had much in common— Adrienne lived on a horse ranch and Mike wanted to. We found a blind date for Jim, who was slightly nearsighted himself.

Dad gave Jim and me five dollars to buy corsages, but Mike had more exotic tastes. He bought Adrienne a baby alligator! Thwarted, trying to pin this glassy-eyed gremlin to the front of her dress, she coaxed the cuddly creature back into his wire mesh cage. Enchanted with her new friend, she named him Norman, in deference to a distant uncle with a scathing skin disease.

When we arrived at the Diplomat I warned the parking attendant about Norman in the back seat but neglected to mention Charles Atlas rattling in the trunk.

To our surprise, Vic Damone wasn't the only celebrity listed on the marquee. Sophie Tucker, billed as "The Last of the Red Hot Mamas," also appeared! She sounded like a typical Wheaton dorm mother to me. Karen was appalled at my conclusion.

I scurried the pack past the scurrilous hawker in the lobby, who was peddling Sophie Tucker's "Little Lover Pills."

By the time we reached the neon-rimmed nightclub, "The Last of the Red Hot Mamas" was red hot—parading all over the stage spewing out double doses of vitriolic venom like a jumbo Joan Rivers. Sophie picked apart her prey with ribald rhetoric and shifted into a sensual song.

Karen cringed under the weight of this wayward warbler wiggling her way across the stage. Sassy Sophie's last act was espousing the vixenish virtues of her "Little Lover Pills" as she tossed red-hot samples to the crowd. She would be selling them in the lobby after the show.

Sophie has to be "The Last of the Red Hot Mamas"—the rest had been locked up or lowered into the ground by now. I wanted to flee this flea market faster than a funeral director faced with a resurrection in Parlor "B"! However, a character flaw kept me glued to my seat. It was my wallet! Too cheap to shell out a shipload of shekels and be sunk by this shrew, I was determined to hear Vic Damone.

Sophie sashayed off the stage and gave ground to the renowned velvet-voiced singer. Vic Damone was not a drone. His agent should be canned for booking him on the same show with Sophie.

Upon exiting we spied Sophie peddling her "Little Lover Pills." Her face was plastered with mounds of pink powder. She got into a shouting and shoving match with a guy who called her "a beatout old bag." We split before the cops came.

If Karen's mother got wind of this she would strangle me with my North Park sweat shirt. Imagine, taking an other-worldly Wheaton girl to witness Sophie Tucker on a first date! This Red Hot Mama act was wilder than any forbidden fruit outlawed under "The Pledge." "The Pledge" was a signed binding agreement protecting Wheaton students from the devious darts of the enemy in case there were cracks in the armor. The cinema was sinful, cards corruptible and dancing was degradation. Hootenannies were allowed at alumni reunions only. Alcohol was for Catholic kids and if a student smoked, his destiny was to smoke in the hereafter, also. At North Park the only activities frowned upon were necking and necromancy, which many claimed to be one and the same!

Upon returning to the Kenilworth we ditched our siblings and headed for the veranda parallel to the pounding surf. The moon's hazy glaze blanketed the beach. Karen was kind about the Diplomat debacle. Neither Norman, Charles Atlas, Sassy Sophie nor "The Pledge" possessed enough power to put us asunder!

## Will the Real Fred Fruehauf Please Stand Up

The ensuing evening we confined our activities to the conservative Kenilworth. Karen joined us for dinner in the main dining room.

The Diplomat Hotel was history as a topic of conversation. We weren't' telling my parents about the "Little Lover Pills" either. Having been happily married for 32 years, they were good for another 50 without the pills anyway.

It came as no surprise when Dad popped up and greeted a middle-aged couple passing by. As a proud father he often went out of his way to introduce us to people. We all took turns shaking hands with Mr. and Mrs. Fred Fruehauf before they continued on to their table.

Dad promptly informed us that Mr. Fruehauf owned the Fortune 500 - Fruehauf Trailer Co.. A few seconds later he wasn't so self-assured and seemed to be searching for a second opinion. Finally he blurted out, "Who were those people?" We obviously didn't know, even though we had just been introduced. We had taken Dad's word they were the Fruehaufs!

Meanwhile the couple was sneaking peeks in our direction. They looked as confused as comic strip characters plucked off the printed page and suddenly subjected to real life.

After minutes of deliberation, Dad decided this couple was not the Fortune 500 Fruehaufs. They belonged to some other cloned clan. Dad downed his two desserts and then approached their table to offer apologies. He was an old pro at smoking the peace pipe.

The Glen Banks forgave Dad's mortal mistake and wanted to know all about the Fruehaufs. Knowing his knack for making long talks off of short piers, we left; leaving him in spirited conversation with his newfound friends. Dad had an uncanny way of drowning the darkness of defeat and rising again with the new dawn of victory!

The week went faster than Arthur Godfrey could fire another TV family member. It was time for the tears of tearing apart. Karen headed back to Mad City with her beach booty bagged up in a boxcar. I flew to the Windy City for my internship with Arthur Young & Co. Mike and Mrs. Mulberger returned to the Beer Capital, while Mom, Dad and Jim carted Charles Atlas back to Chatham. No one laid a glove on him all week!

# 3

# Wintering At The White House

Living at the Wilson Avenue YMCA on the North side of Chicago wasn't exactly like wintering at the "White House." In addition to the quasi-quacks with peculiar quirks, there were derelicts hovering in dark hallways. I embellished my reports to my parents so they wouldn't make me move in with relatives. I would rather take my chances with this haven of have-nots. Where else could I find a room with running water for two dollars a day?

I visited Karen in Madison four weekends during the two-month internship. The other weekends Arthur Young assigned me out of town work.

One late Sunday night I left Madison in a blinding snowstorm. Even the plows were moving at a pussyfoot pace. Peering through peepholes in the windshield I pulled off I-90 near the state line. While parked on the shoulder, I dozed off in the drafty darkness. Suddenly I was startled by ear-piercing pounding on the window. The snow obliterated my view from this igloo. Not knowing the identity of my night visitor I elected not to open the door.

Maybe it was mean Ed Gein, the gangrene machine from Plainfield, Wisconsin! Not having the heart to end up in Ed's Sausage Shop, I used my head instead. I shouted at my would-be assailant and a gruff voice grunted back, "This is the State Patrol and you are illegally parked!"

Concluding that Ed would have been in my igloo by now, I lowered the window. What a relief to see "Old Smokey" when you are expecting Ed. Of course if the stalker is a wolf in bear's clothing the fun has just begun!

After Smokey's lecture I drove to the next wayside where I had a fighting chance of escaping annihilation from a side swiping.

I arrived back at the Wilson YMCA in time to crawl into my monkey suit and take the elevated train to the Loop. Arthur Young & Co. was entrenched on the tenth floor of the Harris Trust building. Thank God they didn't send me out on an inventory. What would Swift & Co. think when I informed them they owned 10,000 sheep?

That night, after a sulfur-scented supper with the boys at the "Y," I slept like a scarecrow sedated by sleeping pills. I would have rivaled Rip Van Winkle if I wasn't rudely awakened by repeated raps at my door.

It was a devilish case of "deja vu." The busted bolt was as tight as a tattler's tongue and there was no time for prayer or fasting. The intruder treated my door like I was Noah and there was another flood. With holy boldness I demanded the proper password. It was Les Barnes, a balding buddy from the "Y" who wanted to return a book he borrowed. This bookworm must be suffering from an acute case of cirrhosis of the cerebrum! He claimed his conscience was keeping him awake all night. I demanded Les to march his conscience and my book back to his room and I would redeem my reading material sometime after sunrise—besides, I wasn't charging fines!

Les brought it to breakfast and requested to keep it until he was finished. Tempted to hit him over the head with the book, I gave it to him instead. I could always buy another copy but I could ill afford to squander any more sleep.

After two months I was out of the Wilson "Y" and back in "The Garden State" attending Rutgers. If I wasn't weeded out by June, July would be joyous. With a coveted MBA, maybe I could capture a CPA by November. Eluding Uncle Sam might be the biggest challenge of all.

## Summering at the Outhouse

After graduation, Karen and I visited my parents summer home in Northern Wisconsin, six miles from Iron Mountain, Michigan. The Spread Eagle Chain of Lakes was a cherished childhood sanctuary. It was our family's refuge for a few weeks each summer from the humidity hovering over New York's nastiest neighbor.

Swedes from Chicago flocked to this "Promised Land of the New World" in the early 1900's. Spread Eagle put the immigrants in touch with the territorial trappings of the Old Country, such as crystal-clear lakes, pine-scented forests, rocks, rills and other thrills. My grandparents built a bungalow big enough for the entire brood to bandy about. The clan included cousins, aunts, uncles and black bears on occasion.

There was always an avalanche of activities readily available— fishing in a creaky, leaky old wooden rowboat, picking blueberries while being picked upon by ravenous red ants and night fights with curious creatures out at the dark, dingy outhouse.

Eight lakes composed the secluded Spread Eagle Chain. Its borders contained ample breezy bays and isolated islands to explore. A quiver full of fun-loving friends were only a channel away as we raced from lake to lake in Penn Yan boats energized by Evinrude.

Swedes were too weighted down with the side effects of smorgasbords to indulge in big bashes. Among the Christian contingent, caffeine and gluttony were in, but sniffing glue and chugging glug were far out. A Swede's idea of a blast would make Frenchmen frown and Irishmen irregular. Nature and restless natives provided all the excitement.

One silent night our sleep was put on hold by an enormous explosion in the kitchen. It sounded like the start of WW III. I envisioned boatloads of nationalistic Norwegians seizing this Swedish stronghold! By the time we arrived in the kitchen, most of it was scattered all over the woods. It looked as if Paul Bunyan had bludgeoned his blue ox with a ballistic missile. It was an Act of God that no one was cooking or there would have been instant spaghetti.

The real culprit was an LP gas tank in the basement with an uncontrollable temper. The entire crew was put on KP and cookouts were in order until Uncle Harold could repair the extensive damage. One of my relatives was brained by a falling rain gutter, which made a lasting impression on him.

Next summer lightning struck again at the same spot. This time it wasn't Paul Bunyan, but Jack Lundbom, the Maxwell Street manhandler, who was into heavy metal by now.

He stopped at our cottage after giving his 1951 Oldsmobile a rigid road test by racing it from Chicago in five hours. He parked it on the hill above our place and while walking towards the front porch, the Olds passed Jack on the right. The Rambling Wreck ran roughshod over every foe and slammed head-first into Grandma's recently resurrected kitchen! The bumper ripped through the siding like it was sawdust before giving the stove a cross-body block. The kitchen, beaten beyond recognition, reflected the distress on Grandma's face. Her eyes had seen the gory of the coming of Jack's car as it trampled through the kitchen that would need to be restored.

Jack grimaced in pain at the sight of his grounded graven image. We concluded that his Olds hand brake had a bad day as the wrecker hauled another load away. However, Maxwell Street Jack didn't suffer a total loss. He gained a new nickname—Jack the Ripper!

Uncle Harold, our family hero, came to the rescue once again, as he exercised all his seasoned skills on our stricken kitchen.

## Gaylord Nelson's Headquarters

Karen fit into this exciting Spread Eagle experience like a fresh flower in a fertile field. Her contagious spirit of adventure cunningly coaxed the clan into clandestine activities that would have never entered their innocent minds.

Her first expedition involved our neighbor's outhouse, which had been abandoned for many moons. It was in prime shape to be plucked and placed in more prestigious surroundings. Karen envisioned this architectural gem to grace downtown Iron Mountain, Michigan, a city of 10,000 people six miles away.

My duty was to dig up the necessary manpower to maneuver the outhouse off its moorings and onto Uncle Harold's trailer. Rounding up the rowdies was no problem, but securing a getaway car was another matter. Top secrecy needed to be maintained for a successful mission. At the midnight hour, Jim Miksa, whose family owned the lumber yard in town, commandeered his dad's white Cadillac convertible. This crew was going to cruise in class!

We plotted to take advantage of the political profundities of the time by turning this treasure into Gaylord Nelson's headquarters. Gaylord Nelson, a badger bigwig, was engaged in a battle for the governor's office in Madison. We were convinced it would accentuate the candidate's courage to open a headquarters of mysterious origin in a neighboring state. Our hindsight proved to be as forthright as our foresight.

The moonlit night cast shadows on the stark surroundings as we approached our prey. When I knocked nervously on the outhouse door to make sure it was still abandoned, a chipmunk came scampering out. A skunk would have been more appreciated to neutralize the odor in the area.

It took ten minutes of tugging to pry the privy loose and tote the trophy into the rear end of the trailer. Everyone climbed aboard as Jim Miksa jumped into the Cadillac. Two miles down the highway he turned onto a gravel road and came to a grinding halt.

Karen mounted the privy and painted "Gaylord Nelson's Headquarters" in big bold boxy letters on all sides. For good measure, she plastered, "Gaylord for Governor" posters on any empty spaces.

The caravan re-entered the highway and headed downtown. The paint was still wet when we crossed the tracks and quickly dumped our cargo at the west end of the deserted depot. After propping up the privy we hurried back to Spread Eagle for a few winks of well-earned sleep.

By dawn we returned downtown to make sure Gaylord Nelson's newest headquarters was contributing positively to his campaign. The Dickinson Hotel was our headquarters for observing Gaylord's.

Just like a Candid Camera Caper, puzzled people stopped and stared at the odd-looking outhouse. Slowly they inched closer, as if high-powered explosives were ready to blow Gaylord's headquarters to smithereens! One bold soul, sporting a bushy beard, entered and emerged a few minutes later looking flushed. The next visitor that ventured in didn't stay as long, which was probably a direct reflection on the first visitor. No one else braved this barrier in the brief time Gaylord's Michigan Headquarters was open.

An hour later, an army of sanitation workers arrived to officially close his Michigan campaign. Seizing this American Gothic with the gusto of a Miller Lite ad, they stuffed it in the dark regions of a dump truck. Grieved in our spirit we paid our last respects on the spot. Following the funeral procession to the privy's final resting place could have led to reprisals. This is what's wrong with America! We tear down our most outstanding architectural achievements under the guise of progress.

Gaylord was never given a chance to host an open house at his U.P. headquarters. However, its sudden demise didn't darken his political career. After Governor, he served many terms as a US Senator from Wisconsin. Gaylord also got in the Guiness Book of World Records as the only Governor in US history to operate a headquarters in a neighboring state!

## Uncle Sam's Billion Dollar Band

As a young man in the 60's, no matter how small your clan, you had at least one uncle who took special interest in you. You could count on him to attend your commencement. Seated near the speakers' rostrum in his patented red, white and blue, "I want you" regalia, he grabs your arm and escorts you off the stage.

Uncle Sam's insatiable concern was confirmed by an invitation to his induction station on the west side of Chicago to get better acquainted. Warned about my health, he scheduled a physical.

Seeing the red flag, I turned down his request. Knowing my Great Uncle was a confirmed nepotist who never gave up on his nephews, I rushed to the Army Reserve Headquarters on Peterson Avenue. When I told my tale of woe to the 1st Sergeant he produced a list of two hundred harrowed homo sapiens who also wanted to become weekend warriors. By the time my name floated to the top I would already be fidgeting in a foxhole.

I immediately played my trump card and he snatched it like the last slice of sausage at Oktoberfest. Desperate for a payroll clerk, he prepared my papers for a physical to enter the Reserves.

The induction center reminded me of the lard refinery at Swift & Co. where I once took an inventory. Uncle Sam and Swift had much in common—they both wanted to get the lard out. The lineup looked like beef cattle being led to the slaughter—some had been grazing far too long. If these guys weren't declared 4F, any foe could destroy our country!

I breezed through the tests except for the eye exam. I couldn't see the big "E" on the wall chart. The examiner swiftly stamped "simple myopia" on my form and ordered me to the next station. If I had "simple myopia," the poor guy with "mega-myopia" would need a seeing-eye dog!

Six weeks later I was riding on the rocky roadbed of the Gulf, Mobile and Ohio Railroad headed for Fort Leonard Wood. This post, fondly referred to as "The Outhouse of the Ozarks," was considered Uncle Sam's most revered vacationland.

Arriving in St. Louis at 6:00 a.m., we were herded on buses and transported to a worn-out warehouse. There the tired troops were treated to a breakfast of greasy bacon and green powdered eggs.

One train ride and two buses later, we arrived at the Fort and were greeted at the Reception Center by two sergeants who boarded the bus. Acting as if they were suffering from the same breakfast we had, these leather-lunged clones of Legion barked out commands to get off the bus and fall in formation pronto! If this was the Reception Center, we wondered with bated breath what boot camp had in store.

Our march to the base barbershop for hair styling became hair raising. Raw recruits were nervous in the service as they shuffled forward in the fast-moving line. Cliptomaniacs were paid piece rate to shear somber soldiers at the pace of two a minute. City slickers with DA's and Elvis impersonators had the most to lose. Within thirty seconds their entire identity floated to the floor!

With our craniums reduced to raw rounded relics, the next act of skullduggery was the cadre marching us to the supply center for outfitting in the latest fall fashions. Supply sergeants, acting more like Field Marshals than anyone associated with Marshall Fields, threw gravy green getups at us. It was a freak of nature if anything fit. Our destiny was doing duty in the duds we were dealt.

Four days later we were delivered to boot camp in the back of army trucks and indoctrinated by cadre competing for the swearing swine award.

The boys in the barracks were like a Who's Who at a werewolf roundup! The Sons of the South couldn't read or write and the Northern Nasties were pen pals with their parole officers.

Cordoned off in rooms of eight, I had the fate of being saddled with a bucking bronco for a bunkmate. Russell Suverkrubbe, a large lummox from Lubbock, Texas, had never wandered off the ranch. His phobia for heights projected me into the upper bunk opposite a broken window. He shook the bunk so bad that motion sickness overcame any homesickness.

During the second week we tackled the terrain of the infiltration course. Live ammo sails over your head as you crawl cradling an M-16 rifle. If you jump up and get blown to bits, Uncle Sam charges you with destroying government property! Your best buddy defends you at the trial.

Two weeks of marching to the rifle range to shoot at pop-up targets should satisfy anybody's inane interest in slinging lead. I never felt at home on the range. After firing for a few hours I concluded the real enemy was behind the lines. It was a pack of Dobermans dishing out decibels of overkill. "Kill or be killed," was their cry, barked out to the beat of their bestial drummer.

Once when my rifle backfired, my left contact lens catapulted into the new fallen snow. Simple myopia was about to be tested on the front lines. While searching for my lens, my M-16 waved around aimlessly. Suddenly a vicious voice yelled, "Point that weapon down range!" The voice grabbed the revolving rifle in one hand and me in the other and marched both of us to the warming tent. Another red hot voice took over the tent. When the coals cooled, I pleaded my case in an ashen state. Convinced that my presence on the range was more serious than turning a serial killer loose at a turkey shoot, he committed Uncle Sam's unforgivable sin by permitting me to return to the barracks.

Five days later our entire company marched to the field for a winter's week of bivouac in the bosom of Mother Nature.

Russell was my tent mate which meant quarters would be tight. After the ten-mile trek we were ordered to pitch our tents and dig a trench. Entrenching tools were tested by trying to penetrate the frozen tundra. A pitched battle of man-made metal against Mother Earth raged until the once-proud implements bit the dust and were dutifully ditched.

That night my sleeping bag revealed its true nature—its zipper got stuck. Russell tried to remedy the situation with the abandon of a draft horse in a tug of war. On the third yank he ripped the zipper from its moorings! To compound the calamity the air mattress sprung a lethal leak in its lungs causing God's frozen chosen to shiver for three nights.

Meanwhile, Russell, who could sleep standing up, snored like a sputtering seismograph.

By the third night there was sizable slippage in the ranks. Of the 130 stout-hearted men who strutted to this isolated iceberg, 46 remained. The others dropped out like lemmings who had overdosed on laxatives! Frostbite and pneumonia cases went to the hospital. Many suffered from the severe bivouac malady— barracks fever. Grown men pleaded to go on KP! On the fourth day Russell and I lucked out—the KP list hit the low S's.

The mess hall was a Finnish sauna compared to the field area. Sun peeked through the window as I warmed up the water at the back sink. For 16 hours I placated cantankerous cooks by turning out spic and span pots and pans.

The duty to be avoided was "Mop Man." Recruits moved around the mess hall like revolving doors off their rockers, mopping every form of slop imaginable.

"Pot and pan man" did double duty at the loading dock. We filled lawless-looking vehicles to the gills with Uncle Sam's food rations. It was reminiscent of rum-running days as civilians fled with the contraband. The mess sergeant was as silent as a sick seer at a seance concerning these shady shenanigans!

Behind the back door was a Who's Who collection of garbage cans. The KP's needed Ph.D's in waste management to figure out the system. Beyond eatable and non-eatable, the garbage was grouped in sub-classes according to its final destiny.

Suddenly I was parted from the pots and pans by a portly cross-eyed cook who pulled me into the storeroom. Seizing a large sack of potatoes, he ordered me to peel them by pouring them into a monster machine. I turned on the hose and put 100 lbs. down the portal. As the spuds spun in a cyclone motion, I felt flying objects ricocheting off my feet. I realized I had forgotten to close the escape hatch as the naked potatoes skidded all over the kitchen floor.

The livid-lunged mess sergeant sidestepping the AWOL army attacking his feet waded my way to wage war. He ordered me down on all fours to fetch the scalped escapees. I was joined by the mop man and two other petrified potato prototypes.

After 16 hours of pampering pots and pans, delivering stolen goods and playing potato hockey, I was released to return to the barracks. In spite of Russell's snoring, I slept as sound as the stone statues on Easter Island.

Two weeks later I was sent to Finance School at Fort Benjamin Harrison near Indianapolis. Fort Ben was like a college campus compared with the "Outhouse of the Ozarks." I attended class during the week and visited Karen in Chicago on weekends.

Upon graduation I had one month of active duty remaining. Some saintly soul made me a bookkeeper in the Officers Club. I read newspapers in the morning and played golf every afternoon. Uncle Sam paid me 67 cents an hour for this heavy duty. After this type of treatment I would need time to re-acclimate before going back to work at Arthur Young & Co. However, I knew that Uncle Sam's Billion Dollar Band would keep marching along. He would never have a problem finding bookkeepers for the Officers Club!

# 4

# Two Can't Live Cheaper Than One

Karen and I were engaged on December 23, 1962—a year from the day we met. Before making it official there was the major matter of locating a ring. Maxwell Street was off limits but any other place was fair game.

Once again I was wintering at the White House on Wilson Avenue. Les Barnes, the bookworm, still resided there. When he wasn't reading he was working at Harrison Bros., a wholesale warehouse on the North Side.

According to Les, Harrison's diamonds had no rival this side of Elizabeth Taylor's. Born with one hand in my mouth and the other on my wallet, I was willing to wager that Les was right. Karen wasn't! She wasn't real fond of Les, and this proposed diamond deal didn't cement the relationship. I convinced her there was no downside to sneaking a peek at these gems.

Harrison's was as humble as a Haitian hovel. Les lugged out an old wooden box which held the glistening goods. These deadbeat diamonds, with their yellowish yeast casts, looked to be in the last stages of yellow fever! He presented the next gem as having a slight flaw in its character. A few seconds of my scrupulous scrutiny revealed its imperfection was a crack that rivaled the Grand Canyon!

I informed Les we had seen enough of these jaded jewels—they were real rocks! With a hurtful hang-dog look he bowed his bushy brows over his basset brown eyes to hurl one last-ditch pitch. Les made his appeal to our pocketbook but we passed. If I had given in to the guilt I would still be at Harrison's!

We escaped out a side exit, got in our getaway car and proceeded to Peacock's Jewelry store on State Street.

Peacock's had a polished operation. They weren't in any danger of hitting rock bottom like Harrisons. It didn't take long for Karen to pick out a winner. If only I would learn to depend on her discernment I could live a stress-free life!

I slipped the ring on Karen's finger at Chalgels Restaurant at the Cudahy Towers in Milwaukee. This romantic candlelight night was followed by an engagement party given by Karen's mother at the Wisconsin Club. Les couldn't make it. He was too busy with books, bangles and beads!

## Haunted by the Hollows

My parents treated us to a trip to the Greenbriar Hotel in White Sulfur Springs, West Virginia. The five of us, including brother Jim, left on the night train from Chicago.

At 6:00 a.m. there was a loud rap on my compartment door. Thank God it wasn't Ed or Les. Karen couldn't sleep. She was in awe of the hollows. Candlelight flames flickered in the cabin windows as the train wound around the Appalachian villages. The tracks nestled so near the canyon walls that a leap would land you on a mountaineer's porch. It was a sociologist's celestial bliss.

Upon arriving at noon, we were transported to the Greenbriar by a horse-drawn wagon. We lunched with the Kimball Colemans, friends of the family from Chatham.

Fascinated by the morning's folkloric feast we desired to drive up in the Allegheny Mountains. Devoid of any vehicle, Karen used her charm to commandeer Kimball's 1963 Cadillac.

We left at 3:00 p.m. with the sun still bathing the surrounding beauty. Twenty minutes later we turned up a snow-slushed mud-rim road. Karen, oozing with obsessions of meeting mountain folk, spurred me on.

Five miles later we hadn't encountered any living thing. Even a raccoon refused to reveal its real nature. We had already forded more streams with Kimball's Cadillac than Conestogas did on their way west. It was like spending the afternoon at a car wash!

The only reason I quit talking about turning around was it was too narrow. Mud was the menace at the moment. Kimball's oil pan was filling like a bed pan! It was dark and we were due for dinner shortly.

Visions of my mother's frantic face flashed in front of me. Thank God I couldn't see Kimball's! Karen's courageous curiosity showed signs of crumbling—she started to refer to mountain folk as a way out of the Promised Land, rather than the avenue in. Our prayers remained silent so we wouldn't scare each other. Kimball's Cadillac didn't come equipped with sleeping bags. This engagement trip was so filled with thrills, I could hardly wait for the honeymoon!

Finally we sighted our first ray of hope. Cautiously we crept up to a light on the right a few hundred yards ahead. The stark stillness was interrupted by a barking barrage. Cowering at the sound of cannibalistic canines, we remained incarcerated in Kimball's car. Suspecting we had stumbled on a moonshine maniac's munitions works, we moved out of range. We found a turn-around and barreled down the mountain faster than the Cadillac would carry us. Once we were airborne the pull of gravity quickened our trip to the bottom.

Two hours late, we reported to the dining room where the wounded worriers were diving into their dessert. Gallantly, I let Karen do all the talking as they were less likely to be upset with her. There was no wrath—they were just glad to have us back. Karen related a rousing rendition of our mountaintop experience. Kimball laughed as if he had forgotten whose car was borrowed for this adventure. However, I noticed that he clutched his keys like a kid latching on to candy!

Not wanting to press my parents' patience, we restricted our rambling to the Greenbriar grounds. On New Year's day we watched Bucky Badger's last blast in the Rose Bowl. Bucky put up a fierce fight but lost to the USC Trojans in the waning moments of the game. It would be 31 years before they would find the path back to Pasadena.

The next day we all returned to real life. Trading in my tux for army gear, I returned to Fort Leonard Wood to finish basic training. Going from the Greenbriar to "The Outhouse of the Ozarks" was like falling out of favor with the king and catapulting into catacombs to wage war with an unruly rat pack!

## A Near Miss at Wedded Bliss

We planned for an evening wedding on September 7th at the Zion Evangelical Lutheran Church on Capitol Drive in Milwaukee. This date coincided with Karen's Mother's fiftieth birthday. We asked our friend Dr. V. Raymond Edman to officiate and give us his spiritual seal of approval. Dr. Edman was President of Wheaton College and a Director of the Billy Graham Evangelistic Association.

The rehearsal started upbeat but during the dinner the cuckoo emerged from his clock and brought the nasty news that Dr. Edman wasn't licensed to marry couples in Wisconsin! In Illinois you were in, but in Wisconsin you were living in sin. Apparently there were hidden hang-ups when a man of the cloth crossed the border. It was the biggest mix-up since the margarine mess!

Forewarned about the wages of sin, we searched for a stand-in. Suddenly one of Martin Luther's most valiant vicars vaulted out of the vestry. The shepherd at Zion Lutheran, sizing up the seriousness of the situation, agreed to sign the Certificate. Dr. Edman, the spiritual patriarch, could perform his planned function.

On the crisp cool early autumn evening guests gathered in the sanctuary. Candles hugging the center aisle cast a glorious glow on the bridesmaids walking down the aisle. My anxiety evaporated the moment I saw Karen escorted by her Dad, Hank Mulberger, who lived in Colorado Springs with his second wife. Her mother, Lorraine, was so caught up in the ceremony she stood the entire forty-five minutes! So did the fatigued faithful following her lead.

Glenn Jorian, a soloist for "Songs in the Night" radio program, sang two selections. When Dr. Edman asked if anyone knew of a reason why we shouldn't be united in holy matrimony, I feared he had gotten wind of Gaylord Nelson's headquarters, or worse, Sophie's "Little Lover Pills." Thank God, everyone held their peace.

At our reception in the garden of the Wisconsin Club, Gabriel DiPiazza, a concert pianist, provided the music. I was extremely disappointed he didn't play the "Caisson Song!"

During the planning stage there was a lively debate surrounding the spiritual sensitivity of serving champagne at the reception. In honor of Jesus' first miracle we popped the corks and let the bubbles effervesce past midnight.

After a sleepless night at a secret rendezvous, we boarded a Denver-bound train in Chicago. Karen's dad, Hank, loaned us his station wagon. He also handed us two tickets to the Air Force Academy vs. University of Washington football game.

This smashed our pre-nuptial agreement to smithereens. We covenanted that I wouldn't be a sports fanatic and Karen wouldn't become a shopoholic. The morning of the big game we hit the stores. At least we tore this agreement asunder, together. Neither of us has transgressed this turf since!

The aspen were arrayed in their golden glory as we neared Estes Park. We found a cozy cedar cabin near a swift flowing stream. Leisurely walks during the day and flickering fires at night was our paradise gained. Then it was on to Aspen, Mesa Verde and the Black Canyon of the Gunnison.

After the two weeks slipped away we returned what remained of Hank's car and went back to the Windy City.

## Pounded by Pancakes

Our two and one-half room apartment on North Sheridan Road was a high diver's dream—Lake Michigan loomed directly below our bedroom window. However, we weren't allowed to catch our dinner, as fishing was forbidden above the third floor.

The kitchen became Karen's playground, as she created her culinary concoctions like a researcher on a roll. Her most infamous inspirations were plump pancakes that could pass for sandbags. Tons of fruit, nuts and novelties were poured into each batch. Then whip cream artistry took over.

Dollar signs dangled in front of my eyes. We could revolutionize the supermarkets. Envision skipping down the aisles and spying "Karen's Portly Pancakes" packaged in oil drums! Station wagons would be at a premium.

Pancake euphoria was no blessing in disguise. Tantalized taste buds gave way to blatant bulges. As the girth grew at an alarming rate, I turned over my entire wardrobe to my tailor and went shopping for suits at two-for-the-price of one sales. I also sentenced myself to lifelong aerobic activity.

Karen's entrepreneur plans were put on hold. She had a higher calling. Employed as a case worker for Illinois Children's Home and Aid Society, she worked with unwed mothers and placed babies with adoptive couples.

A couple of times she wanted to bring her work home, but I wasn't ready for dirty diapers and sleepless nights. At that age they couldn't even help me eat the pancakes.

However, we weren't childless. Kids in our building were turned loose to fend for themselves. Bobby, age three, was given a dollar each morning and then put out to pasture by his parents. He crossed six-lane Sheridan Road by himself to blow his bonanza on candy at the corner store. The wandering waif waited at our door at night and joined us for dinner.

## JFK Blown Away

Two and one-half months after our marriage, President John F. Kennedy was assassinated in Dallas and the nation was plunged into mourning. The thousand-day reign of Camelot came to a crushing close, and the word went forth from that time and place wounding the hearts of the people. We wrestled with the word, but it wore us out. Denial danced with delirium and disbelief dissolved into tears. Shell-shocked by pain and confusion, the soul of our country stood still for four days.

Was this the work of one wounded spirit named Lee Harvey Oswald or was there a cataclysmic conspiracy to kill us all? Would revenge run rampant and push people beyond the point of no return? Sobering thoughts surrounded the loss of our fallen leader.

When I heard the word I was working on an audit of John R. Thompson Co. on Clark Street. I was numbed by the news and devastated by the reaction of its bearer, Ron Burris. His only concern was whether LBJ would ruin the country! Couldn't Ron find one ounce of grief for our Commander in Chief who had been murdered in the back seat of his car? Wasn't it possible to bypass bias for one brief moment of mourning?

Reconciling bank accounts was no way to respond to the event wrenching the world! I hurried home and watched the story unfold on the networks, including the demise of the Dallas assassin. Karen and I shared in the shame as well as the sorrow.

## The Newport of the West

Often on weekends we escaped Chicago to drive to Oconomowoc Lake, thirty miles west of Milwaukee. As a child, Karen spent summers on this lake where her grandparents had established a homestead. One hot Friday afternoon we headed for the border in our first car—a classy 1956 two-tone Chevrolet coupe pushing 100,000 miles.

Two miles after entering Edens Expressway, the roof caved in! It had help from the hood, which dislodged and wrapped over the windshield as I struggled to keep tempo with the sixty-mile-an hour pace in the passing lane. The terrorizing thud on the top of our car made me as tense as a lightning rod with thunder phobia. With visibility reduced to two inches, I jerked the veering vehicle towards the shoulder of this six-lane expressway.

Sounds of irritability resonated from the rear—there was more honking than roundup time at the Horicon Marsh! Couldn't they see that this four-wheeler was a wounded duck with a blind driver? Karen was hanging out the window warding off cars as if we were quarantined.

Safely arriving at our highway haven I was faced with a car resembling a pit bull that lost its jaw in a barroom brawl. I peeled the metal off the glass and wrestled the hood back to its roots. Latching it to the grill with my leather belt, we were ready to hit the road again.

We arrived in Oconomowoc only a half hour late. However, with our faith in the Chevy fading fast we sold it sight seen for two hundred dollars.

The following summer we learned about a large Victorian house we admired, on the south shore of Oconomowoc Lake, that was for sale. We had inspected this palatial property as best we could on many of our Lewis and Clark canoe expeditions into the inlets.

This time we paddled past the vast frontage and skimmed under the bridge to a lagoon with a wooded island in the middle. Perched on a lofty ridge, the Queen Anne house of twenty gables stretched out like a luxury liner riding the high seas.

We had dreamed of moving someday. Chicago was exciting, but breathing was brutal, solving pollution was political ping-pong and traffic always tangled itself in a tight web. Our friends and church would be missed but visions of tiny tots on the distant horizon led us to pursue the possibilities.

The Victorian was vacant for six months because of the untimely passing of its owner, A. D. Braun, who died of a heart attack in Mexico on January 25, 1964.

This one-man Milwaukee business conglomerate had interests in real estate development, investing in fine art, operating a bottling company and raising prize Holsteins. His plans for a sixteen-million dollar downtown Milwaukee Convention Center never materialized due to his death.

A. D. Braun's vast collection of paintings, tapestries, sculptures, coins, jewelry, jades, Orientals and furniture were sold at a four-day public auction on the premises. Buyers appeared from all over the nation to bid in the largest auction of private treasures in the history of Wisconsin. A New York art dealer dealt for John Singer Sargent portraits, and the Mexican government purchased the valuable Oroscos, Tomayas and Diego Riveras paintings.

A. D. Braun and his wife lived on the property for only three years. They purchased the 152-acre estate in 1961 from Herbert Dickinson, the chauffeur of Levi Merrick, a Chicago tobacco merchant who built the house in 1882 as a summer home. It was designed after a stately Queen Anne overlooking the Hudson River in New York.

At the turn of the century, the Merrick estate was one of many mansions built around the lakes by wealthy Chicago, Milwaukee and St. Louis residents. Oconomowoc rivaled Lake Geneva as "The Newport of the West."

The Merricks had to find a new chauffeur when their daughter Zella married Herbert Dickinson during World War I. The children had over one hundred Shetlands to choose from for their pony races. Not to be outdone by the younger generation, Mr. Merrick built a track on the farm for harness racing. The sulkies were a popular sight until the zoning zebras caught up with them! Upon the death of Zella, Mr. Dickinson sold the estate to A. D. Braun.

A. D. was dead, so we settled for dealing with his handpicked executors. The farm portion had been sold but there was thirty-five acres on 1800 feet of lake frontage remaining. However, a conquer and divide developer was darkening the doorstep. The executors told us on the phone about a picture in the Milwaukee Sentinel captioned, "Last Look at Lake Home," which detailed the proposed massacre of Merrick's monument to a bygone era. This wasn't mercy killing—it was the mauling of his mansion! Pained by the mental picture of graceful gables being ground into dust, we requested a meeting. Like prisoners on death row we were granted our last request.

The mile-long driveway was silhouetted by stately American elms that survived the deadly Dutch invasion. Partially blinded by the setting sun, we set foot on the porch where we were greeted by the executors.

Inside it appeared as if a gang of ghosts had been granted asylum. Alfred Hitchcock must be setting up for Psycho II! The fine arts were long gone, and even the kitchen sink was among the missing.

We were ushered to the study of the vacant Victorian for a serious session with James Frisch and William Churchill. They stated that A. D. Braun, who was their buddy as well as business partner, always desired that his property remain a single section. With the intestinal fortitude of a funeral director resting his case, we assured them we would keep the body of the property intact. The demolition demons would never get their clutches on this elegant edifice. Rigor mortis recoiled as we painted a picture of a resurrected residence full of new life. After reminding us a rapid reply was required to ward off the army of Earth-beating machines, we were given twenty-four hours to submit a serious bid.

Part of the day was spent digging up the down payment. When our shovels hit rock we were granted another day of grace. Praying like a parson about to proof preach, we sensed the Lord had set this property aside for a purpose.

That afternoon we submitted our offer and on the third day received the call that changed the direction of our lives. The executors executed the designs of the developer and handed us the house on a silver platter. They accepted a lower offer so we could carry out a higher calling!

The house remained haunted until April as we cleared up commitments in Chicago. With no furniture, we put the heat on hold and stayed with the Clyde Shaws on weekends. Clyde and Eugenia Shaw's house was situated on Beach Road at the foot of the old Valentine Estate. Their daughter Nancy was Karen's best friend during her teenage years. The Shaws were radiant role models for us, and their warmth and hospitality will never be forgotten.

## Beetlemania

After New Year's we received notice from the Village of Oconomowoc Lake that the Dutch had done in the aristocratic American elms. Beetlemania was running rampant around the lake and it had nothing to do with Ringo.

It would take more than a "Hard Day's Night" to cast out these demons which were deadlier than Legionnaire's Disease. With exorcisms proving ineffective, we spent weekends cutting these tall timeless trees down to size and burning them at the stake. I can still hear the beetles bawling at the dump, as they pleaded in vain for mercy!

I hired David Miles from Stone Bank to carry out the sentence. Bearing the smirk of a seasoned executioner, he was the best beetle beater in the Midwest.

One Saturday afternoon when Dave and I were disposing of dead elms by the bridge, we were distracted by a squad car. The officers bore bad news—Karen's car had careened down a fifty-foot embankment landing wheels up in the water! The cop wouldn't give any more details except that she slid off a curve on Pabst Road and rolled into a wet inlet called "Granny's Gully."

Dark thoughts muddied my mind as we drove to the scene. By the time we arrived, curiosity seekers were gawking over "Granny's Gully" as if it was the Grand Canyon. Our new 1964 Chevrolet station wagon was treading water as Karen was carried up the steep incline on a stretcher. I raced to her side and the first thing she said was her back felt broken. Next she wanted to know where our basset hound Winston was.

Caked with mud crud, Karen was put in the ambulance and driven to Oconomowoc Hospital.

She was diagnosed as having broken vertebrae in her back and would have to wear a brace for a few months.

After being wheeled to her hospital room, Karen related the riddle of her ramshackle ride. Halfway through the hairpin turn she applied the brakes which locked, causing the car to skid to the brink of the embankment. The wagon rolled over twice until it was bottoms up in a couple feet of cold water.

Winston, our beleaguered basset, crashed through the window like a wincing wildcat! Adrenaline flowed freely as Karen forced open the door and crawled out to the crunch of collapsing ice. Winston's aerial artistry propelled him into deeper water. Karen in cold pursuit of her prize pet finally collared him and dragged him to higher ground.

A woman who heard the hubbub, but wouldn't offer any direct help despite Karen's persistent pleas, must have alerted the police. Another lady took care of Winston until we could reclaim him.

After Karen was released from the hospital we borrowed a car and drove back to Chicago. Acting bionic, she shunned the back brace and barged ahead with packing for the big move. Because her bones never knit properly, her back became a burden.

Many years later Karen's back was restored through the healing gifts of a house guest from Zambia, Africa. Archbishop

Emmanual Milingo laid hands on her afflicted area and it was made whole in the name of Jesus.

Winston recovered without reconstruction. His main pain was psychological—he had a fear of flying! His beer belly still swept the floor as he swayed from room to room.

The car even tried to make a curious comeback, but we lost all love for this wayward wagon. The prodigal son would have to start his search for a new set of parents.

The insurance agent, the car dealer and General Motors all displayed disinterest in dealing with this dilemma. We gave each prophet of doom his day but they pleaded not guilty and pointed the finger at each other. The labor negotiations lasted for weeks before they produced an identical twin. We wagered our bad breaks were behind us—lightning never strikes a wagon twice in the same spot!

April, 1965, was the appointed time for the big push from the Land of Lincoln to the Promised Land. We exchanged the greening of the Chicago River for milk and honey minus the margarine.

The advance party included a platoon of painters who doctored up the dull grays before we hung the damask drapes—the only legacy left from the A. D. Braun era except three crystal chandeliers.

When we moved our furniture into this fifteen-room high-ceiling hermitage, it resembled a smattering of peas in a giant pod. In the months ahead, Karen's mother donated some family furniture to wean us from our wilderness.

Meanwhile, every spare moment was dedicated to the momentous task of resurrecting this relic. The kitchen was the most noticeable nominee in need. Restoration was out of the question as there was nothing left to restore! A new birth was in order. We hired Bob Mologne from Milwaukee to create a custom kitchen, while we went on a forty-day fast at fast-food factories.

## From Here to Maternity

I took another public accounting position with Michael Mulligan from Mequon who operated a firm out of his home.

Michael Mulligan & Co. was so small I was its only visible employee. Mr. Mulligan's idea of out-of-town work was driving to Menomonee Falls for the afternoon to balance the books of the local butcher.

Michael Mulligan was a mystery. He was a shriveled-up chap suffering from emphysema who still smoked like a scrapyard of smoldering tires. With his wad of weeds wedged in his shirt pocket, the whiff was always with him. When he wasn't puffing, he was panting or cussing! As cranky as a Model T Ford, his forte was mouthing malice and shouting sarcastic replies to anyone with the courage to ask questions.

By mid-morning Mr. Mulligan rocked the room with his oxygen deprivation routine. Under these cataclysmic conditions I kept one hand on my working papers and the other on the phone in case he didn't surface. Some days I was so distracted I couldn't distinguish a debit from a credit. I empathized with the man but I detested the way he was dealing with his affliction.

Meanwhile, Mr. Mulligan kept me in camp with subtle hints of my impending superstar status. A month later he greeted me with a grim message—his doctor commanded him to cash in his accounts. The weary warrior's marching orders spelled retreat.

When I confronted him about the chances of taking over his business, he dashed my hopes into eternal darkness with a distressing diatribe about dealing his clients to a competitor. Remaining as hard-nosed as the Mt. Rushmore four, Mr. Mulligan refused to give me a second chance. I would have to chisel out another niche for my career. Ten days later I landed a job with Reilly, Penner & Benton, a CPA firm in Milwaukee.

Michael Mulligan met his maker six months later. I hope his credits exceeded his debits. It was definitely in his favor that I wasn't conducting the final audit!

## The Stork Strikes at Midnight

Proving that actions speak louder than words, Karen became pregnant in May. Our joy was tempered six weeks later when Karen came down with German measles. This nemesis sweeping the nation was devastating for those with child, as the magazines featured negative articles and grotesque pictures of deformed babies.

If German measles were Hitler's last hurrah, he was still hailing havoc on the human race. Many knowledgeable people were promoting abortion as the answer, including Karen's obstetrician. He had seen firsthand the results of these fetal malformations.

Discussing abortion as an intellectual exercise is a shallow substitute. Faced with real facts, our former words were washed away by a flood of newfound feelings. God blessed us with a child, and the strength of our childlike faith would be the catalyst to carry us through.

We prepared for our first Christmas in our new home by cutting down a Norway pine at a tree farm. The pine looked smaller in the field, but now that it was finally secured to the luggage rack it resembled the Jolly Green Giant. We could have passed for a float in the Arbor Day parade as the only visible vestige of the vehicle was its tires. If this wagon rolled down "Granny's Gully" we would at least have a soft landing.

Lugging this woodland wonder home was only half the struggle—yanking it through the door in an all-out tug-of-war was the other. This tall piece of timber was relegated to the two-story stairwell. We felt very close to nature over the holidays—we were living in it.

Karen's due date was near her January 20th birthdate. As the day drew close there were outward signs of the inner work. If kicking was the clue, we had a kangaroo about to leap out at the first sign of labor. The 20th passed and no papoose.

My brother Jim, who worked for IBM in Milwaukee, was living with us for a few weeks. By the 25th Karen was a week overdue. It was twenty below and winter winds were whipping.

Jim and I were watching television in the living room when suddenly there was a stir at the top of the winding staircase. Karen shouted that the water had burst! I was so shook I started to phone Sterling Mainz our plumber, when at the last second my sixth sense told me to call Dr. Verch instead.

It was thirty miles to Milwaukee Lutheran Hospital—any less and I would be put to the test. I wrapped Karen in a blanket and we disappeared into the dark garage. If the engine didn't turn over I would be pressed into an instant deliverance ministry.

After a few wimpy wails, the wagon erupted as I floored it. When we reached I-94, Karen wanted me to find a closer hospital. In five seconds we hit 90 M.P.H. This was one night I craved a cop's attention. The two of us could collaborate as a roadside MASH unit!

As we approached the Waukesha exit, the contractions got closer. Karen continued to suggest an alternate but I vetoed her proposal. A bitter cold night was no time to embark on a Ponce de Leon expedition. The Fountain of Youth was easier to find than Waukesha Hospital, as the dude who designed the road system must have been a victim of vertigo.

When we arrived at Milwaukee Lutheran, Dr. Verch was among the missing. His staff acted as cool as canaries chirping catcalls. If they wanted their waiting room turned into a delivery room it was okay with me—just don't charge us the full rate!

They finally assigned Karen a room. I stayed and prayed with her through every piercing pain. An intern bounded in with a case of bad bedside manner. He kept reminding us of the chances of deformity. This drove us deeper into faith that the Lord would complete his creative work.

Dr. Verch arrived and decided it was time to wheel Karen to the delivery room. I was relegated to the worry and wonder area where a smiling Dr. Verch appeared a couple of hours later. Either our child was all right or this man was a sadist! I knew it couldn't be the latter—after thirty years in the baby business any shadow side would have surfaced by now. He delivered Karen twenty-six years before and she was still kicking.

We were blessed with a beautiful black-haired baby girl. Dr. Verch declared her perfect except for a slight strain of stubbornness. Tears of joy welled up inside as Karen and I celebrated like lifers released on a full pardon.

The intern was nowhere in sight. I peeked through the glass partition at our pink-cheeked present. I told everyone she waved, but I flunked the polygraph test.

We named our firstborn Krista Lorraine Swanson. Later on when I got to hold her I realized I was embracing the warmth of a loving God. Our burden had lifted.

Karen, concerned Krista might get cold, asked me to bring her some warmer clothes. Putting faith to the test she had previously purchased an arsenal of baby girl attire.

Convinced it was unconventional to cart a newborn's wardrobe to the hospital, I snuck up the back stairs with Krista's ensemble stuffed under my coat. I crept down the corridor like a cat burglar on a mice heist and slipped into Karen's corner room. Even she looked surprised at the size of Krista's classic collection as I stuffed it in a drawer before it was confiscated by a nosy nurse.

Every time Krista was brought in the room Karen garbed her in a different outfit. It didn't matter that she drowned in the dresses as long as her proud mother got a large charge out of the fashion show.

## Vaudeville Visits the Victorian

The show closed down after a four-day run. New attire got scarce and the model protested the hours. Musicals don't survive long with the same audience! We packed our bags and took the show on the road.

When we arrived home the baby nurse was waiting. Karen's mother, insisting we needed assistance, hired Ipha Sutter from an agency. She wore white attire but her demeanor was straight out of central casting's comedy classics. Ipha's lean five-foot frame hunched over at the shoulders. Weathered wrinkles said she was on the far side of seventy. I upped the ante five when she insisted we call her Granny.

Granny's lithe limbs allowed her to leap from room to room like a leprechaun. She lugged Krista under her arm as if she was carrying a pigskin. Karen got concerned Granny might fumble our baby down the back staircase.

Granny's incessant smoking set off our internal alarm. With one weed after another listing from her lower lip she looked more like a blackjack dealer from Las Vegas than a baby nurse.

With our home and baby on the line, we checked Granny's credentials. Born Nov. 21, 1879 in New York made her three years older than our house! Her parents were vaudeville entertainers which accounted for Granny's acrobatic antics. At 87 years young, she could do soft shoe and tell spellbinding stories. Granny outlived three husbands including a symphony conductor.

The way Granny bonded to babies in her brood, the new mother might as well fly south for the winter. Possessiveness may be nine tenths of the law but it was not pleasing to Karen's caring instincts. Why suffer through morning sickness and miss motherhood?

The three-ring circus short-circuited our sleep. Not wanting the circus to move on, we provided an alternate arena. We put Granny on permanent KP so we could cuddle our kid! Attacking her chores like a chimney sweep, she cooked, washed clothes and climbed ladders to clean kitchen cabinets.

Granny Sutter never folded her tents. She lived in her own house in Oconomowoc until she hit one hundred years. She rode a bike and carried groceries home.

In 1979 she moved into Shorehaven Nursing Home in town, so she could help wheel the old folks around. She could still shuffle soft shoe and relate amusing stories. She cashed in her cigarettes for fear it would stunt her growth, but Granny always grabbed Krista under her arm like the good old days.

At 108 years old she failed some but hung on as tough as a settler supported by squatter's rights.

The following December when our prayer fellowship sang Christmas carols at Shorehaven, Granny was stretched out on a lounge chair in the front row. She was out of touch physically but her spirit synthesized the sound. I was expecting her to rise from the recliner and render one last rousing rendition from her vaudeville repertoire, when I realized Granny was going to miss this curtain call. She was saving her dancing shoes for her next engagement.

Karen kissed Granny on the cheek and whispered, "Jesus Loves You." The next day Granny Sutter put on a command performance for the King of Kings. She was 109!

# 5

# From Religious Roots to the Rapture

Karen was baptized as an infant in the Roman Catholic Church. Her maternal grandmother, Mrs. Harry John, was the guiding light. However, Karen's parents rejected organized religion and gravitated towards metaphysical philosophies. As a result her religious roots were never enriched and she was raised a churchless child. Karen's only contact with Christianity was occasionally attending Mass during her brief student days at St. Jerome's grade school in Oconomowoc.

Karen's chances of having a happy childhood were clouded by her parents' divorce when she was seven years old. Her mother, Lorraine, withdrew from the world, and fears filled their home. Except for school, Mike and Karen's only contacts were visits with their grandparents. Harry John Sr. was the bright star on the bleak scene during the kids' formative years. His passion was growing flowers in his greenhouse. Karen helped him share the fruit of his labor with everyone they met.

By thirteen, Karen's spirit was tormented to the point that she was planning on ending her life if God didn't reveal himself.

The following day as she and Grandpa Harry were fishing off the pier at their Oconomowoc Lake home, they were hailed by a hearty middle-aged man in a canoe. Tony Reno was his name and Karen would never be the same. Bubbling over with a heavy Italian accent, Tony told them how the Heavenly Father put his fishing pole on hold and prompted him to paddle across the lake.

This fisher of men pulled out his work card which had John 3:16 printed on the back and testified about his terrible struggle with tuberculosis as a teenager. Tony was about to darken death's door when a Pentecostal pastor, Rev. Joseph Wannemacher, prayed for his physical healing. Shortly thereafter Tony walked out of the hospital with new life and has been spreading the good news ever since.

Tony tossed his nets out to catch Harry John. However, Harry became part piranha when faced with spiritual matters and managed to chew through! Karen, the next candidate, was too tired to put up a struggle. A fishnet serves as a life preserver for someone who has been treading water since the day they were born. Tony was no intruder—he came armed with the answer to Karen's lonely search. The faith-filled fisherman's missionary journey across the lake netted a real keeper. Karen joined her future to Jesus and has never looked back.

Karen tuned into Youth for Christ programs on the radio. The second time she attended a Youth for Christ Club at Wauwatosa High School they elected her President. Her crash course in Christianity was on-the-job training. Her joy for Jesus escalated into contagious charisma as she fed on the Word of God and drank living waters.

Karen's first encounter with a consecrated Christian family were the Robert Simons from Elm Grove. Bob and Esther graciously opened their home and their children Sandy, Carol and Jim became Karen's good friends. Through their loving example she discovered that health in the home was not an anomaly.

After Karen graduated from Milwaukee Lutheran High School in 1957, she enrolled in Milwaukee Downers Women's College.

During this period she met Dr. V. Raymond Edman, the President of Wheaton College. He was a kind soft-spoken saint who served in the mission field for thirty years. As a member of Billy Graham's board, Billy referred to Dr. Edman as his right arm. The next semester Karen joined the Wheaton College family.

The bleak days of Karen's confining childhood were over. Wheaton was a winter wonderland. Before long she had more friends than the Friends Society and they weren't limited to students. In addition to Dr. Edman, her sociology professor, Dr. Gordon James, and his wife Dorothea, opened their lives to her.

Gordon found field training for Karen with Evangelical Child Welfare, an adoption agency. His pet project was setting up summer adventures for Wheaton students in Spanish Harlem in New

York. The program, called Youth Development Inc., was headed by Jim Voss, a former wiretapper for Mickey Cohen, the West Coast gangster. When Jim became a Christian he converted his talents to ministering to teen gangs.

Karen signed up for Harlem as if it were her heavenly reward. However, her mother was not amused by her daughter's sudden gravitation to gangs and gangsters! She knighted Norman Klug, the President of the Miller Brewing Co., to act as her special agent. His assignment was to fly to New York and bring this wild Wheaton Crusader back alive.

Norman Klug, at 5 ft. 5 in., 135 lbs., proved to be no match for the mettle of this mission-minded maiden. Wooing this warrior with candlelight dinners at exclusive clubs and Broadway shows turned into fun and run games—fun in Manhattan and a mad dash back to Harlem.

As a hardened, lifetime lawyer, Stormin' Norman countered with legal persuasion. Karen, refusing to be corralled, dodged his lariat and headed for Harlem to grapple with the gangs. Norman was forced to lick his wounds and fly back to Milwaukee to meet with Mrs. Mulberger. Both were in big time danger!

## The Bogeyman of Braidburn Goes Bananas

My faith venture, which began in the Evangelical Covenant Church, was tested in my teen years. My parents, their friends and church youth counselors provided me with a firm foundation but now it was time to find Jesus on my own.

At thirteen I caddied at Braidburn Country Club, a five-iron shot from our Florham Park, N.J. home. Shagging wee white balls in the weeds on weekends wasn't my picture of paradise, but I discovered there was gold in "them thar hills." Thirty-six holes could clear sixteen dollars a day, carrying double.

The worst combo was to caddy for two hackers that included a hooker and a slicer. Caddies had to be cross-eyed to keep up with this chicanery. Lost balls triggered tongue-lashings—the rewards for lugging hundreds of pounds of leather and heavy metal over twisted terrain on the eternal search. Meanwhile, the foul-mouthed foursome from behind is spraying the course with drives designed to put the whole pack out of the picture.

One humid August afternoon, as I was carrying two bulging bags that were clearly clones of their owners, tempers started to rival the temperature. The foursome was waging an uphill fight against shanked shots, lost balls and four-putt greens. As we approached the eighteenth hole all I could think of was a cold Coke in the caddyshack.

My divot-digging duffers had been swinging as if they were breaking ground for an irrigation project. They both needed a hole-in-one on the 430-yard eighteenth to break 110! However, what was really ruining their day wasn't the raw score but the $100-a-hole wager with their opponents.

Mr. Portello, with three hundred dollars down the drain, was desperate to salvage the last hole. He had such a huge hitch in his swing he was capable of hooking a putt. Despite his flawed flailings, his second shot landed only seventy-yards from the pin. Straightening his sand-colored safari hat, he called me aside to advise on club selection. I gave him a nine iron to make sure he would clear the mean ravine in front of the green. He shanked the shot short and slammed the iron to the turf.

Now it was wedge all the way as the ball sat precariously near the edge of the ledge. With nerves of steel Mr. Portello took another swipe and the ball bounded into the bubbling brook as if it were dying of thirst—the wedge went next. He assassinated my character with cuss words as he charged the ravine like a rabid buffalo. When I tried to retrieve his club, he ripped the bag off my back with such force I felt I was being separated from my shoulders. Fifty pounds of paraphernalia sailed through the air with the greatest of ease, landing ten feet from his golf ball in the brook. The bag was well-stocked but lacked scuba diving equipment!

Mr. Portello refused to let me reclaim his rubbish but by the time we reached the clubhouse he changed his mind.

I returned to the ravine as another foursome was fast approaching. They appeared as bewildered as bats running low on radar until I shed some light on the litter causing this landfill. They laughed and helped me get a grip on all the goods.

Meanwhile back at the clubhouse, Mr. Portello was belting down brews, so I boycotted the bar and brought his heavy artillery straight to the locker room. I had no worries about my fee—being free of this firecracker was reward enough.

The next day the caddy master handed me an envelope with fifteen dollars in it. Either the beers had buoyed Mr. Portello's spirits or he was afraid I would report him to the Humane Society!

I caddied for the Bogeyman of Braidburn numerous times again. My motivation for this masochism was money—his was the fear of linking up with a caddy who couldn't swim. His hitch still put a glitch in his game but his temper got more tepid with time. Losing $100 a hole left little in the budget for buying new bags!

Braidburn bustled on weekends but often fizzled during the week. Many caddies killed time by shooting craps or playing cards while others grazed on the hillside like sheep or fell asleep.

I enjoyed meditating on the magnificence of nature and dreaming of faraway places with strange sounding names. Awed by the Master's stroke of splendor, I envisioned Him coming on the cotton puff clouds drifting across the skyline.

I always believed Jesus was on my side but I sidestepped Him on many occasions. Now was a great opportunity to meet him face to face. Jesus was gentle as I poured out my problems. I questioned him about my perception of being shortchanged on Creation Day and secretly stitched together on the seventh.

Enraptured by the real presence of His Spirit, I laid down my lawyer leanings and came as I was without any further pleas. Repenting of my pop-up target tendencies, I promised to press on for the prize pronto.

I hurried home before Mr. Portello appeared with his bag. I had just experienced a glorious salvation—baptism by total immersion could wait for another day!

Witnessing about my faith wasn't easy as I was often panicked by the primal pretenses of my peers. When traveling evangelists read the religious riot act, I headed for cover. I pounded baseballs over right field fences but had problems knocking down doors and dragging people away from the snares of the devil. I prayed that "The Rapture" would take place so I would be spared—my witness would be rising to the occasion as part of the biggest air show in history!

Fortunately Jesus didn't have the same agenda as some of His dash-and-dare disciples. I found out I didn't have to perform for Him—He had already seen all the shows. His Father always provided Him with season tickets in the front row. Jesus took away my guilt and set me free to be a witness not a religious robot.

Karen and I traveled different streams but we came to the same river. Jesus answered our spiritual thirst with His oasis of living water. We drank a minimum of eight glasses a day and He kept us afloat in the raging rapids. Many times we branched out into untested tributaries to add a breath of fresh air to our forging faith.

## Kicks, Flips and Spiritual Side Trips

College chapel was a challenge for most students and sometimes presented a problem for speakers also. Live doves were often released to quicken the spirit. Nothing awakened North Park students faster than an activated alarm clock in the middle of the message. The most electrifying chapel service I witnessed was the morning the choir sat in their seats and the chairs were wired for shock. Three rows jolted up in unison like they were auditioning for a hemorrhoid ad. This was student unrest at its best!

Some Sunday nights we ventured down to First Church of Deliverance near 42nd and Wabash on the south side of Chicago. First Church was black but welcomed whites for their 11:00 p.m. service broadcast live on WCFL radio. The narthex of this large tabernacle had a huge painting depicting Jesus with skin a few shades darker than Warner Salman's Swedish Covenant version.

The ushers dressed in stunning black-and-white outfits with white gloves. The center aisle was reserved for their pastor, Rev. Clarence J. Cobb, whose Cadillac pulled up in front of First Church at exactly 10:55 p.m. He jumped out of the back seat and greeted the gathered throng as if it was opening night on Broadway. As he made his grand entrance down the center aisle, parishioners arose to pay him homage. The instant Rev. Cobb sat down the choir wisped in from the wings like a rushing wind.

Reminiscent of the white-robed remnant from Revelation, this mighty fortress burst forth with "Jesus is the Light of the World." Goosebumps trickled down my tailbone as the 200 power-packed voices climbed to a celestial crescendo rocking the foundations of the church.

Next came a rousing rendition of "Joshua Fought the Battle of Jericho." The choir vociferated with so much volume it would have been anti-climactic for the walls to come down! Impassioned parishioners, keeping a perfect beat with thumping feet, sent back a barrage of "Amens," "hallelujahs," "sing it," and "I feel it." Some of the flock "feeling it" left their feet, slumping back into their chairs. Two sopranos, seized by the Spirit, landed on the stage floor. Ushers rushed down the side aisles to assist these supine saints.

Those still standing eased into "The Lord's Prayer" as Rev. Clarence J. Cobb came to the microphone. His patented preacher style was long on oratory and short on content. He never minced words nor did he change any—after attending a few times I could recite his entire sermon. "Brothers and sisters, those on the airwaves, the highways and byways; our brethren in prisons, institutions and hospitals all over this city; let's gather in tonight, let's gather in to crush the power of sin! Let's atone! Let's atone tonight, brothers and sisters—close to the throne. Close to the throne, my brothers! Close to the throne!"

Dr. Cobb continued this cadence for ten minutes and then took an offering. After a few more upbeat numbers the choir marched out the side doors singing, "When the Saints Go Marching In." The happy throng regrouped in the basement for refreshments and fellowship.

I visited First Church of Deliverance to hear the music and mix with the brothers and sisters. First Church was a far cry from North Park Covenant, but the Lord meets us where we're at.

Karen attended First Church many times with her Wheaton friends. She claims she saw me leave on a stretcher one night, but I categorically deny it!

## Snake Handlers at Scrabble Creek

Karen and I had so much fun together, the Lord must have felt guilty for not letting us search for seashells sooner. He atoned by sending us to Charleston, West Virginia, to visit Dot and Gordon James.

In 1963 Gordon took a leave of absence from Wheaton to head up a poverty study in Appalachia for Bobby Kennedy.

The night we arrived, Gordon shared many exciting encounters—his life was inundated with intrigue. He asked us if we were up to witnessing snake handling in the hollers of Scrabble Creek. He knew he had a soft sell—the snakes couldn't shake us any more than Sophie Tucker.

After a thirty-mile trip over tail-busting terrain, we passed a row of ramshackle shacks on the edge of town. Leaving a trail of tears for anyone allergic to gravel dust, Gordon bludgeoned the brakes as we slid to a screeching halt in front of the church.

The Scrabble Creek Church could never be confused with the Crystal Cathedral. It was a patchwork of wooden folk art put up in an era of moonshine madness—each generation added its appendage.

Darkness dumped its blanket as we approached the paint-starved steps. The sounds of electric guitars pierced the peaceful valley with the twangy tune of "Thank God I'm Still Alive." Hand hewn benches provided our perch for the proceedings.

Rev. E. P. Priestly and two sidekicks attacked their guitars with such frenzy their duds were drowning in Scrabble Creek sweat. If "Thank God I'm Still Alive" had more lyrics, they were saving them till Labor Day—there was no need for a teleprompter.

Tambourines and foot stomping rattled the serpents' cages as a young lady leaped to her feet to perform a disjointed dance—every joint was jumping in a different direction. Her jutting jaw and cobra contortions caused a stir as this whirling dervish spun around the sanctuary. The real message of "Thank God I'm Still Alive" was starting to arrive.

Meanwhile, a Burl Ives beardnik was hopping around the church like a perennial pogo stick. It's good this guy wasn't passing the plate or coins would disappear down the cracks faster than crickets! Gordon introduced him as Jumping Charlie. He had more bounce to the ounce than a kangaroo with caffeine fits. Shaking hands with Jumping Charlie was like priming a pump—he had mastered the ancient art of bouncing, bobbing and conversing at the same time. Playing the perfect host he invited us to join him— we politely passed up this once-in-a-lifetime opportunity!

After two hours of faith-building fervor, the rattlers were still rattling in the shadows of their secluded sanctuaries. The only thing that separated them from us were wire meshed wooden boxes with carved crosses resembling serpents. Maybe the church roof had to be blown off before they were released.

Gordon got antsy. Seeing him pace like a panting panther convinced us it was time to pull out. Thank God Gordon didn't desire to handle the snakes—I had no license to drive a hearse through the hollows!

Gordon shared startling facts as he stomped on the pedal. Snakes have smitten Jumping Charlie seventeen times over three decades and he is still leaping. He often sips strychnine for an encore!

On a previous visit, Rev. E. P. Priestley warned Gordon, "Ya can't read Mark 16:17-18 and skip over the serpent part. If ya lay hands on the sick, ya have to handle snakes. Some say we're temptin' God—ya can't tempt God doin' what He says ya should do! For those that think this is a show, let them thusly reach into the serpent box!" Gordon added, "There were no takers that night."

Not persuaded by the pedigree of E.P.'s degrees for interpreting Scripture, I continued to distance myself from reptiles. It's true that the number of reported deaths among snake handling sects since 1909 is minimal, but the few who flunked their test of faith are too far gone to retake the exam! Back then these agonizing deaths were blamed on backsliding—in this enlightened age the reasons have been elevated to lack of faith. Either way it's a grave situation for the family.

The aftershocks of "Thank God I'm Still Alive" were still shaking me when Gordon hit me with another revelation. The Girards,

New York sociologists, studied snake handlers in the state for six months and published an unsettling report—the punchline was, Jumping Charlie and his clan are more stable than the average mainline church member!

How could this be? Were the Girards flakes or were they sounding the alarm? Were silent pew sitters more of an anomaly than Jumping Charlie or the Whirling Dervish? Maybe we were Christian cripples who couldn't crawl to the altar for help while our bodies burned with emotional pain! Was there anybody up front who could put out the fire? Water pistols would never work when we needed the river of living waters!

Questions came easy, answers were agony. We were heading west towards the Windy City but I couldn't shake the Scrabble Creek dust from my feet. Maybe Dick Daley could deal with this dilemma—"His Honor" had handled a few snakes in his day. He should join Rev. E. P. Priestly in "Thank God I'm Still Alive!"

## Identifying The Antichrist

Karen's mother made peace with the Lord after many years of spirited struggle. Her longing for the light was launched by Karen's Christian walk and the witness of many friends of Jesus. Shortly after, Lorraine sold her stock in the Miller Brewing Co., which her grandfather Frederick Miller started—the High Life and Spiritual life didn't mix.

Lorraine attended a fundamental Bible-believing church in Waukesha where the word of the Lord was law and order. Their spiritual ladder leaned so far to the right that an unwary visitor could get clobbered by it.

The first Sunday we heard Rev. Phil Forthright, his sermon centered on the identity of the Antichrist. After an exhausting exegesis from Daniel to Revelation, he revealed the real Antichrist to be our esteemed Secretary of State Henry Kissinger! Why he didn't eliminate the middleman and go straight for Dick Nixon's jugular, I will never know. Three weeks later it was the Pope. Fearful of saying his full name, Pastor Phil left us to guess which one. We assumed it was Pope John XXIII unless it was the position he was assailing.

So far he had nominated one Jew and one Catholic. If I was I gambler I would wager that Martin Luther King was next. Rounding out this field of candidates was like playing Christian "Clue"—who was the culprit? What weapon would he use? Under which dispensation would he do it??

The next time we heard Pastor Phil preach on his favorite subject, the villains' vehicle was the United Nations, which he called a Communist front to take over the world. Would Däg Hammerskjold hammer us home or would Trygve Lie trigger off the insurrection? Either way it appeared as if the Vikings would vault into the end times arena—Uff da! At least this UN connection took the heat off the World Council of Churches, a former target of his hit list.

If Pastor Phil had anything positive to preach he was saving it for another dispensation. Feeding on his sermons was like eating shredded wheat without milk—it left wounds on the way down. If this flock was searching for solid food it would never stomach it as long as the Shepherd was passing off paranoia as pure spiritual milk!

## Getting Old Hogan's Goat

We were churchsick for North Park Covenant in Chicago. Pastor Douglas Cederleaf preached the power of Jesus with a beautiful blend of salvation and social responsibility. He called forth your faith and covered you with compassion. Loving Jesus wasn't a chore anymore—it was a natural expression of friendship.

Dr. Oscar "Ockie" Olson's choir sang stirring hymns but no one passed out or passed on. The trustees never needed to start a stretcher fund.

Occasionally we traveled the 250-mile round trip but discovered that God's arms are longer than ours. We relinquished the grip but will always be graced by the spiritual growth we experienced at North Park Covenant.

After a few months of "check 'em out church hopping," we landed at Our Savior's Lutheran on Fowler Lake in Oconomowoc. This ALC was short on Swedes and long on liturgy, but its redeeming features included an opportunity to work with youth groups. We eventually joined Our Savior's, even though we believed Martin Luther's claim that man was a wretched worm was groundless!

We befriended Alan and Jan Olson through an ecumenical discussion group that met once a month in various homes. Alan had recently graduated from Luther Seminary in St. Paul and was starting his first parish assignment as the assistant pastor at Our Savior's. One of his visions was to pour vitality into a struggling youth group. He conscripted Karen to teach Junior Lutherans and enlisted both of us as honchos for the high school hellions.

Eternal teenage turmoil, the shifting social scene of the sixties and the liberal leanings of Rev. Alan Olson caused a collage of confrontations in the congregation.

Most seminary students are two paces to the left of their potential parishioners. Upon arrival, the young pastor's first mission is to sharpen his chisel and chip away at those plastered in a state of placidity. Doses of the social gospel are dished out daily to cure the small town souls of crippling conservatism. After the friar frees a few parish progressives the fragmented flock start knocking heads in the narthex.

Being new members, most people assumed we were part of Alan Olson's Norwegian Army from the North. Doctrinally we were orthodox and hadn't delved into the demons of demythologizing. Politically we were progressive and fought for fair housing and championed civil rights. We couldn't match Alan's intellect but we supported many of his ideas.

Alan brought in speakers from diverse backgrounds such as Bill Wetzel, a black Episcopalian seminarian from Nashotah House. Bill was part of Jesse Jackson's Operation Breadbasket in Chicago. As a tonic for teens he pounded the pavement day and night helping kids in Oconomowoc. His underground network was as expansive as the New Deal. Bill's biggest challenge was convincing parents there was a drug problem—the burbs still believed all the downing and dealing belonged to the big cities. Bill brought so many kids to our home that he finally moved in.

Meanwhile Alan organized hunger hikes in Milwaukee, but the parents pulled the plug on a planned Civil Rights March with Father James Groppi on the south side.

The possibilities of broken bones on ski trips to the north country were considered safer. On our first trip to the Porcupine Mountains on Lake Superior, Peter Swan, a teen with jumping beans in his genes, fractured his leg on the third run. After being mangled on a mogul, he traded his skis in for crutches and spent the weekend in the Ontonagon Hospital.

Another youth with a yen for adventure hit new heights by poking multiple holes in Hogan's motel ceiling with a cue stick! Three weeks previously I convinced Mr. Hogan that Our Savior's was a civil lot and would cause his motel no harm.

Mr. Hogan summoned me to the pool room to view the carnage. By the time I arrived Mr. Hogan, the peeved and grieved party, was tongue-lashing Sam Turnbull, the turncoat who took his temper out on the acoustical tile. After necktie negotiations, Sam was handed a note to show his parents. The punchline was, "He who plays pool by his own rules must pay the price of being a fool!" I assigned Sam a bodyguard to protect him from himself.

My energies turned towards talking Mr. Hogan into taking us back next year. The selling point was Sam is a senior whose number was already retired. Mr. Hogan put us on probation for a year providing his pool room was patched up pronto.

On our way home our rear right tire blew—the patchwork was a snap compared to what I performed at Porcupine.

# 6

# Swept Away by the Swell
# of the Second Wave

We joined a lively discussion group that debated timely topics monthly. Abortion, civil rights, Christianity, the Vietnam War, drugs and countercultures were all dissected during these sizzling sessions.

Participants in these rewarding repartees from diverse religious persuasions included Brian and Mary Steinke, Alan and Jan Olson, Babs and Ralph Magnus, Barb and Dan Miller, Ted and Sue Cheney, Ken and Ann Chandler, Joe and Cindy Weix and Bill Wetzel. It took us two years of grappling with these issues to solve all the world's ills—with nothing left to discuss we disbanded until further notification of any problems. During this time, Mrs. Eugenia Shaw opened up her rambling ranch home on Oconomowoc Lake for a Women's Bible Study. Every Wednesday morning the Scriptures were studied religiously in the shadows of the Valentine estate. This grand Victorian with its vast verandahs fell victim to a Valentine's Day massacre many years before. The only remnant to escape the carnage is a regal red brick wall which still casts a glimpse of the golden age. The Shaw's house framed the formal gardens.

Karen gave scriptural structure to the sessions. She was amply supported by Krista, who was only five months short of fruition at the time. Among the members of the group were Mary Steinke and Kay Fink. Mary became the local manager of Wauwatosa Realty and Kay was a state leader of the Jehovah's Witnesses prior to her conversion.

Occasionally husbands were allowed to attend this sexist society. Special guests were invited to share at evening sessions. Dick and JoAnne Casper, a young Catholic couple, told of the miraculous cure of their infant daughter who had devel-

85

oped cancer throughout her entire body. They passed around pictures that showed the extent of the disease—the doctors offered no hope. The Great Physician healed their baby in short order through prayer and made her a loving witness of His power and compassion.

The Caspers mentioned Friday night meetings in Elm Grove where faith-filled followers of Jesus gathered in His name. Bill and Lorna Toll, an Assembly of God couple, had the vision to open their home to mainline Christians to share about the current move of the Holy Spirit. The spiritual gifts outlined in the 12th chapter of I Corinthians were manifested in their meetings.

We had heard tales about the Toll's gatherings from Rev. and Mrs. Edwin Ziemann, Assembly of God missionaries to Ghana, Africa. Karen's Elm Grove grade school friend, Lowell Pritchard, introduced us to his in-laws, the Ziemanns. Karen solicited Bernice Ziemann's help in undergirding the Bible study when she was home on furlough.

When the book of Acts study started, Mom Ziemann, as we reverently called her, shared from "They Speak With Other Tongues" by John and Elizabeth Sherrill. Devouring the pages like prophets at their last supper, we were amazed that seemingly sane people were speaking in unknown tongues. If John Sherrill, the editor of Guidepost Magazine, was gripped by glossalalia, who else could be grappling with these grass root gifts?

The book claimed these utterances were intelligible languages to which linguists could trace the origin. Discontinued dark age dialects were being restored by the Lord for full-scale revival. If this boom ballooned, Berlitz was doomed!

I had read "Cross and the Switchblade," the story of Rev. David Wilkerson's passion to preach the power of Jesus to notorious New York ghetto gangs. The book told about teenage toughs turning to the Lord, being baptized in the Holy Spirit and speaking in tongues.

Having enough trouble with tried and true English at the moment, I chalked tongues up to teenage trauma on the big turf.

Karen challenged this phenomenon from a different angle— the psychiatric social worker's sophisticated approach to spirituality. Paraphrased it means, "Better led by the head than leave the ranks of the living dead!" As long as the dead in Christ are slated to rise first at the Rapture, there is no immediate cause for concern. The evangelicals had always taught that the dead in Christ were the mainline churches.

Karen, caught in a crisis of faith, bombarded Mom and Dad Ziemann with every spiritual question conceivable. They never ducked the barrage, but stuck boldly to their beliefs—their faith was built on nothing less than Jesus and his righteousness. The essence of their answers were down to earth.

Jesus, the same yesterday, today and for eternity, provides salvation for the whole person—body, soul and spirit. If we clear the clutter that cuts us off from Christ, the same Spirit that raised Jesus from the dead will quicken our mortal bodies. Two-thirds of his earthly ministry was healing the sick and setting the captives free. His compassion was never eclipsed into celestial bliss— He left his people a Comforter. The fire of the Holy Spirit is forever falling on His flock.

In our hearts we knew Mom and Dad Ziemann were right. Pride glued our shoes to the floor—it would take backbone to bend over and deal with the double knots. It's comforting to read God's word, but it takes courage to respond to it. Mark Twain nailed down the nitty gritty when he said, "It ain't those parts of the Bible I don't understand that bother me, it's the parts that I do understand!"

We understood the message—the still small voice doesn't produce silent partners. Hospitals don't send surgeons into the operating room without instruments—the patients would take a real pounding! Warriors don't reject weapons in the heat of battle. The Great Physician isn't so heavenly minded that He's no earthly good—He equips his saints for surgery and spiritual warfare.

We were challenged to the core, but the apples needed more polishing before we bit off more than we could chew.

## Labor Pain's Eternal Gains

Meanwhile a crisis of faith occurred at Our Savior's Church. Laurie, a blue-eyed blonde, asked the unforgivable question in a

Luther League buzz session—"As a teenager, how can I relate to God personally?" Laurie's leap of faith took a few lunges backward when Bradley Dirkson, the adult sponsor, replied, "Maybe someday when you are about to be a mother, God might meet you in the long suffering of labor." This male chauvinist pain in the brain missed the mark by a mile.

Karen helped Laurie pick up the pieces by offering to host a Tuesday evening teen discussion dedicated to the dynamics of the Christian life. Faith doesn't need to wait for wedlock on Jesus' walk—He already paved the way and has no heart left for labor negotiations!

Laurie rounded up five of her friends to fortify the ranks. Questions popped faster than sparks from the fireplace, as Karen seasoned her answers with salt and the Spirit.

Within a few weeks Laurie, Jan and Sue invited Jesus to live within. Instead of pain there was spiritual gain—instead of new borns the old borns were born again—instead of new names the old names were written in the "Book of Life." Shortly after, Darlene Toll, the teenage daughter of Bill and Lorna Toll, joined the group to undergird their growth.

As the girls shared their newfound faith they became the forerunners of the youth explosion which shook every shingle on our house in the late 60's and early 70's. Laurie married a pastor from a Four Square Gospel church and they cut a musical album called "Simple Again." We sent Bradley Dirkson an autographed copy!

## For Whom the Bell Tolls!

We were told it would take twenty-five minutes to drive to Bill and Lorna Tolls' house in Elm Grove. The first night it took us ten minutes extra—five for getting lost and five for fear of what we would find beyond the front door. There was no need to ring the bell at Tolls as their friendly greetings always awaited their guests.

Bill is a gentle giant with a soft smile and down-home drawl. When he wasn't resurrecting wrecks on his used car lot, he was redeeming lives in his living room. As President of Full Gospel

Businessmen's Fellowship International, the Milwaukee Chapter, he joked, "the only thing longer than the name is the meetings." Lorna helped start the female counterpart called Women's Aglow.

Our anxiety abated a bit as Bill introduced us around the room. We met Jay and June Dalton, a Southern Baptist couple; Sally Redmond, a Catholic housewife; Jeff Siegal, a young Jewish man who recently had met his Messiah; Betty Hall, Edna Reynolds and Nancy Kuzmick from the Pentecostal persuasion. Dick and JoAnn Casper were also present.

The evening began with informal sharings about miracles in Milwaukee and beyond. People were being baptized in the Holy Spirit, speaking in tongues, prophesying in the name of Jesus and being healed physically, spiritually and emotionally.

There were reports of teeth filled without fearful trips to the dentist. The infilling of the Holy Spirit was hard enough to fathom, but teeth filling was far out. It wasn't clear whether it was silver or gold, but either way it was a crowning achievement!

Jay Dalton told a tale about a lady whose car ran out of gas in a California desert. She laid hands on the tank and it supernaturally filled to the gills. It's delightful to drink from the rivers of living water, but to tap into the source that puts the tiger in the tank is out of sight. No Visa is required when the Master is in charge!

These stories rattled me but I felt secure as long as there weren't wooden boxes in the corner. Bill was too relaxed to be related to Jumping Charlie and the room size restricted any serious Holy Rolling.

Bill articulated about the origins of the outpouring of the Holy Spirit. It started in 1908 in a converted warehouse on Azusa Street in Los Angeles. "It was so powerful even the warehouses were converted," he added. Tough times in rural America forced people into the big cities, which resulted in rabid crime and moral decay. Seminarians captivated by the heresies of "higher criticism," spread the bad news to novices. The field was ripe for the Holy Ghost fire which fell on the faithful.

The Azusa Street revival, characterized by consuming evangelistic zeal and manifestations of the gifts of the Holy Spirit, fulfilled the words of the prophet Joel as recorded in Joel 2:28-29,

"And it shall come to pass afterward that I will pour out my Spirit on all flesh; your sons and your daughters shall prophesy, your old men shall dream dreams, and your young men shall see visions. Even upon the menservants and maidservants in those days, I will pour out my Spirit."

People came from all corners of the world to partake of this prophetic promise. Many believed the time was short and soon the sound of the trumpet would announce the Savior's return to rapture the saints. With these expectations, holiness was not a hard sell.

Undergirded by this urgency, prayer vigils lasted all night, night after night. Preaching, prophecy and repentance brought people to their knees, salvation sent them to share the good news. Baptized in the Holy Ghost with tongues of fire illuminating their lips they leaped for joy and danced in the Spirit. "We know they all spoke in tongues," Bill interjected—"What else could they speak with?"

Denominational doomsdayers, shaken by this sudden surge of the Spirit, exercised the left foot of fellowship on this fired up flock. With the Rapture on hold, the excommunicated enthusiasts were forced to form their own folds. The Assemblies of God, the Foursquare Gospel and many other Pentecostal groups were organized in the ensuing years.

The mighty winds which flamed the Azusa Street fire were blowing once again. The gentle breeze of the late 50's had whipped into a full force gale by the 60's as it swept across the land. Now people were preparing for a Holy Spirit hurrah of hurricane proportions!

Jay Dalton broke in with Acts 2:1-4 to support what Bill was saying—"When the day of Pentecost had come, they were all together in one place. And suddenly a sound came from heaven like the rush of a mighty wind, and it filled all the house where they were sitting. And there appeared to them tongues as of fire, distributed and resting on each one of them. And they were all filled with the Holy Spirit and began to speak in other tongues as the Spirit gave them utterance."

Jay said, "People from every mainline denomination were experiencing the same personal Pentecost. I recently attended a

United Church of Christ in Elk Grove, Illinois, where over three hundred people are filled with the Holy Ghost, speaking in tongues and prophesying in the name of Jesus."

Suddenly the Toll's meeting shifted from sharing to prayer and praise. Shouts of "Thank You Jesus," "Praise You Lord" and "Hallelujah" filled the room as petitions were placed at Jesus' feet. Charged by the Spirit, native tongues grew restless and speech beyond space took over. This heavenly language had traces of Spanish and Italian mixed in with more distant dialects. My faith would have fallen if the tongues were tied into just German!

After a few catchy choruses sung to the timbre of tambourines, Bill asked if anyone desired prayer for healing or to be filled with the Holy Spirit. As Jerry Banks slid into the chair in the center of the room, eager believers converged on him as if he might make a run for it. Some knelt and others stood as Bill placed his huge hands on Jerry and asked Jesus to fill him from his crown down to his feet with the Holy Ghost.

I sensed a powerful presence of the Spirit from the safe sanctuary of where I was seated. After some stammering starts, Jerry spoke smoother, with repetition. Soon he was speaking many strange words in succession. This gift of the Holy Ghost gave him a peaceful glow.

Jerry's tongues tailed off as the group sang heavenly harmony in the Spirit. Choirs that practice perennially could never compete with this celestial chorus. The singing subsided in unison and gave way to prophetic words of encouragement. Bill gave another invitation, but there were no takers. We were prime candidates but weren't ready to take the plunge.

After a time of fellowship, we went on our way rejoicing. I knew someday I would have the same spiritual experience but it would take time. That night at Toll's I was edified by my brothers and sisters, but the real call from the Lord is person to person. Jesus never calls collect—He always operates toll-free!

## Full Gospel Fans the Fire

We returned to the Toll's Friday night meetings many times in the months following. Bill and Lorna are Pentecostal pioneers possessing a vision of victory for Christians of all persuasions. During the 60's these forerunners of the faith ran interference for hundreds of Milwaukee area mainline monastics imprisoned in their own partitioned prayer towers. Recluses were released to form friendly forces for waging spiritual warfare.

Religion was on a holy roll and Bill and Lorna were resplendent role models. In addition to launching Full Gospel Businessmen's Fellowship International (FGBMFI) and Women's Aglow, they hosted the first Charismatic Conference in Milwaukee. Called Inter-Church Team Ministries, they featured Father George Pattison, an Episcopal priest, and Rev. Ed Gregory.

A few years later the Tolls helped usher in the Jesus People era by providing love and leadership for these former flower children.

Bill inducted his Charismatic clan into the FGBMFI like a recruiting officer—the second time I attended he put me on their Steering Committee. The committee, comprised of Classical Pentecostals and Charismatics, contacted speakers, located meeting places and promoted attendance. Whenever our wheels went out of alignment, Bill steered us in the right direction.

The Charistmatics were riding high on the crest of the second wave while the old line Pentecostals, weather beaten by decades of persecution passing through their pores, were the last of a brave breed. These first generation believers had been labeled everything from devil's disciples to holy rollers by insecure pseudo-saints and heathen highbrows!

These patriarchs understood the spiritual significance of the second wave of God's Spirit. After being swept away by the first wave, they were booted out by the bastions of the belfry. Now they were bellhops bringing in the mainline brethren. Meanwhile, their descendants sat on the sidelines puzzled by this parade of pumped up Charismatics passing by. They weren't as eager to march with the new kids on the block.

The Full Gospel businessmen were more mellow than macho—only men are eligible for membership but the meetings are open to all ages and genders. It was started in 1951 by Demos Shakarian, a dairyman of Armenian descent. Constituents consist of local born-again businessmen blessed with the Baptism of the Holy Spirit. FGBMFI is akin to a Charismatic Christian Lions Club.

Back in the 60's the Milwaukee chapter met on Saturday nights with the featured speaker well-advertised. Bill ran the meetings like a world championship heavyweight boxing event. He raced around the room lining up additional luminaries, vocalists and verbalists right up until the big bell sounded.

Each preliminary participant was instructed to confine their contribution to five minutes. This produced the same results as telling a legion of lumberjacks to go light on the evening meal after a long day in the forest! Bill introduced each person with wide-eyed anticipation. They shared about conversion experiences, the infilling of the Holy Spirit, physical, emotional and spiritual healings, and miraculous manifestations of the gifts of the Spirit. After the preparatory rounds of rhetoric ended close to 10:00 p.m., it was time for the love offering.

Five minutes of sanctified stewardship jokes preceded the passing of the Kentucky Fried Chicken buckets. Bill's favorites included, "The Lord loveth a cheerful giver but He will even accept money from a crank." His follow-up was, "Last month we got a lot of love, but very little offering. Please be generous tonight." Finally, he said, "With a guy named Toll in charge, you didn't expect to get in free, did you?"

The main event usually lasted fifteen rounds. One night the prize pugilist was Wendall Wallace, an evangelist from Portland, Oregon. He packed such a wallop with the Word that even the devil shook each time Wendell delivered the knockout punch. Wendall's aim was to win the whole world for Jesus.

Bill introduced him with the following story, "Many years ago Wendall was the featured speaker at a FGBMFI convention and using Revelations 22:7 as his text, preached on the Second Coming of Christ. 'Everybody better get ready for the "Rapture" because the Lord is coming soon,' he shouted as he paced back and forth from the podium. Suddenly the Spirit seized Wendall with such a powerful prophetic word, that every cemetery in the city was in peril of losing its paying customers. 'I am coming! I am coming soon! I am coming real soon!' he bellowed. As he roared 'real soon' he lost his balance and fell forward with the podium into the audience, knocking an elderly lady to the floor. As Wendall frantically applied first aid to the flattened woman's head, he apologized profusely for his clumsiness. In her fallen state she shouted back, 'It's all right! It's all right! It's all right! You warned me three times!'"

Fortunately Wendall selected a different text this night—his topic was "Waging Spiritual Warfare." By 11:00 p.m. Wendall was so arm weary he hit the devil with a sucker punch and yielded the microphone back to Brother Bill Toll.

Bill asked everyone to remain ringside to receive information about the post-meeting ministries available. The prayer teams shifted into a four-corners-of-the-room offense to attack everything from arthritis to evil spirits. Not yet a card-carrying Charismatic, I was assigned a traditional task of counting cash—it didn't take long. In spite of Bill's tongue-in-cheek teachings on tithing, there was a lot of love but very little offering!

FGBMFI put Ringling back into religion. It sure beat Bultman, Barth and Brunners demythologizing derbys. I envisioned them pacing around the campfire in the cool of the evening deliberating over which miracle to debunk next. If only they had drawn closer to the flames, the Holy Ghost would have set them on fire!

Full Gospel gave me a fresh perspective of Pentecost and a roadmap for living a faith-filled life. My main concern was whether they could live up to their name. Wouldn't Part Gospel Businessmen's Fellowship International be better? Even Peter and Paul fell short of living the full gospel at times!

It's the nature of man to brand bands of believers—spiritual security demands delineation of doctrine. If we join First Baptist Church we can expect to get wet, but how about Fourth Baptist or Last Baptist? Do they have a higher revelation or are they merely moody mavericks who couldn't mingle with the First Baptist brood? Or maybe it's a simple case of bathtubs vs. baptismal tanks.

How come Lutherans, Anglicans and Catholics all claim St. Paul? This is enough to make Martin mad! Is the Great Apostle part of the original remnant or has he reformed? Is Paul pleased to have his stamp of approval plastered on these doors or has he been misrepresented by Madison Avenue? No matter what brand inside, if Paul's name is out front we should expect mighty miracles, missionary journeys, persecution and prison!

## Taming the Tiger in Tony's Tank

Tony Reno, the fisherman who led Karen to the Lord, always came to our house unannounced. This short jovial gent never suffered in silence—when he wasn't feeding on the Word, he was feasting on food and talking a ton at the same time. Still sporting his Sicilian accent, he challenged our Christian commitment as if we were heathens from the hut who had never heard the Word. If I had a ten spot for every time I heard Tony's testimony I could retire.

Tony was a health nut before it was considered healthy to be one. He carted fifty-pound sacks of assorted produce into our kitchen and crammed the contents into his juicer. Apple and carrot cocktails weren't so bad but onion juice was like tying into tear gas at tea time!

Not desiring to crush Tony we told him his concoctions were tasty. One day he hauled in a monstrous Atlas juicer for us to purchase. It looked like an Air Force model from the missile program. Our kitchen was filled with fuel to fire up this contraption.

Despite our decision to buy this beauty, even if it detonated during the demonstration, Tony insisted on giving us the full sales pitch. Standing by the sink with rolled-up sleeves he spouted his spiel in vintage TV style. Passionately pointing out every redeeming feature, his pitch intensified when he shoved pounds of various veggies into the juicer. With V-8 sloshing all over the kitchen like someone was bleeding to death, I managed to corral three full glasses of the carnage.

After one swig I knew the secret of TV hawkers' success—there was no taste test. When Tony stopped to breathe I shouted, "I'll buy it," fearing he would start in again. Mom Ziemann, who had joined us, was in no mood to outbid me, so I became the proud owner of this awesome Atlas juicer. Tony threw in the bags of unused produce as part of the deal.

Tony's theatrics switched to the music room where he told us old-time stories in between piano selections. He attended revivalist tent meetings along the Sawdust Trail. His itinerary included Oral Roberts, William Branham, A. A. Allen, Jack Coe, Kathryn Kuhlman and myriad other miracle workers.

Tony's favorite was William Branham, who would challenge any foe attempting to disrupt his tent meetings. One night a crazed character with a drawn dagger charged Branham on the platform. Branham, drawing on the Sword of the Lord, took authority over him in the name of Jesus and his attacker wilted to the floor like wet spinach before the enthralled throng.

On another occasion William Branham and a friend were walking on a ranch when suddenly they were faced with a large bull bearing down on them. Branham commanded the bull to halt in Jesus' name and it bit the dust like a wounded warlock. I warned Tony to steer clear of revivals that attracted bulls!

William Branham finally met his match in the form of a wayward vehicle. Plucked from this Earth in the prime of life, his faithful followers were crestfallen. With no resurrection in sight, they were forced to fold his tents. Although many theories surfaced to explain Branham's abrupt departure, the most convincing was the Lord spared him the stress of dealing with deification. His flock had placed him on such a supernatural pedestal there was only one way to go!

Once Tony became convinced we were genuinely saved, he started stressing the Baptism of the Holy Spirit.

One Saturday morning he brought out a tape on "Holy Ghost Fire" by John Osteen, a Southern Baptist preacher ignited by the flames many years before. As Tony set up shop, Karen slipped up the backstairs for a higher calling.

By the time I realized it was only the two of us, Brother Osteen was exhorting all believers to be baptized in the Holy Ghost—"There is no time for tarrying," he shouted, "Your appointed time is now!" Responding on cue, Tony leaped from his chair and lunged towards me with fire in his eyes. Fortunately for him I didn't possess the holy boldness of Branham!

Seizing my skull he yelled, "Do you want the Holy Ghost?" Asking turned out to be Tony's tactical error—it gave me time to make a move. I twisted free of his grasp faster than Branham subdued the bull.

When I apologized for ducking out on my Divine appointment, Tony gave me a huge hug and said, "The Holy Spirit is really after you." I wasn't sure who was chasing me, but whoever it was must be winded by now! Please, someone tell me if I am resisting the Spirit or merely taming the tiger in Tony's tank!

# 7

# Tongues and Tambourines

Jay Dalton raved religiously about the meetings at Church of the Good Shepherd in Elk Grove, Illinois, where two hundred spirit-filled believers from mainline denominations met twice a week to worship the Lord. Karen was shaken by the revelation that among these New Testament neophytes were Wheaton College professors. She reasoned, if Wheaton profs were parading Pentecostal gifts the Rapture was just around the corner!

We put Jay off a few weeks until our curiosity caught up with us. Halfway down to Elk Grove he revealed that there would be a special speaker that night from South Chard, England. Knowing our allergies to electric guitars, Jay quickly added, "There are no electric guitars, but Rev. Harry Greenwood plays a mean tambourine."

When we arrived, the place was packed with people singing glorious songs of praise. Fifteen minutes later Rev. Lloyd Weber, the pastor of the church, presented a synopsis of the charismatic gifts the Holy Spirit was manifesting among the flock. Spontaneous praise gave way to singing in tongues, which sent a shiver of spiritual ecstasy through my body. Praise was supposed to be a sacrifice, but here it seemed more like a reward!

If I hadn't given Tony such a hard time, I could have joined this celestial chorus. The singing slowly subsided in unison and a soothing silence ensued. Suddenly the quiet was broken by a modern-day Micah with a booming voice. I sneaked a peek at the prophet standing next to the pastor. With hands raised and heaven filling his face he exclaimed, "My children, come into my presence with an open mind and spirit. Let me remove the barriers between us so I may minister to your hungry heart. The work I am doing in you and among you brings me great joy. You are precious to me. I am your shelter. Come into my arms and experience my love and my peace as I pour out my Spirit."

Shouts of praise and thanks filled the church, followed by a reading of scripture to confirm the prophecy. Then a lady from the back of the church brought these words of comfort, "My beloved one, you are agonizing over whether these manifestations are of me. I assure you that my Spirit is among my people. I am pleased that you are searching for me with all your heart. Let go of your fears and doubts. Humble yourself and let me fill you with my Spirit. I will pour my gifts within you and through you to others. I love you, my beloved child." This message ministered directly to Karen's concerns about coming to the church.

Rev. Lloyd Weber introduced Harry Greenwood, who stepped forward with his tambourine to teach choruses. Harry, with his rugged rugby physique, attacked the tambourine like a tiger testing a toy drum. Flashing mischievous blue eyes he belted out, "In the name of Jesus, in the name of Jesus, we have the victory, in the name of Jesus, in the name of Jesus, demons will have to flee!" Keeping the beat with his toe-tapping feet, the tambourine reverberated as he ran his fingers across its face.

In between choruses Harry produced prolific puns. He said, "I learned most of them from a Mother Superior at a Catholic Punnery." Groans surfaced among the saints. With his Dennis the Menace demeanor, he snapped back, "A pun is the lowest form of humor—when you don't think of it first."

With one flick of the wrist, Harry tossed his tambourine on the chair and grasped the microphone to tell his testimony. He joined the Queen's Royal Navy as a teenager. Whatever entertainment was needed on board he could supply—singing, stand-up comedy and acrobatics were all within his repertoire. It was never fear, Harry is here. However, in port the scene changed to drinking, carousing and brawling.

A Plymouth Brethren brother, who was hot on Harry's trail, led him to the Lord while he was home on leave. When Harry returned to the ship the swabbies sensed something strange about the old boy—there was a new man in the old uniform. When he shared his salvation with his shipmates he was often mocked and ridiculed.

On one occasion, a longtime nemesis needled Harry about his new life. His old blood boiled as onlookers snickered. His antagonist reminded him that as a "Jesus boy" he wasn't allowed to retaliate. Harry replied, "For such a bloody bloke, you have a great grasp of scripture which I agree with. However, being a baby Christian the Lord isn't finished with me yet," as Harry hit him with a full fist to the forehead, sending him sailing across the upper deck! The not-so-innocent bystanders were shocked at the power of Harry's evangelistic thrust. Getting from the head to the heart was another matter, but at least it was more peaceful on board. After studying the book of Acts, Harry concluded he was long on head knowledge but lacked spiritual power. A Pentecostal evangelist baptized Harry in the Holy Ghost, which separated him from the Plymouth Brethren Church where they taught that tongues were taboo.

Harry joined a New Testament church at South Chard, in southeast England. Rev. Sid Purse and Harry shared the vision to send trained evangelists all over the world to teach, preach and demonstrate the faith-filled life with signs following.

Anointed by the Spirit, Harry junked the jokes and tore into the meat of his message. He hammered home, "The just shall live by faith, not by hope or fear. If the same Spirit that raised Jesus from the dead dwell in you, it will quicken your mortal bodies——." He held his Bible but never looked at it as he reeled off scripture after scripture giving chapter and verse. Holy Ghost power fell on the flock as Harry was energized anew by his own preaching. Forty minutes later his lungs still supplied enough fuel to fire up the crowd.

Suddenly he switched into ministering healing by the gift of the word of knowledge. As the Holy Spirit supplied the information, Harry exhorted the person to respond. If the sick saint resisted, he pointed to the area where they were sitting. If this didn't draw them out of seclusion, Harry addressed their fear but never pulled them out by the ear.

Everyone who came forward was prayed over in the name of Jesus with the laying on of hands. If appearances were proof, all the sick received a full loaf of the Living Bread.

Jay Dalton introduced us to Harry after the service. Satisfied Harry was human, we drove on our way rejoicing. We arrived home at 2:00 a.m., drained physically but awake spiritually.

Six hours later I was at Reilly, Penner and Benton in Milwaukee, balancing books.

Two weeks later, we met Jay Dalton at a shopping center parking lot in Waukesha and drove down to the Church of the Good Shepherd again.

After a time of praise and prophecy, Kevin Ranahan from Notre Dame arose and spoke in glowing terms about the outpouring of the Holy Spirit among Catholics at Duquesne University. This grass roots spiritual revival spread rapidly to Notre Dame, Ann Arbor and other Catholic citadels.

Jesus was pouring his Spirit upon Catholic believers by the thousands while feisty clenched-fist fundamentalists believed a Catholic couldn't be a Christian. The bastions of the Bible Belt suggested that even the elect were deceived by this neo-pentecostal phenomenon. Meanwhile their eternal security ship was sinking fast with this flood of Romans running on board!

Kevin and Dorothy Ranahan, Bert Ghezzi, Ralph Martin and Bishop Kevin O'Connor were early leaders of the Catholic Charismatic movement. Their immediate task was to interpret tongues. prophecy and the gifts of the Holy Spirit to Catholics who equated these manifestations with Protestant fanaticism.

Kevin suggested church history as a good starting point— the lives of the saints were filled with the dynamic dimension of "duminus," or Holy Spirit power. Canonization qualifications included performing miracles.

In the 1960's, there was conjecture that Catholics who mixed with miracle workers would be forced to leave their church. The Lord had an alternate plan—Pope John XXIII's encyclical on the Holy Spirit at the Second Vatican Council. Subsequent popes recognized Charismatic Renewal as a resource to infuse the lifeblood back into the church. Pope John Paul talked in terms of "evangelizing the baptized."

Meanwhile, some have fled from the Roman ranks in search of a freer form of worship. Protestant replacements have been found who are drawn to Jesus through the sacramental life.

On the way home, Jay updated us on the pockets of prayer groups popping up all over the country. As a well-traveled businessman, he knew the who, where, what, why and how of anything resembling religious revival and charismatic characters.

Jay's car pulled into Arlan's parking lot at 2:30 a.m. Before I made a move for the door he asked us if we would like him to pray over us for the Baptism of the Holy Spirit. Karen readily replied, "Yes," and they laid hands on me before my planned leap of faith into the front seat of our station wagon! The only vision I saw was a soft warm bed in a large Victorian home.

When Jay prayed, my jaw quivered like a queasy Quaker encountering quicksand. Quickened by the Spirit, I succumbed to His peaceful presence. Jay urged me to give voice to these supernatural promptings. Confused, I thought the Lord would perform the speaking also—if Jesus could vibrate my jaw He could certainly come forth with a few foreign words! Minutes passed and I was still tongue-tied. There was mounting evidence that Jesus wanted me to get out of the boat and stretch my limbs a little. I was so limp I couldn't get out of Jay's car, much less walk on water!

Jay gave up on me for the moment and shifted his attention towards Karen. Seconds after he laid hands on her head she poured forth in foreign tongues. Her language was so heavenly I suspected Berlitz might be Bible-based!

It was 3:00 a.m. What would I tell my boss if I showed up for work with bags under my eyes, spouting a strange language with my jaw jerking like it was on an all-night jam session? After thanking our Christian brother for his holy boldness, we climbed into our car and went on our way rejoicing down the dark abandoned interstate. Upon arriving home I collapsed on the bed and fell into a deep sleep, knowing I had been swept away by the swell of the second wave.

## The Legend of Living Waters

Three weeks after our personal Pentecost in Arlan's parking lot, Rev. Harry Greenwood visited our area. After speaking at the FGBMFI Saturday breakfast in Milwaukee, he came with us and shared that same evening at the Clyde Shaw home.

The ladies from the Wednesday Bible study had been working for weeks on their husbands, pastors and friends to come and hear Harry. Saturday night arrived with forty adventurers slipping through the shadows of the Old Valentine Estate to get to Shaw's. Some looked more curious than courageous.

Harry, with his patented command of faith and power persona, presented an overview of the Holy Spirit's moving among His people. Next came timber-shaking tambourine time. The look on Clyde Shaw's face when Harry belted out, "In the Name of Jesus, demons will have to flee" was worth the price of admission.

Then Harry hit them with a full frontal faith message—"Jesus spent two-thirds of his earthly ministry healing the sick, driving out demons and performing mighty miracles. Jesus said, 'According to your faith be it on to you.' Two thousand years later we have turned this truth totally around—faith is only for the frail, frazzled and faint-hearted while miracles are for the maladjusted Monks of Madagascar! In the cupolas of Christendom a fly would have no chance of being healed of a headache! Doubt and Rationalism are in like sin as seminaries are being emptied by degree."

Some were warming up to Harry's message while others looked hot to hit the road, or even Harry. A morose Madame perched near the fireplace was eyeing the poker. This lady's Lutheran pastor didn't appear pleased either—acting as if his nutritionist put him on a diet of worms and he wanted to wiggle out.

Harry, discerning the spiritual warfare, shortened his sharing to fifty minutes. Opportunity for personal prayer and fellowship followed. The freaked folks disappeared down the driveway like the devil was pricking them with his pitchfork. However, a nucleus of novices remained to explore more about the move of the Holy Spirit.

Later that evening we told Harry about our parking lot experience. When he heard I got tripped up on tongues, he snapped to his feet and laid hands on my head. When my jaw started jumping he said, "Give voice to those words," and I burst forth like a river freed by a damaged dam! Karen was amazed at the language looming from my lips.

I have spoken in tongues thousands of times since with the same presence of the Holy Spirit. However, I have never again encountered the miraculous movement of my jaw—the Lord reserved this manifestation at a special time for a stubborn Swede who needed a jolt in his jaw to get his spiritual juices flowing.

Harry encouraged us to open our home for Charismatic meetings. Sensing God's peace on the property, he said that the pruning was already taking place to produce ripe fruit for the flock to feed on.

We asked Harry to return in six months after his extensive teaching and preaching tour in Great Britain, Sweden and New Zealand.

We continued attending Toll's Friday night meetings. However, their living room got so packed with people even Weight Watchers couldn't remedy the situation. With no quick fix in sight, we took the Holy Spirit's hint and opened our doors.

The first Friday night in November of 1966, ten of us set sail on the high seas of Living Waters. Many were called to this spiritual excursion but only a few chose to show. Leaving behind more no-shows than Noah's Ark, the fearless who filed in two by two the first night were John and Bev Reishus, Jane and Rich Rizenthaler, Jane and Bill Schneider, Avis Miller and Rev. Andrew Ulrich.

There was prayer and praise choruses, Bible teachings, testimonies and fellowship. Jay Dalton came out occasionally to give brotherly support and tell supernatural stories. Rev. Lloyd Weber and his elders from Elk Grove came every third Friday night to teach and give powerful prophetic words. Dr. Bill Oberg from Wheaton College participated once a month as a Bible teacher, while his wife Ruth played the piano.

The Lord blessed the gatherings and added weekly to the fold. One night Ann and Ken Chandler, from the Congregational Church in Oconomowoc, came to the meeting. Ken, a prominent advertising executive, wanted to see what we were promoting. The Chandlers, like ourselves and others testing the tide of this second wave, approached this phenomenon with shades of skepticism. However, they possessed one common denominator that pulls people beyond religious complacency—the desire for spiritual strength within.

We drove Ken and Ann down to the Church of the Good Shepherd on a Sunday night and they were awed by the Holy Spirit's presence and freedom.

A few weeks later at a meeting, as Ken was sitting on our music room couch, he felt a hand on his shoulder. There was no one behind him but the healing hand of Jesus! Ken appeared so peaceful I thought he had been Raptured and we were gazing at a sanctified silhouette.

Later that night, while kneeling on the kitchen floor, Ken stammered with the strangest language I had heard in my brief Charismatic career—his tongues had an Oriental twist capped off by a Chinese cadence!

Ken witnessed to his miraculous encounter with the Master many times in the ensuing weeks. Attendance exploded after the episode as the faithful got fired up to bring the fearful to find new faith. Where else could you go in Oconomowoc on a Friday night and drink in a dialect straight out of the Ming dynasty?

The Good News spread faster than a prairie fire fanned by forty-mile-an-hour winds. Curiosity seekers turned into Charismatic Christians, the tongue-tied spoke in heavenly languages and the sick were healed in the name of Jesus. Old men saw visions and former dropouts experienced dreams. Words of wisdom flowed fluently and prophetic utterances electrified the elect as the depressed, oppressed and possessed were delivered from the devil's dark dungeon.

People poured in from Fond du Lac to Ft. Atkinson, Milwaukee to Madison, Kenosha to Baraboo. Our music room resembled the main floor of the New York Stock Exchange! The subtle difference was people put their stock in a sure situation, dividends were dished out daily, souls were saved instead of seats sold and the only crash that could cause concern was a fallout with the Final Judge.

Meanwhile, some of the natives were getting nervous. Gossip isn't one of the gifts of the Holy Ghost but it can sure get a firm grip on the gentry. Rumors ran rampant throughout the region—

They ranged from operating a house of ill repute to disguising a drug distribution center. The story spread that the sisters were sordid and the big wheelers were dealers!

Thank God this was before the days of the National Enquirer or Inside Edition! We didn't mind being fools for Christ, but why were we flogged flagrant sinners? This development was particularly devastating to Karen with her Wheaton College background. It was as if she was smitten with a Sophie Tucker syndrome!

When we talked out our feelings with Dr. and Mrs. Edman, who were visiting for the weekend, they shared similar experiences. Dr. Edman read Jesus' persecution passages from the 10th chapter of Matthew. Jesus was at his best when belittled by bigwigs. The 25th verse says, "If they have called the master of the house Beelzebub, how much more will they malign those of his household?"

With no desire to mix ministry with masochism, we moved onward, comforted by the confidence we were in good company. These episodes proved to be a sneak preview of the spiritual warfare ahead.

The youth ministry at Our Savior's went smoothly until we told Rev. Alan Olson we had been baptized in the Holy Spirit and spoke in tongues. Our spiritual experiences challenged his intellect.

Some church leaders treated us like lepers about to leap on poor paranoid parishioners—others were spiritually hungry to hear more. Our senior pastor, Rev. Holland, was pleasant but took the lukewarm approach—neither hot nor cold. As long as we didn't rock the boat we could stay on board. After coming to our meetings a couple of times, we took him to a FGBMFI meeting in Milwaukee that was livelier than a firemen's picnic on the Fourth of July. He wasn't moved—he was Mt. Rushmore material. With lines extended along his listless face he lamented, "I have seen this all before and it isn't any different." Pastor Holland remained a friend to the end and had enough faith in me to share his pulpit one Sunday morning. My predetermined text was Ephesians 4:1-3—"maintaining the unity of the Spirit in the bond of peace."

To say exercising the gifts of the Holy Spirit produced varied reactions in people would be the ecclesiastical understatement of twenty centuries. Responses ranged from aggressive anger to unholy indifference to jumping for joy jubilation. Some said, "The devil did it;" dispensationalists claimed the party ended with the canonization of scripture; others exclaimed, "It is Jesus, the same yesterday, today and forever!" Meanwhile, many pent-up Pentecostals came out of the closet to march with this Charismatic army while reactionary right-wing Christians crawled in the closet to shut out all the shouting. Others who had never taken a stand for Christ were ready to be counted when confronted with the loving joyous Jesus.

One such candidate was Brian Steinke, the track coach at Kettle Moraine High School. In 1960 he was named to the National Modern Pentathlon Team and participated in the pre-Olympics in Rome.

Brian was raised Catholic in Janesville, Wisconsin, but fell away from formal religion. His spiritual awareness led him on a search of eastern religions and experimentation with yoga.

Karen witnessed to Brian's wife Mary when Mary was waitressing at the Red Circle Inn. Mary's first reaction was disbelief, but as the Holy Spirit drew her she made a decision for Jesus. She has been a dynamic Christian ever since—tearing up the town with her powerful testimony and unbridled enthusiasm for her Lord and Savior. Mary attended the Bible studies at Shaw's and the Living Waters meetings.

Mary's prime target was Brian, who was suffering from severe asthma. After a tenacious tug of spiritual warfare, this macho-Marine finally loosened his grip for a trip to see the architectural attributes of our Victorian house on a Friday night. Brian, bound by fear and doubt, heard Rev. Lloyd Weber preach on the power of Jesus to set people free.

Lloyd extended an invitation to receive Jesus afterwards and Brian responded with a big "Yes" on that sultry summer night. Things got worse—his marriage was troubled and his mind muddled, his asthma became more acute and his finances were fading fast.

Desperate, Brian traveled to Elk Grove, Ill, to be baptized in water by Lloyd Weber. When a man got up in the service and gave a message in tongues, a Greek professor from Northwest-ern University gave the English translation and confirmed the messenger had spoken ancient Greek. Another lady gave her heart to Jesus immediately after and joined Brian and others in the Baptismal tank.

Brian was immersed in water, raised in newness of life and felt the Lord bathe him with warm oil over his entire body. With the peace of Jesus in his heart he offered praises of gratitude to his new found Friend.

The spiritual warfare was far from over. Later that night Brian had a flat tire in the freezing rain on I-94. Mental attacks of the devil distracted him in prayer meetings. However, the night he was baptized in the Holy Spirit he prayed in tongues for forty-five minutes and the oppression lifted.

Brian told me about a letter he wrote to God when he was 18 years old asking Him and His Holy Spirit to live within. The Lord blessed Brian with the desires of his heart.

Brian and Mary built their "Miracle House" in 1969 out of old barn lumber.

Hundreds of people came to their Wednesday night prayer meetings over the next twenty years and multitudes moved in.

Brian and Mary undergirded the rapid expansion of the Jesus People movement in Southeastern Wisconsin in the early 1970's. The Jesus People publication "Cornerstone" was started by Sue Polassari in their living room.

Mary went from waitressing at the Red Circle to Manager of Wauwatosa Realty. Among her many other responsibilities are setting up Leadership Prayer Breakfasts in the area that draw hundreds.

Brian completed his long career of coaching at Kettle Moraine and received a barrage of outstanding achievement awards for his efforts. He is still convincing kids that the Jesus life is the only way to survive in this twentieth century. All of their children are in active Christian ministry using the gifts of preaching, teaching, art and music to make a difference.

# 8

# Harry the Healer

Harry Greenwood returned twice a year to conduct meetings in the greater Milwaukee area. He always brought an associate from South Chard—Terry Barge, Andrew Culverwall, Tony Nash and Vic Dunning were among Harry's comrades who crossed the seas to convert the colonies.

Taking responsibility for their evangelistic itinerary, we set up three-day crusades, weekend seminars, one-night stands and one-hour power programs. The sites included such diverse spots as St. Monica's Seminary, St. John's Military Academy, the War Memorial, Ethan Allen School for Boys, the Eagles Club, radio and TV stations, homes and churches.

Harry's ministry personified power evangelism the way the apostles taught it. As bold as John the Baptist bearing a beard of killer bees, he challenged people to repent and surrender their lives to Jesus. After baptizing believers in water and the Holy Spirit, he launched them on a lifetime of ministry with signs following. Faith was Harry's forte. He was completely convinced that God would back up His word.

Harry practiced what he preached. He was a teacher, preacher, prophet, evangelist, chorus leader, tambourine player and could take a terrific offering. He exhorted every believer to answer the Charismatic call. Leading by example he taught that all Christians should be ready to minister the gifts of the Holy Spirit at a moment's notice.

At Faith Tabernacle in Chicago, Harry Greenwood and Derek Prince exorcised a woman named Jill who was involved in every imaginable evil including a baby sacrifice during a Satanist rite. Demons were cast out in Jesus' name, setting Jill free from her former life.

Once when Harry was here, Jill came to visit. We marveled at her sweet angelic spirit. She possessed a divine appointment with destiny to do mighty things in the power of the Holy Ghost.


## A Ten-Pin Attack at the Eagles Club

We scheduled a three-night city-wide evangelistic thrust at the Eagles Club in Milwaukee. The room seating 400 people exceeded our faith, but was 1,000 short of Harry's! With Karen's power of persuasion we posted 2,000 flyers in places even angels fear to tread. Ads placed in papers and radio announcements rounded out the publicity.

On opening night, October 29, 1967, I was alarmed by the noxious noise in the next room as we set up for the meeting. Whatever the Eagles Club splurged on splash they saved on soundproofing! There was more than wailing going on behind that wall—a boisterous bash was blasting into our empty chamber.

I asked God's man of faith and power if he felt led to pray for Jericho gymnastics and annex our separated brothers. Harry replied with a sly grin, "I like your evangelistic enthusiasm, but I have tested the spirits at that party and they wouldn't mix well with my message. We'll save the souses until later and descend on them for a midnight deliverance service!" This was shaping up like the first Pentecost!

Fortunately Harry hadn't lost his humor because I heard another racket in the region below our room. It sounded as if Goliath was hurling heavy metal across the floor! When I went down to investigate, a cool cat crashed through the swinging doors with a bowling ball slung over his shoulders. No more clues were necessary—I didn't want to know how many alleys we were up against!

By the time I resurfaced, Karen and Harry's faces told me they knew the name of the game also. No wonder we were charged such a small fee! This was like holding a revival in an Army Officers' Club. Weeks before, Karen had opted for the War Memorial on Lake Michigan for the meetings and now I was receiving a friendly reminder!

'Harry's booming voice had never been tested against this type of competition. He tuned up his tambourine to a foot-tapping tempo and belted out, "In the Name of Jesus, In the Name of Jesus, We have the Victory," as the folks filled the room. Fired up by fifty minutes of spirited choruses, Harry charged into his message with both barrels and let the devil have it. Despite all these strikes against him, he was in no frame of mind to be bowled over by Beelzebub!

Tenpins pounded the floor below as Harry prayed for the sick. Many were set free in the name of Jesus. The news traveled fast as the last two nights the joint was jammed with an expectant crowd.

Harry came out of this crusade as hoarse as a hyena high on laughing gas! We kept Harry humble by calling him, "Harry the Healer." When I asked him if he ever wanted to test the tenpin turkeys at the Eagles Club again, he said, "No thanks. I have seen what it's done for others!" This was Harry's favorite caustic comeback. When asked if he desired dessert at a meal, he always rolled his eyes and replied, "No thanks. I have seen what it's done for others." Karen never warmed up to this response, but I added it to my repertoire.

The moral of this Eagles Club story is—don't buy land in Florida for retirement before sinkhole season or you will be eternally retired. You can't collect Social Security sealed in a sinkhole!

## Ecumenical Enlightenment

The following fall we held a seminar at our home with Harry Greenwood and Kevin Ranaghan as the featured speakers. Gordon and Dot James from Wheaton helped us sponsor this two-day session centering on the second wave of the Holy Spirit. Included in the invitations was a clip from the Milwaukee Journal entitled "Charismatic Revival Growing."

We invited hundreds of clergy, laymen and leaders from numerous denominations, but concentrated on the Evangelical Jet Set. Far exceeding our faith, but not Harry's, we had sixty positive replies. We provided housing in our home and elsewhere and served buffet-style meals.

Harry and Kevin's contrasting styles worked well among these participants, most of whom had never taken part in a Charismatic gathering. Kevin, the theology professor from St. Mary's of Notre Dame, had a liturgical lilt to his lingo, while Harry, the independent Pentecostal from South Chard, was "Living in Hallelujah Land," which is the title of one of his favorite choruses.

The first night everyone reacted like dromedaries in the dark, but by morning most made it over the hump and were headed in the same direction. Some split on Saturday in the same condition they showed up—amused, confused or short-fused! For others the seminar was a launching pad for a new dimension to their spiritual life.

A month later we started a three-night outreach at St. Monica's Seminary, south of Oconomowoc on Highway 67. St. Monica's occupied the old Gustav Pabst mansion, the most palatial estate in the entire area. The 1928 chateau with forty-five rooms was now a haven for high school boys called to the priesthood.

Two of Harry's sidekicks from South Chard conducted the crusade—Andrew Culverwell the elder at 23, and Terry Barge the younger at 20.

Before Andrew came to Christ in his later teens, he grew despondent over perpetual problems and attempted suicide by overdosing on pills. Unsuccessful at ending his life, he formed a pop gospel group called the "Four Kingsmen" that traveled throughout Britain for four years playing theatres and coffee bars. Terry played the drums, while Andrew, a vocalist, also composed the music. Eventually they left the group to join Harry on his worldwide crusades.

Today Andrew is a well known gospel singer and composer living in Los Angeles. He is working on his seventh album. Terry is presently an international businessman headquartered in the Mother Country.

This was their first trip to the colonies and they were excited by its ministry potential. St. Monica's gym wasn't Carnegie Hall but it was better than battling bowlers at the Eagles Club.

As the large group of seminarians, teenagers and adults settled in, Terry, a dark handsome lad, gave a few opening remarks in his broken British accent. Then he introduced Andrew whose pixieish appearance resembled a blond Beatle.

Andrew, short of stature and long on talent, belted out an upbeat number on the piano called "Climb a Mountain." The room rumbled as the teens throbbed to the tempo. However, some adults suffering from the souped-up syncopation, appeared more chilled than thrilled. Many marched out to the beat of a different drummer during the third number. Meanwhile, Terry barged ahead on percussion while Andrew kept bopping his head to the boogie bounce.

Suddenly Terry abandoned his drums to take center stage. After giving a brief evangelistic message, he challenged the crowd to commit their lives to Christ. Terry possessed fervent faith but seemed startled when the entire St. Monica's student body rushed to the front like it was round-up time in the old west. As others joined, the converts outnumbered the counselors five to one. Couples were conscripted from the crowd to ensure that everyone had someone to talk to.

We arrived home after midnight feeling we had climbed the mountain Andrew sang about. If this was opening night what was going to happen the next two nights? Only the Lord had a clue and He wasn't telling! "The curious shall live by faith," was his cry whenever He was consulted.

The next morning a large van pulled up in front of our house filled with people on a mission. It was Father Bob, the dean at St. Monica's Seminary, and his students.

Father Bob amicably requested a powwow with our tribe. He said, "The seminary was embarrassed when their students responded to a Billy-Graham-type altar call last night. Catholics get confused by this approach because they are not sure what they are agreeing with. They are baptized as infants, confirmed as teenagers and now someone claims a further commitment is required to be a real Christian!"

Two of the kids parroted Father Bob's remarks and the rest looked uneasy to be caught up in this situation. We understood Father Bob's dilemma—he had graciously allowed us to hold these outreaches at St. Monica's and now internal heat was heaped on him for what happened.

We didn't ask questions or offer solutions. This was a time for temperance and healing, not thrashing out theological distinctions!

Father Bob granted us the use of the facilities for the final two nights as originally planned. However, due to the evangelistic thrust the seminary would officially distance themselves from the proceedings.

We provided food and fellowship as a peace offering. After the kids demolished two dozen doughnuts I took them on a tour of our house.

The next two nights the gym was jumping with teens. Seminary students congregated near the back door in case Big Brother was watching from the wings. In talking with a few, it was evident that the King of Kings had passed them keys to the kingdom. Whether it was reaffirmation of baptism, reconsecration of confirmation, or a sudden St. Paul knock down conversion, it didn't really matter—there was no internal auditor keeping count. As long as the Eternal Auditor inscribed their name in the Book of Life there was no cause for spiritual strife!

We returned from St. Monica's marveling at what God did despite denominational differences. We were weary but wiser in working out ecumenical idiosyncrasies for the future. There was only one week to rebound before Harry's meetings started at the War Memorial in Milwaukee.

## Restoration at the Red Circle Inn

Hosting Harry meant entertaining his entourage. Friends from Illinois, Iowa, Michigan and regions beyond bombed in with no warning. Fifteen for a Friday night feast was a frequent event.

Harry's guests always included Marvin Klattwater from the Windy City who wheeled up in his white Cadillac convertible to give Harry a cruise. Marvin's pockmarked face and mysterious makeup was Mickey Spillane material. Many moons later Marvin parked his prize Cadillac on a railroad crossing and neither has been seen since, this side of glory!

Jude Beach rode her motorcycle all the way from Detroit. Harry teased Jude about eliminating a hundred miles if she had the faith to ride on water. She replied, "No thanks, I have seen what it's done for others!"

Big Jim Hoosier came from Iowa to schedule Harry's itineraries for foreign countries. Big Jim needed to be fortified by food to plan properly—he depleted our pantry in 24 hours or less.

Jay Dalton drove out from Milwaukee to delve into doctrine with Harry. The two spent entire afternoons in heated discussions about "Harry's Latest Heresies." Harry envisioned his revelations as straight from the Lord, while Jay's Southern Baptist background saw them as human heresies! The two remained the best of friends, but Jay's calling was keeping Harry humble. Harry always said, "There is no pride in my family, I've got it all." We encouraged him to write a book and entitle it "Harry the Humble Healer's Latest Heresies."

Karen's mother, Lorraine, still attended church in Waukesha. We shared our recent experiences with her, but she dismissed them as something out of the dark ages. Karen kept her informed whether she liked it or not. She told her mom so much about Harry she wouldn't answer the phone anymore.

Finally one Sunday she consented to meet us for dinner at the Red Circle Inn in Nashotah. We positioned Harry straight across from her so she would feel the full effect of his vibrant faith. Impressed with his knowledge of scripture, Lorraine took to Harry like a hound dog hits on hamburger. She even laughed at his jokes as he shared a synopsis of his life story.

Harry prayed for her chronic back problem and the pain lifted instantly in Jesus' name.

Radiant, she retreated to a private parlor and asked to be baptized in the Holy Spirit. The Lord set her spirit free and gave her a glorious tongue. Later, Lorraine asked Karen, "Why didn't you tell me about this before?" Karen restrained herself and smiled.

Lorraine thanked Harry heartily and invited him to lead a crusade in Phoenix in January.

As she pulled away in her white Eldorado we praised the Lord for the miracle he performed at the Red Circle Inn. This quaint 1848 restaurant saw more restoration in those two hours than in its lifetime.

## Montezuma Meets His Match

Lorraine scheduled Harry's meetings at a large tabernacle on the near north side of the city. She never ventures out at night so she recruited us as stand-in hosts.

Uncle Harry, as kids of all ages called him, never needed help once the service started. He was a one-man band with signs following. He even lightened everyone's load by taking his own love offerings. When Andrew wasn't present to play the piano, Harry attacked the tambourine with more tenacity. If Terry was absent, Harry introduced himself and produced a few more puns. His favorite prologue to start a message was, "Unaccustomed as I am to public speaking..." Nothing was farther from the truth. Uncle Harry looked like Benny Hill, spoke like William Jennings Bryan and moved an audience like Billy Graham—forward!

The week crusade started on a Sunday and after four nights Harry was still living in "Hallelujah Land." People were responsive, spreading the word, requesting individual prayer and opening hospital doors for ministry to the sick. Not knowing the word "no," Harry would go with the flow until he felt flushed. He never mentioned tiredness—it was contrary to his concept of living in divine health.

We decided Harry needed a break before he burned out. Thursday morning we coaxed him into coming with us to Nogales, Mexico, to enjoy some comic relief. Initially when he resisted with his spiritual stance, we fired a round at his flesh. After assuring him he would be back for the evening service, we made a direct appeal to his stomach. Visions of a sumptuous lunch to munch at "La Cave" restaurant in Nogales flashed before his eyes. God's man of faith always had room for food!

Harry slept in the back of the station wagon for three hours until we hit the border. After some sightseeing and shopping, we headed for "La Cave."

118

This cool underground cavern with star-shaped twinkling lights illuminating the ceiling produced shivers. Long underwear would have been in order but was mysteriously missing from the menu. Karen settled for a poncho, but Harry and I were too macho to admit we were freezing. A Mariachi band strolled in between tables serenading gringos with south of the border ballads.

We warned Harry that Montezuma owned a piece of the action in every dining den in these parts. We didn't want God's man of faith and power caving in to a case of cramps during the evening crusade. Harry reminded us he was a King's Kid whose cast iron stomach had tested every conceivable culinary concoction on the face of the globe.

Uncle Harry dove head first into greens, beans, fowl and Coca Cola with cubes. Montezuma had met his match. Karen and I chickened out and made safer choices. We had seen what it had done for others! We had a little wine for our stomach's sake, but steered clear of the water.

After a leisurely lunch we returned to the shops to haggle over prices. Karen respected Mexicans but knew border towns expected bartering. Karen was born to bargain! As a new babe she beseeched Dr. Verch not to spank her bottom—she agreed to cry on her own to make it look official. She believes a good deal is worth a day's drive no matter what it costs to get there.

Cashing in a few fins, she cleaned one proprietor out of piñatas. We looked like part of a Mexican fiesta as we paraded back to the car. With so many piñatas wedged in the wagon, Harry had to sleep sitting up on the way back.

A few miles north of Tucson Harry wanted to stop at a service station. I purchased gas while Harry made a mad dash for the men's room. When he resurfaced I reminded him we had to move quickly to make the meeting.

Twenty minutes later he pleaded to pull in a garage again. Uncle Harry and the car had a lot in common—both of them were full of gas! God's man of faith and power looked peaked, peeking out from the piñatas. Karen asked him, "Are you still living in divine health, brother?" Harry denied any discomfort as he bolted from the back seat.

North of Casa Grande Harry was hit hard by more rumblings of Montezuma's ruthless retributions. Finally we made him face up to his infirmity. God's man was grounded until we discovered a remedy. Lacking Lomotil or Kaopectate, I suggested we sing the chorus, "Bind us together, Lord, bind us together," lay hands on Harry and storm the thrones of heaven.

Meanwhile he made another run for the restroom. If this kept up it was going to be a short meeting tonight at the tabernacle. Ten minutes later Harry crawled back in the car looking like a British monarch dethroned by an Aztec attack. Maybe he was allergic to piñatas also. We laid hands on our ailing brother and prayed that he might be delivered of his maladies and restored to divine health.

Bargaining with my guardian angel, I barreled down the interstate. Harry wasn't living in "Hallelujah Land" yet, but color was slowly coming back.

We snuck in the rear door of the tabernacle as the meeting was in full swing. After a quick trip to the toilet, Harry the Healer grabbed his tambourine and found his place on the platform. From our vantage point it appeared as if he was gearing up for another attack. We interceded in earnest for our waning warrior. After two choruses the cramps returned and Harry disappeared. Terry and Andrew looked bewildered but carried on in fine fashion.

When Harry reappeared I knew we were in for a rip-roaring time—victory had returned to his vitals! Sick of the attacks, he started attacking. The devil better hide or Harry would have his head.

Harry paced back and forth on the platform like a panther about to pounce on his prey. "If the same Spirit that raised Christ from the dead dwell in you, it will quicken your mortal bodies," he shouted! The warfare at the Eagles Club was wistful compared to this. People stirred in their seats as he moved in for the kill.

Many were healed instantly by the power of the Holy Spirit as Harry called people forward with words of knowledge. The deaf heard, the blind saw and those needing deliverance were set free as they cried out to Jesus. The Lord's presence was so powerful nobody wanted to return to their earthly homes. We moved from Montezuma's revenge, to revival, to Rapture in the space of an hour.

We arrived back at our hotel in the early morning. Buoyed by faith we left the piñatas in the car until breakfast. Harry was up by 8:00 a.m. ready to meet the challenges of a new day. He was living in divine health with a big "D." When we asked him if he wanted to return to Mexico he replied, "No thanks, I have seen what it's done for others!"

Harry never before experienced miracles to that extent except in Sweden when a bunch of beatniks tried to disrupt his service. He said, "The greater the challenge, the more we are forced to fall back on faith in the Lord to fight our battles. The devil doesn't devour dead works—he tries to pull the plug on resurrection power!"

# 9

# Trading in the Old Nature on a New Model

Harry Greenwood wasn't Baptist, but he sure delighted in dunking the Lord's disciples. He baptized more believers than the Popes produced penitents. He held them under the water long enough to test their faith, but short enough for them to exercise it in the future. Baptism went far beyond producing perfect corpses.

His theology was based on Colossians 2:12—"You were buried with Christ in baptism, in which you were raised with Him through faith in newness of life by God, who raised Him from the dead." Harry concluded that our old nature was buried with Christ in the water and we put on a new nature as we came forth.

We never understood why it was necessary to be re-baptized but the notion of getting rid of the "old man" had real appeal. Who wants to bear a body of decaying flesh, of St. Paul fame, when it can be buried? If Jesus was baptized as an adult, maybe we should follow suit. Assuming the baptizer possesses the strength to pull us out, the worst downside scenario is getting wet!

After Harry preached on believer's baptism at the Elk Grove Church, Rev. Lloyd Weber lined up the local Baptist church for adult immersions. Karen and I opted to take the plunge, along with Gordon and Dot James and thirty others from the Elk Grove Charismatic community.

We made our planned pilgrimage to Elk Grove on a Saturday afternoon. Upon entering the church, the elders provided us with white robes to throw over our bathing suits. The resemblance to the Ku Klux Klan was too close for my comfort—in this neighborhood, even our new nature could be annihilated!

The candidates filed into the front pews as Lloyd Weber and Ern Baxter stepped onto the platform. Ern Baxter, who ministered with William Branham in the 1940s and was pastor at Faith Tabernacle in Chicago, preached on water baptism to prepare our hearts.

The elders led us to a dimly-lit corridor in back of the baptismal tank. Gordon James was frantically wrapping waterproof plastic around the cast on his right arm. He broke it the week before under mysterious circumstances. I suggested it cracked when he shifted his four on the floor too fast while drag racing a student on the Eisenhower expressway. Gordon grinned but emphatically denied it.

All kidding quieted down when we realized we were next in the tank! Gordon was led down the steps and Lloyd offered a few words. Gordon glanced at his arm, cupped his hands over his nose and hit the water with the force of a fallen bridge! Lloyd, small of stature, went partway with him. It was difficult to determine who surfaced first, but as long as the "old man" stayed under it didn't really matter. Gordon looked more relieved than radiant as he trudged out of the tank supporting his right arm.

Nervously, I waded into the water expecting some "old natures" to be nibbling at my knees. Ern Baxter asked me some questions which I didn't mind, as long as it wasn't, "What would you desire for your last meal?" When he asked me if I renounced the devil and all his works my mind said, "I sure do, I have seen what he's done for others," but my lips simply answered, "Yes."

Ern baptized me in the name of Jesus and when he raised me up I identified deeply with Jesus' resurrection. I knew I could never deny Him.

Shortly after, we discovered that our new natures could never be confused with perfection. We possessed no qualifications for casting stones but our feet were firmly placed on the Rock.

## The Reports of Our Deaths
## Are Greatly Exaggerated

Many months later, Elk Grove's "old man" turned into a Loch Ness monster. The original diagnosis was growing pains, but a second opinion revealed advanced malignancy. Praise became passive, joy and peace passed away and prophecy became more directive than edifying.

No new speakers were invited and the old ones were weeded out faster than a victory garden ravaged by rabid rabbits! Harry Greenwood was treated like rotting timber; Derek Prince was placed in pauper status; Kevin Ranaghan turned out to be too Catholic; Ern Baxter earned a prophet's reward and was bumped in favor of Jim Beall, a big deal from Detroit.

When we cornered Lloyd about our concerns, he offered the following scenario: The Lord allowed a free-flowing atmosphere at first but now it was time to settle down so the "second wave" wouldn't toss Elk Grove like the Titanic, with every wind of doctrine. They desired to pattern themselves after a pedigree church where the pure prophetic word would flow. After a serious five-state search for this viable voice, it was revealed that Bethesda Missionary Temple in Detroit was the anointed one.

Lloyd and his elders aligned the Elk Grove church with this "Latter Rain Movement." James Lee Beall, the pastor of Bethesda, brought "America to its Knees" through his nationwide radio broadcast. Elk Grove was the next to knuckle under.

Lloyd envisioned Living Waters as a kissing cousin of Elk Grove, who were full-fledged offspring of Bethesda. This family was in imminent danger of birth defects due to inbreeding!

We were anxious about some aspects of the early renewal also, but much more alarmed about the path Elk Grove chose to protect itself. The cord was cut to other churches and Christian communities. In the process of throwing out the dirty dishwater they destroyed the smoke detectors. An arsonist was moving in for the kill!

We couldn't share the full extent of the fire damage with our flock for fear they would be derailed by the black smoke of disillusionment. We took a few Living Waters leaders to Elk Grove to discern for themselves but no confirmation was forthcoming— the devil camouflaged this fire with cunning, while cannibals boiled their cauldrons in the back room!

A month later, Elk Grove gave Karen and me this ultimatum—either Living Waters becomes kissing cousins with these kindred spirits or Lloyd and the boys can no longer be big brothers. In a last-ditch effort they tried to bury bad breath with Dentyne. Sunday night would be the showdown—at their place!

To avoid embroiling any egos at the Elk Grove Corral we went alone. Knowing indiscreet discernment could dry up Living Waters as well, we kept the door ajar for any ray of hope at the Church of the Good Shepherd. If only this flock could extinguish this deadly fire and rekindle the Light that dissolves all darkness.

We entered the sanctuary to stone silence. They were waiting for a word—when the word came it wasn't good. It was doomsday directed towards those outside the circle being deceived. The prophecy was confirmed by scripture taken out of context. Lloyd Weber, appearing as stern as the rear-end of an ocean liner, preached a profile on the profundities of the pattern church.

After this service our pow-wow took place in the parking lot. It was like school days back in the concrete jungles of Jersey where every scrap was settled in the side lot.

After a short round of plastic pleasantries, Lloyd's elders, looking as grim as groundhogs struggling with their shadow side, suggested we pray. John, the younger elder, brought forth a prophectic vision as I stared at the stark tarmac. He saw a colossal casket slowly lowered under the ground with Karen and me in it. Krista, our three-year-old daughter was frantically flailing at the metallic top trying to get a rise out of us. Refusing to give up she finally flung herself into the grave, clinging to the coffin.

We didn't need an interpretation. We had already been pierced by the pain of this deadly message! However, Bob, the older elder, shaking dust off his sandals, added shock value. Karen and I embodied the Living Waters Fellowship incarcerated in the casket. Krista depicted Elk Grove's final effort to keep us in the fold. If we spurned their pleas, Living Waters' doomed destiny was the cold dark ground!

This situation got graver when some Wheaton friends who had meet us there for moral support vouched for the veracity of the vision. The only upside to this downer was Karen and I bit the dust together in a casket built for two—separate coffins would have been a real drag! Harry's teaching on being buried with Christ in baptism glossed over this possibility.

126

There was no going-away party. It was time to face the next hurdle—how would this separation sell to the saints back home?

We held no press conference but fielded questions on a one-to-one basis as they were asked. We lost a few of the flock but the remnant dug their roots in deeper for the days ahead.

We never passed through the portals of the "Pattern Church" again. Many of our friends still clung on with clenched fists to this fading falling star, hoping for a dramatic climactic change in direction. It was not to be. The devil never released his death-grip as darkness snuffed out the light of its former glory.

All singing ceased. The cross was extracted from the edifice. Teachings challenging the core of Christianity were advanced as avant-garde revelations.

Jim Beall bailed out before the blaze burned the entire body. Many located fire escapes before the last act and were led to other fellowships. Others, too traumatized to test a towering inferno a second time, retreated to the safe sanctuary of their local church. They had seen what it had done for others!

John, the younger elder with the vivid vision, vindicated himself five years later. He made a peace pilgrimage to Oconomowoc begging forgiveness. This gentle soul wept as he recounted the Elk Grove gory years when their body was bludgeoned to death.

As the peace pipe was passed around our meeting room, all festering feelings went up in smoke. John was pleased that his doomsday vision died a violent death in the parking lot, when the macabre was mashed to the macadam. The return of the weeping prophet was a time of rejoicing for all of us.

# 10

# Bombarded by Beer Demons

Leading meetings during the early days of the Charismatic Renewal was like playing Russian Roulette with a chamber orchestra—the leader had one chance in six of being mortally wounded if he wasn't wearing the full armor. It took only one tuned-out musician to turn harmony into a holocaust. With this Juilliard Judas calling the shots, only the helmet of salvation kept the level-headed leader leaning on the everlasting arms. When he encountered a full chamber he was forced to face the music.

In the middle 60's there was a dearth of dedicated leaders who had experienced live combat. Having led nothing more lively than a depreciation debate at an auditors' symposium, I considered myself among the ill-equipped. However, my training at Ft. Leonard Wood came in handy on occasion.

By the process of elimination, Ken Chandler and I were the designated leaders for Living Waters Fellowship. While we were both neophytes in the nudgings of the Holy Spirit, Ken has a natural leadership ability which the Lord elevated to the spiritual dimension. This tall matinee idol combined a caring attitude, a mellow speaking voice and spiritual authority to inspire confidence in people. Of course it didn't hurt that Ken had an oriental twang to his God given gift of tongues.

The average attendance on Friday nights was twenty people. However, Jay Dalton assured a full house when he arranged for Dr. Derek Prince to speak. Derek was our first internationally known guest speaker outside of Harry Greenwood, who was part of the family by now.

Corralling Derek Prince for a Friday night was like landing Gen. Norman Schwartzkopf for a banquet after Operation Desert Storm. The much-maligned Charismatic movement gravitated towards anyone who acted as if they had blue blood pouring through their veins. Buoyed by a British accent and an ambassador's air, Derek's acute intellect imparted prestige every place he went.

Born in India to a British military family, Derek was educated at Eaton College and Cambridge University. An avowed atheist, he was converted to Christ in 1940 and baptized in the Holy Spirit a few days later. In 1968 Derek moved to Ft. Lauderdale to establish a think tank for terrestrial teaching titans called the Holy Spirit Teaching Mission. Bob Mumford, Don Basham and Charles Simpson were his colleagues.

Derek Prince was a proper pioneer without fear. He outclassed adversaries with his quick mind. Once after being attacked by his peers for delving into the deliverance ministry and blasted by the bourgeoisie for becoming a holy roller, he replied, "If rolling makes us holy, let's roll! If holiness comes that easy, what are we waiting for?" As the years rolled on I realized that people's hang-up was holiness, not rolling!

Once an amateur camera addict snapped a shot of Derek Prince dancing in the Spirit with his shirt tail hanging out. The prized photo made the rounds of every neo-pentecostal group in the country. Derek was also the forerunner of a flock of leg-lengthening luminaries who put backs back in alignment through prayer.

With a man of this caliber coming we encouraged people to invite friends and foes alike. John and Bev Reishus were successful in recruiting many students from Nashotah House, an Episcopal Seminary a few miles away.

John and Bev had been an integral part of Father Richard Winkler's prayer group at Trinity Episcopal Church in Wheaton, Illinois. Trinity was one of the first main-line churches to experience the gifts of the Holy Spirit in the mid-1950's. Later, John was led into a delayed vocation of studying for the priesthood at Nashotah House. John and Bev nurtured an unofficial network between Nashotah House and Living Waters that has lasted for thirty years.

The momentous March night finally arrived. When the music room became packed, people poured into the living room.

Jay Dalton transported Derek and his wife Lydia from the airport and they arrived as our meeting was starting.

Lydia, a native of Denmark and founder of a Christian children's home, was considerably older than Derek, who was in his fifties. Wearing her hair in a bun and balancing thick eyeglasses near the end of her nose gave Lydia a rather austere appearance. She was known for hitting Harry Greenwood hard on his humor!

To say I was slightly nervous was the same as saying Abraham Lincoln was a little bit dead. I was sweating bullets and no one was firing yet! Brother Andrew Ulrich rippled the room with his rendition of reworked revival songs. In addition to breathing deeply, I was praying in tongues and pleading the blood of Jesus, knowing the next moment I would have to rise from my respite and greet the gathering.

After the welcome, the Holy Spirit led us in worship for a half-hour followed by a strong prophetic word.

With hands raised high we reached out to the Lord with the chorus, "Oh Come Let Us Adore Him." Suddenly we were interrupted by a loud shout from the back that filled the flock with fright. "Vhen are you going to qvit singing your lullabies to Jesus and let my husband speak?" was the cry. Nobody replied as a silence seized the place that would make a morgue sound like a madhouse. My ticker felt as if its time had terminated!

If this word was from the Lord, He sure changed his strategy! The message had more muscle than Oscar Mayer has meat. The Scandinavian accent gave the prophetess away.

Discerning that this outburst was a camouflaged command I quickly introduced Derek Prince in glowing terms with no reference to the grenade that had exploded. Meanwhile, the launcher looked like the calm after the storm.

Derek didn't add any fuel to the fireworks. He was either too shocked or an old hand at handling live grenades. He shared a brief testimony and then taught on "Repentance From Dead Works" from Hebrews 6:1. All the dead works were blown to bits when Lydia lowered the boom on us earlier.

After Derek finished we dared to sing one last lullaby to Jesus before a time of fellowship and refreshments. Derek and Lydia had to leave due to jet lag.

Dr. Ed Fraser was their designated driver back to Milwaukee. Ed and his dad Russell had been medical missionaries to China with the Lost Tribes Mission headquartered in Wausau, Wisconsin. Russell served on the mission field for fifty years before he was baptized in the Holy Spirit. Ed soon followed his dad's leap of faith. They counted the cost of Pentecost as Lost Tribes Mission was part of a Protestant contingent who believed the gifts of the Holy Spirit ended with the early church. Even holding hands caused problems for courting couples until they consummated their marriage.

While Ed headed east on I-94 Lydia continued to launch live ones from the back seat. She warned Ed that our house was haunted from attic to basement with beer demons and anyone entering the place was a prime candidate to be sucked up by these spirits!

This knee-numbing news hit Ed hard. Lost Tribes tradition taught that all alcohol was anathema. If lovers couldn't embrace, they certainly weren't allowed to belt down beers!

After wrestling all night with visions of burly beer demons running rampant around our house, Ed was led to share the story. Unfortunately, he didn't phone us first.

When he did call, we were horrified to hear our hallowed home was under attack! Reminding Ed that possession is nine-tenths of the law, we swore that there wasn't one ounce of beer on the premises. We even invited him to case the joint! At the risk of being sized up as "Sipping Saints", we neglected to mention the wine stored in the pantry for our stomach's sake.

Rigid religiosity produces personal prejudices. When the demon of alcohol is under attack it is called "wine thrashing" or "selling the grapevine on the grape juice theory of evolution." Never mind Jesus' first miracle. Even the King of Kings is entitled to an off day!

Apparently a fine tarred and feathered friend informed Lydia that Karen's ancestors started the Miller Brewing Company.

Armed with this nasty knowledge, Lydia let her beer bias burst into the thick of the battle. We encouraged Ed to get on his grapevine and plead our case with gusto!

Karen, never one to let a Great Dane do damage and go dormant, called Florida the next day. When Derek answered, Karen shared our distress over the beer demons. Derek lived up to his surname in relating to this eerie episode. He apologized, saying this wasn't his perception of our place and thanked us for the pleasant visit. Derek didn't elaborate on Lydia's leanings.

We informed Ed that Derek had vindicated our vast Victorian. The coast was clear to reappear. Ed was obviously in better spirits knowing the burden of the beer demons had lifted.

A year later the Princes were back in the "Beer Capital of the World." Derek was the featured speaker at the FGBMFI regional conference.

After the Saturday evening meeting, Bill Toll invited us for a late night nourishment at the Jolly Roger restaurant. The Lord placed us in the middle of a long table, across from Lydia and Derek. It was a healing hour—there was no mention of the mayhem from last March's melodrama. We learned about Lydia's ministry of love to the downtrodden children of India. We saw her in a different light—the light of the Lord.

Lydia was in the twilight time of her life and the Lord called her home gently a few years later. The Scandinavian saint who marched in like a lioness on that memorable March night went out like a lamb.

## The Bitter Taste of Tongues

One Friday night a month, Dr. Bill Oberg, a spirit-filled Wheaton College professor, taught at Living Waters. His wife Ruth supplied accompaniment for the choruses. Bill, always low-key, remained seated while sharing, peering with earnest eyes over the rim of his glasses resting on the narthex of his nose.

One Friday night Bill's teaching was rudely interrupted by a thunderous voice stammering in tongues! Bill attempted to continue but the bloke was too stubborn to stop. When Bill was silent the tongues ceased, but when Bill resumed, the untamed tongue lashed out in a tempest that could turn a tea party into a barroom brawl. This wasn't Pentecost, this was pandemonium!

There was a familiar spirit behind this tongue. No, it wasn't Danish—this time it was decidedly Germanic. Genetically it sounded as if it could be traced to one of Hitler's henchmen. Maybe if I screamed "Achtung" the tongues would terminate.

I sneaked a peek at the pack to see their reaction to this renegade. Overall, they appeared ashen. Not a creature was stirring, not even a Living Waters leader.

Bill, giving it the old Wheaton College try, attempted to teach once more. However, the voice hammering home its horrendous harangue cut Bill off with the grace of a potentate on pep pills!

I was about to pounce on the poacher and provide my own interpretation, when Eldon Purvis, visiting from the Holy Spirit Teaching Mission in Ft. Lauderdale, gently ushered the man into the living room.

As Bill started teaching again, the wounded soul sobbed on Eldon's shoulder, pouring out pails full of pain from the past. The Lord sent one of his heavenly hosts to bring healing to this hurting heckler.

When they returned, Eldon introduced his newfound friend as Chuck Updorf. Chuck's shadow side faded as his face took on an angelic glow. Mesmerized by this mighty miracle we invited Chuck to come back. If this was part of the end time's persecution, we had better get prepared—the armor was wearing thin!

The next morning Eldon talked about Chuck's chances of growing in the Christian life. As a victim of child abuse, Chuck unleashed his anger on his family. To reinforce self-hatred he provoked rejection by acting out publicly. Chuck considered the Charismatic circuit fair game because of the freedom of the Spirit format.

Eldon's ministry of love started Chuck's release, but he needed constant prayer, affirmation and counseling to live the victorious Christian life. His days of trampling the troops in tongues were over. He was no candidate for sainthood, but as the Lord healed him his family relationship was restored. Anyone encountering the anguish of Chuck Updorf's pain on that nerve-racking night knows they witnessed a divine transformation.


## Jimmy Swervert

Ecclesiastes teaches that there is a season for everything. Friday afternoons were stomach-churning time in anticipation of what was to transpire later that evening. This Friday was no exception.

Coming home from work I saw a sleek silver Stingray speed down our mile-long driveway. As the car careened around the second suicide curve, its guardian angel bailed out of the back seat, somersaulting into the swamp in search of a safer sanctuary. Who was this heavy-footed hotshot tearing apart the terrain as if the tribulation was at hand?

By the time I caught up, two middle-aged men were ringing the front doorbell. I recognized the redhead as Rick Rodgers, the fun-loving photographer from Kenosha. I assumed his pale plump passenger was Jimmy Swervert, the speaker he suggested for our meeting that night.

On the phone Rick had billed Jimmy Swervert as God's man of faith and power who was ready at any hour to preach to the lost and pray for the sick. In person Jimmy appeared as if he needed perking up himself after exhibiting signs of acute car sickness.

When we entered the kitchen, Karen was shocked to see I had guests gracing my presence. I quickly ushered the early birds into the living room and returned to the kitchen for a confab.

My first attempt to convince Karen that I hadn't invited these two turkeys to dinner went over like a live grenade in a love offering bucket! As the scene simmered down, we were free to face the real foe—a food shortage. Frantic for fill-in fare, we spied some Spam which Karen miraculously resurrected to look like a fancy French pâté. I placed this choice culinary concoction on the table next to the chicken.

Taking a leap of faith, I served our guests first. They spurned the Spam and dove into the chicken as if it was about to take flight.

Faced with Spam or famine, I chose the latter—I was too nervous to eat anyway.

Meanwhile, Jimmy Swervert ran afoul of any fellowship as he chomped on the chicken. Karen asked him what his topic would be. Acting more like a monk masking moonshine than an energized evangelist, his only answer was a blank stare. How could this shushed-up servant slip out of his shroud and deliver the keys to the kingdom?

We separated Jimmy from the chicken and led him to a large upholstered chair in the music room. Ten minutes later the room was packed with people bubbling over on the new wine.

Brother Andrew Ulrich ignited the ivories of the baby grand with a pulsating rhythm of saintly syncopation known as "Reformation Roller Rink." Any deadwood in the crowd was quickened back to life by Andrew's keyboard capers honed on the south side of Milwaukee. Brother Andrew was in no known danger of being mistaken for Van Cliburn. However, he had been likened to Liberace as he bounced his body back and forth like a rocking horse on a roller coaster.

Brother Andrew was the pastor of Church of the Risen Savior in Milwaukee, a holiness church in the classic Pentecostal tradition. Pentecostals were as dumbfounded as other denominations in discovering that some of the Lord's most frozen chosen had slipped out of their iceberg image. Flames of Holy Ghost fire sparked a worldwide grass roots revival, rekindling charismatic gifts and a fervent love of Jesus.

Meanwhile, Jimmy Swervert sat in the corner suffering from the Lazarus Syndrome. I was tempted to poke him with a toothpick to make sure he was still alive. Nothing deadens the spirits of a lively crowd faster than introducing a mummy!

Hit by a divinely-inspired idea, I introduced Rick Rogers instead, and asked him to present his buddy Jimmy.

Rick raved about Jimmy in such glowing terms I feared the people might think the Messiah had returned! Rick mentioned mighty miracles, hundreds of healings and thousands of converts under Jimmy's ministry. Meanwhile, our star of the silent screen sat with his eyes transfixed on a suspicious spot on the Oriental rug—Winston, our old basset, was a Baptist with a bad bladder.

Suddenly Jimmy sprang from his chair and charged around the room like a caged lion reacting to newfound freedom! The booming behemoth shouted with a raging raspy voice about the Culpepper Crusades where he preached under huge tents to thousands. I entertained the idea of interrupting Jimmy's itinerary with a cross-body block to remind him we were only forty fearful people crammed into a small room.

Jimmy was sizzling faster than a French fry fortified by another round of grease when suddenly he dropped the knee-knocking news that recently he had been released from the back ward of a mental institution—this was his first outing since the separation. I was tempted to call his shrink and tell him he made a dreadful mistake—we would cooperate fully in Jimmy's safe return.

Rick's smile had soured and I heard rumbling in his solar plexus. If ruddy Rick was sounding the alarm we were all in trouble!

Jimmy waved his big black Bible in the air and started a harangue on holiness. He told us to quit compromising with the world and get right with God, before He wiped us all out. Jimmy bellowed, "A lukewarm Christian is as pleasing to the Lord as a partial circumcision!" I didn't know whether I was in the world, of the world, or under the world, but I knew I wasn't on top of the world! My head was pounding like it was a stake in a hotshot horseshoe match.

Jimmy paused for a penetrating peer into the evasive eyes of the beholders. His steely stare was scary enough to cause "Sipping Saints" to switch to prune juice! If Jimmy was God's gift to humanity, I wanted to join another race.

Jimmy worked the fearful faithful for an hour when the ranks started to slip away. Every time he elevated his eyes heavenward, one or two of the flock made their break. Moving faster than a speeding bullet, they flung open the front door and raced to their car. It was as if poison gas had been released on the place and this was their last chance for survival. Jimmy caught one of the creeping creatures out of the corner of his eye and called her back for repentance.

A few of the escapees retreated to the kitchen, barricaded the door and stormed the gates of heaven.

Taking a mental inventory of the remnant remaining in the room didn't take long. The meeting had taken on a Western flavor—foot stomping and wide open spaces. The fearless forty had dwindled down to nine.

Brother Andrew baby-sat the baby grand as if Jimmy was going to demolish it for his next demonstration of Holy Ghost power. Rick was so pale even his freckles looked freaked. A new couple huddled in the corner hung on to each other as if they were still on their honeymoon. The others were weather-beaten Charismatics cringing under this one-man crusade.

Jimmy ended his message and shifted into one-on-one ministry. This realization met with gas chamber silence. Sensing I was his first victim I prayed that Karen's kitchen brigade was still on their knees.

Jimmy tossed aside his maligned microphone and grabbed my head in a vise-tight grip. His style of laying on of hands was more like a strangle hold at the Friday night fights. As he moved my neck around like a gear box in a stick shift car, I developed renewed empathy for LBJ's dog. Now I knew why scripture warned, "Lay hands on no man suddenly!" Apparently Jimmy hadn't meditated on that verse for a while.

Jimmy prophesied that the Lord was pleased with my faithful shepherding of this flock. Meanwhile, two more sheep drifted away—the cute couple in the corner. That left only seven in the fold!

Having worked me over, Jimmy moved towards Brother Andrew at the baby grand. I raced over to rescue him from Jimmy's gymnastics and the others joined me. We laid hands on Jimmy, suddenly! My hands wanted to squeeze his neck, but I couldn't support it with a Bible reference.

Patience prevailed as we placed our hands on less sensitive parts and pleaded with the Lord to take control of this charismaniac.

Slowly Jimmy crawled back into his safe solemn shell. He slunk back in his chair as if he was hibernating. At the first twist of his torso I was prepared to stuff him with more chicken. However, Jimmy didn't twitch an inch—history had repeated itself in four hours flat.

I rushed Rick to the kitchen where Karen's contingent was still holed up. Convinced that Jimmy hadn't joined us they let us in. We shot Rick with suggestions for salvaging Jimmy's life. He promised to get help for his friend. If Rick didn't slow down his Stingray they would both need a resurrection before they hit Kenosha.

Rick walked his wasted warrior to the parking lot for their midnight ride, while the rest of the remnant retreated to their cars. Too keyed up to sleep, Karen and I returned to the kitchen for a catharsis session.

Answers didn't come easy that night, only questions. Who destroyed the dike and dumped the floodgates of hell on our assembly? Did the Devil do it himself or did he have help? The Holy Ghost wouldn't go Hollywood! Maybe man's carnal nature turned the meeting into a carnival. The shrink has to shoulder some of the blame for letting this cat out of the bag prematurely!

The freedom of the spirit suffered flesh wounds and we had to administer first aid to prevent infection. The body of Christ can't be built up when gangrene gets a good grip. We resolved to dig deeper for the days ahead. With the harvest on the horizon there was no time for hibernation. Flinging our future at the feet of Jesus, we jumped into bed to claim any remaining reward of rest in the wee hours of the morning.

## Taming the Tomah Tigress

We received a two-year reprieve from renegades ruining our meetings. However, lulled into believing that this could never happen again, we were living on bartered time.

One Friday night, after our large family room was built onto the back of our house, we were worshipping the Lord with a lively spirit of praise when a holy hush hit the room. I sensed a strong prophetic word was coming. Hopefully some sidewinder wouldn't quench the Spirit by shotputting a pound of flesh. Folks out of the flow get nervous in the service where there is no noise!

If only we could worship in a hermetically-sealed solarium where every breath was directly from the Son. The Light of the World would lift us up to look in His brilliance. The lion would lay down with the lamb, leaders wouldn't be lambasted by Lone Rangers, and all spiritual warfare would cease.

Suddenly my dwelling on this impossible dream was brought down to earth by an ear-splitting scream. Next an unidentified flying object soared through the air with the greatest of ease, landing two feet from the fireplace. From my vantage point it appeared to be a Bible but I wouldn't swear on it. Feeding on the word is fruitful but flying it could be fatal.

Then came the crash. The missal's mistress somersaulted backward into a table of books with her folding chair still attached! The bug-eyed brethren severed her from the debris and deposited her in front of the fireplace.

Her friends, Bill and Fran Furman, who brought her from Tomah, Wisconsin, identified their acrobat as Janice Germaine. The Furmans explained that Janice suffered from mysterious seizures that weren't diabetic or epileptic in origin. They requested our discernment as to the nature of her difficulty. At the moment I was leaning towards a Legion linkup!

I suggested some stout-hearted men remove Janice from the floor and carry her to the couch in the next room. The Furmans plummeted the plan with a down-home discourse on the dangers of disturbing this damsel in distress. They warned that Janice reverts into a screaming rage when moved prematurely!

Lacking the faith to test the spirits of this Tomah tigress in front of a full house, we proceeded with plan B—two team members kneeled next to our twisted sister and silently saturated her with soaking prayer. Janice produced a few faint utterances during the teaching but no more sonorous sounds.

Once the meeting ended, Janice jumped up like a gymnast, mingled with the amazed multitude, and carried on a coherent conversation. Either we had witnessed a mighty miracle or were dealing with an imposter of imponderable proportions! The Furmans remained mum on the subject as they prepared to return to Tomah.

Five weeks to the night a nervous knock at the door interrupted my meditation before the meeting. One of the brethren, Jon Van Dingstee, was the bearer of bad news—a young lady with light brown hair collapsed in the corridor. With deja vu dancing all over my brain, I needed no further information—I knew it was Janice!

Proving she was no creature of habit, Janice picked a new spot—the dark blue tile in the entranceway to the family room. The Furmans were feverishly huddled over their friend curled in the fetal position. People arriving for the meeting were forced to take a leap of faith to hurdle this barricade.

Bill and Fran Furman insisted that Janice could not be moved, but I bristled at this response. In my estimation there was no downside after this displeasing demonstration. So what if the Tomah tigress tore the place apart with her lungs! I called in the troops to transport her to the couch.

However, our mission was impossible as Janice was always one jump ahead. Her smoke alarm warned her there was fireworks. Discerning there was no future on the floor, she vertically revived with no vestige of her malady. Switching on her saintly smile she talked in tender tones that would make a tough guy tingle. Her aura was so ethereal, it was doubtful she was still in this world.

I took the Tomah trio into the music room to test my theory. I suggested that taking a dive, creating a tempest and casually coming up for air was too cunning to be coincidence. We would admit defeat in this contrived chess game if they would pawn off their attention-getting aspirations elsewhere. Satan's surrogate sapped our strength faster than Wimpy wipes out hamburgers!

The Tomah trio rejected my revelations and maintained that the seizures were a mystery. We wished them well, but asked them to stay away until these strange encounters of the third kind could be cleared up.

We haven't tripped over the Tomah trio since. We trust the Lord has raised their vision. It's hard to send wounded warriors on their way but sometimes tough love gets them back on their feet.

## Pressing on Toward the Prize

All these animated antics were a far cry from the safe sanctuary of our evangelical Protestant heritage. Back then we were surrounded by WASPS whose stingers had been seared. Their most potent attack was to hit the pocketbook on Stewardship Sunday. Now we had knocked down a huge hornets' nest and the inhabitants were beyond the buzzing stage.

It would be easier to pack it in than press on towards the goal for the prize promised in Philippians 3:14. What is this prize? Is it some spiritual lottery with one winner and the rest sent away empty-hearted? Is it to strive on Earth to obtain a front row seat at the great white throne?

This passage is better understood by taking our mind off the prize and turning into the pressing on portion. The plea to "press on" was not the deathbed desires of a Ming monarch to a gathering of Chinese laundry luminaries! These are the immortal words of the great Apostle Paul exhorting all Christians to move beyond the secure spiritual walk and join Jesus at the pinnacle of the temple.

Paul, as the first coach of the Philippian Flyers basketball team, prompted his players to exert full-court pressure. Stepping beyond mid-court opens up fertile ground for testing new territory. In Philippians 3:16 he also tells the team to hold on to what they have attained. The Flyers arch rivals, the Corinthian Carnals, might flip out over some far-out fads but they ultimately pay the price for their prodigal pursuits!

Our persecutions were pale compared to coach Paul's—tea parties in contrast to tempests. For every Jimmy Swervert there are six thousand unsung saints. For every Tomah Tigress there are tens of thousands turning to Jesus. For every battle over beer demons there are battalions baptized in the Holy Spirit. And for every Chuck Updorf utterance there is untold heavenly music ministered to the multitudes. Even Dow Jones would rejoice over these returns!

# 11

# A Mighty Wind Breathes
# Upon the Windy City

Boredom was a stranger at Holy Ghost events. The Full Gospel Businessmen's Fellowship International convention at the Hilton Hotel in Chicago was no exception. Fifteen of the faithful attended from the Oconomowoc area, including Brian Steinke and Scott Soergel.

Scott is the oldest son of Mary and Normal Soergel, members of the Congregational Church. Mary attended meetings at Living Waters in the spring of 1968 after a friend, Carolyn LeSac, informed her we were praying for Scott's healing.

Scott was diagnosed in 1965, at fourteen, as having a malignant brain tumor. In the course of three operations, the bulk of the tumor was removed along with most of his pituitary gland. His hypothalamus gland was damaged which at times made him ravenous, lethargic, forgetful and prone to lose emotional control. The doctor concluded that Scott would not live beyond his eighteenth year.

By seventeen Scott was so depressed about his condition he gave up on life. Living Waters committed itself to praying for his complete healing, body, soul and spirit.

The first time Scott attended a meeting was on a Friday evening when Harry Greenwood was the speaker. Shortly after Scott sat down he felt the warmth of a hand on his right shoulder, but there was no one visibly pressing his flesh. As the healing hand gradually pulled away, Harry gave a powerful prophetic word that started with, "My Son, I have placed my outstretched hand upon you to draw you to myself..." It ended with more words of comfort that left Scott with only one conclusion—Jesus loved him!

From that point Scott got progressively stronger. He still had some symptoms of his sickness but his spirit was alive with the love of Jesus. We soaked Scott with healing prayer as he attended every fellowship function. Ken Chandler became a big brother to this beloved child of God and brought him to the meetings when Mary couldn't come.

Convinced that Scott would benefit from the healing ministries of Kathryn Kuhlman and others at the FGBMFI convention, we arranged to take him with us.

Upon arrival in the Windy City we went directly to the auditorium where the miracle service was to take place. Two hours before the doors opened there was already a sizable crowd camped outside exhibiting a contagious expectant atmosphere. Bearded brothers with bare bony knees rubbed elbows with Michigan Avenue fashion plates, as they sang worship songs that moved the spirit and alleviated sore feet.

Kathryn Kuhlman, born in Concordia, Missouri, was ordained Baptist. She shepherded a congregation in Franklin, Pennsylvania, where spontaneous healings took place as she preached on "the Power of God." As word spread about the signs and wonders, she was led to rent the Carnegie Auditorium in Pittsburgh to accommodate the growing crowds. The power fell for fourteen years before she branched out to other spots, such as the Shrine Auditorium in Los Angeles. As the foremost faith-healer of the times, thousands from all over the world attended her miracle services to be touched by Jesus. Kathryn taking no credit for herself said, "I am a woman with a little faith in a great God."

At 2:00 p.m. the doors swung open and the eager believers rushed in like a mighty wind to capture the cherished front seats. Mania momentarily blocked the biblical admonition that the first shall be last.

The handicapped had a helping hand in this mad dash—they slipped in the side door a half hour before. Wheelchairs were lined up like the latest models on a car lot.

The two-hundred voice choir sang "He Touched Me" as the presence of the Holy Spirit permeated the place. Twenty minutes later a smiling Kathryn Kuhlman walked in from the wings with her white silk dress flowing a few inches from the floor. Electricity emanated from her as she glided across the stage calling out conditions that were being healed. As she named them, people popped up all over the auditorium and claimed them.

A lady with a gigantic goiter growing in her neck had it instantly vanish. Asthma and allergies were under attack from above. Ears opened and vision was restored. Wheelchairs were abandoned as their occupants walked to the front.

Kathryn, pointing to a young woman in the balcony who was healed of cancer, shouted, "There is healing in the name of Jesus." As she returned to center stage to greet those parading towards the platform, I prayed she would add brain tumors to her list for Scott's sake.

Kathryn quizzed each one and asked them to say something about their miracle. Before they could finish she placed her right hand on their heads and they fell backwards under the power of the Holy Spirit. Ushers catching the falling faithful guided them to the ground. They rested motionless for many minutes until moved by the Spirit to rise. Kathryn decked some with a double dose, while the rest walked wobbling back to their seats aglow with the Spirit.

Towards the end of the service Kathryn called the clergy forward for an anointing. There were more collars in this cluster than in all Cook County kennels combined! The shepherds looked sheepish as the ushers lined them up side by side across the stage. As Kathryn touched the clerics they crumpled to the floor like trees in a twister. A couple of resisting redwoods needed a second shot before they toppled over to join their fallen comrades. The Holy Spirit's presence was so powerful even the catchers collapsed under the anointing.

Kathryn cleared the deck of clergy and invited the Catholic nuns forward. None of them made a habit of this in the convent but they appeared ready for the same experience the apostles had on the Mount of Transfiguration when their feet failed them. Moments later the sisters were sprawled on the platform like penguins at a pajama party!

We exited the auditorium with mixed emotions—rejoicing over the miracles, but wishing Scott could be counted in that number. However, touched spiritually, he remained upbeat and hopeful there would be more opportunities for prayer.

## Stalking the Jesus Man from Jessup, Georgia

After registering at the Hilton, we took a short siesta before attending the evening meeting in the ballroom.

After a lengthy round of Full Gospel testimonies, Rev. Wendall Wallace was introduced. When Wendall finished preaching he jerked his jacket off, rolled up his sleeves and called people up front for ministry. When asthma was mentioned, Brian Steinke went forward. Wendall laid hands on Brian and he hit the floor as if he was struck by lightning. He laid on the floor so long I was tempted to cancel his room and save him some cash. Brian was still "slain in the Spirit" when the service ended an hour later.

In the 1960s, this falling phenomenon was called "slain in the Spirit." Subsequently the experience was renamed "resting in the Spirit" by Ladies Illuminated International, a splinter group of Women's Aglow, who were appalled that this manifestation was described by such violent terminology. A macho wing of FGBMFI put up a floor fight but eventually succumbed to the wishes of LII.

Meanwhile, Wendall was ministering a marathon. Aided by a word of knowledge, he proclaimed there was a Catholic sister present who was skeptical about this falling phenomenon. If she would step forward, God would prove to her it was of the Holy Spirit.

A small habitless sister walked to the front to confirm her doubts to Wendall. Ten seconds later she was flat on the floor where she remained for fifteen minutes. When Sr. Francis Clare Schares got back on her feet she testified about the peaceful presence of the Lord while prostrated. This launched her on a worldwide Charismatic teaching ministry including resting weary warriors in the Spirit. Sr. Fran has written many books including "Wow God" and speaks at Living Waters Fellowship periodically.

The next morning I woke up with renewed determination to pursue a preacher who would pray for Scott. While Karen attended a ladies luncheon, Scott and I slipped into a side room in the Hilton where a slight man with slicked-down hair was directing a healing session.

Rev. Joe Poppel from Jessup, Georgia, with a deep southern drawl, was calling people forward with back pain. He seated a woman in a chair and grabbed her heels in his hands to demonstrate that her left leg was an inch shorter than her right one. As Rev. Poppel prayed in tongues, her left leg slowly stretched forth until both legs were of equal length. After he went through the same procedure with her arms the back pain disappeared and the delighted lady walked back to her seat without a hitch.

We moved closer as the next candidate came up on crutches. As a result of an auto accident, his right foot curled inward and was visibly shorter than his left. Proving that length was no handicap for the Lord, the man's foot straightened and pushed forward as Joe Poppel prayed. Gasps filled the room as he made it back to his seat minus the crutches. He wasn't Boston Marathon material yet but he was already a moving miracle!

If only the Milwaukee Bucks could latch on to this leg lengthening—they would tear up the league with seven-footers.

Leg lengthening stretched the flock's faith to believe for other miracles. Brother Joe named many maladies, but not a brain tumor. In desperation I told Scott we were going forward for anything above the neck—even dandruff would do!

Meanwhile I had a brainstorm. When Brother Joe tried to exit we would block his path and plead our case. Unless he vanished via the fire escape there was only one way out of the room.

Brother Joe asked everyone to bow their heads while his associate Bill Bellows led in a closing prayer. With every eye closed Brother Joe made a beeline for the door. By the time I tuned in to this chicanery he had twenty paces on us. As a lifelong evangelical I finally found out why Catholics never close their eyes. From now on it would be watch and pray as the Bible suggests!

When Bill Bellows concluded his lengthy benediction we begged him to arrange for Brother Joe to pray for Scott. With pain in his voice he explained it was not possible. Brother Joe was drained and couldn't pray for people privately.

Scott seemed sad but perked up when I assured him King Jesus was in charge and wasn't limited by his loyal subjects! We were pressing on for the prize of a higher calling.

When Karen returned to the room we related our leg lengthening stories. After accusing us of pulling her leg, she trumped us with tales of the deaf and blind being healed and varicose veins disappearing at the Kathryn Kuhlman ladies luncheon.

We conscripted Karen in our pursuit of prayer for Scott. With her persuasive personality she could convince a native Californian that Gary, Indiana, was the Garden of Eden!

We had dinner that night with relatives who were so distant we couldn't even prove we were all descendants of Abraham. The link was Stanley Lund, a tall, friendly Pentecostal preacher from Zion, Illinois. Stanley was related to Arthur Swanson, a cousin-in-law of mine, who was a well-known architect from Park Ridge, Illinois.

Stanley wore many coats on his Christian journey and was well-suited for all occasions. Smooth as silk, he sat impeccably dressed in pastel Palm Beach attire. His genes geared him for business or politics but the Lord placed Stanley in the pulpit.

Stanley, switching into his Scotland Yard mode, offered his services instantly. Popping a few mints he dashed off to make contacts and returned twenty minutes later with some valuable leads.

Stanley enlisted Larry Hammond, an Episcopal layman from Florida, to assist him. Larry's enthusiasm for this mission was bolstered by his wife desiring prayer from Joe Poppel for her malformed foot.

The FGBMFI foreign intrigue escalated. Stanley and Larry leaped around the Hilton like lunatics on their last lark before lockup time. Somewhere along the line they quit leaning on the everlasting arms and resorted to strong-arm tactics in an all-out effort to crash Brother Joe's room. Karen and I considered contacting Dick Daley to see what pull the old pol might have with Poppel. Meanwhile Scott remained as calm as a cosmonaut navigating a canoe, convinced that the source of living waters would restore his health.

The big break in the case came during Conference checkout time. Stanley's super sleuth style rendered Bill Bellows breathless. Stalking him like the Shadow, he popped out from pillars to plead his cause. After mouthing another mint, Stanley suddenly spied Bill in the lobby and blocked his path to the cashier's cage. Bill finally took pity on the poor man and arranged to meet him on the eleventh floor.

Taking no chances, seven of us camped out at the elevator until Bill arrived. He herded us down the hall and rapped on room 1164. The Jesus man from Jessup invited us in. Formalities faded fast as he was all business. Faith filled the room as he prayed a fervent prayer for Scott's healing.

While Scott basked in heavenly sunshine, we turned our attentions to Larry's wife who needed a reconstructive miracle. As Brother Joe held her ankles, her right foot straightened and changed shape. Holy Ghost excitement was released as he encouraged her to rise and walk. She was the first lady I had met in ages who really needed a new pair of shoes—the old right shoe wouldn't fit on the new right foot!

We praised the Lord for his healing love and thanked Brother Joe and Bill. This time it was our turn to exit knowing we had witnessed the message of Mark 16 in our midst.

Packing presents no problems when your mind is mesmerized by miracles. Even the luggage seemed lighter. The final proof that the supernatural took place was I paid our hotel bill with a smile.

Our silence ceased as we crossed the state line. Scott, who was growing spiritually, became visionary—he described in detail how the Lord held him in his strong loving arms as Brother Joe prayed for him.

Jesus, who is the same yesterday, today, and forever, changed his style. Knowing we were incapable of keeping quiet, He never told us to clam up about these miracles. Our phone bill ballooned the next few weeks!

During our drive home we decided we would ask Brother Joe Poppell to include Oconomowoc on his next trip north. If we turned Stanley Lund loose on him he would be barreling down our driveway by August.

However, the super-sleuth wasn't needed. Bill Toll wanted Brother Joe for Full Gospel in Milwaukee and included Living Waters on his itinerary.

The word spread like peanut butter on an oil slick as people packed our porch to its portals. He called forward three candidates with back pain and each one had one leg shorter than the other. Krista and her little friends were nose-to-nose with the feet as the legs grew to equal size. After Brother Joe granted Krista's request to pray for more legs, he moved on to other ailments.

After the meeting he lined up my legs. Presently I wasn't in torment, but often I suffered back pain so severe I crawled up the stairs like a baby on a second floor explore game. After determining that my left leg was a half-inch short, Brother Joe prayed and my left knee numbed as if it was shot with Novocain. When I snuck a peek to make sure there was no pulling I saw my left leg extending.

Brother Joe declared me healed and gave me a "holy hug." The main aim of this game is to discern which side of the head the huggee is heading for. If the hugger and the huggee choose the same path it can produce pain and busted beaks!

Assuming bad breath doesn't bother you, the only other hazard with "holy hugs" is when a huge hugger yanks you off your feet as if a hanging is about to take place. Never battle a known bone crusher who rearranges your ribs like he was preparing you for the Saturday night barbecue!

Since Brother Joe prayed for me, back pain has been a pittance compared to previous episodes. I can walk tall instead of crawl. Exercises performed religiously are also part of God's provision.

"Leg lengthening," which in upper-crust Charismatic circles is known as "back adjusting," was the "in" ministry in the late 60's. Every self-respecting shepherd added this dimension to his ministerial repertoire. Even princely Derek Prince included "leg lengthening" on his liturgical list.

The mystery surrounding this ministry may never be solved. Almost every person prayed for experiences positive results instantly. In some instances the pain reappears when the person becomes stressed or refuses to release resentment. At that point a repeat of the prayer is in order along with any further ministry required.

"Leg lengthening" might be simply the Lord's way of using the foolish of this world to confound the mighty. When kneeling on a hard floor lining up legs, you'd better be sure the Lord is with you or you will be left facing defeat!

## A Heavenly Symphony Visits Vatican West

Scott Soergel's physical condition continued to improve. He spent the summer working at a Christian camp called Cross Acres near Hustisford, Wisconsin. Cross Acres, run by Don and Erma Sandeen, brought core kids from Milwaukee out to the country for a two-week camping experience. In addition to traditional camp activities, the kids were confronted with the person of Jesus Christ. Scott contributed his skills by teaching leather crafts. It was great therapy!

All of Scott's family came to our meetings except his dad Norman. Norman was in hot pursuit of another spirit—the spirit of alcohol. After dropping his family off at the fellowship, he shook the dust off his wheels on the way to worshipping at his own temple—the nearest tavern.

The entire family was adversely affected by Norman's dysfunctional behavior. Mary, his wife, found prayer support at Living Waters where she was able to be honest about her feelings during this dismal period.

In 1971 the family moved from Oconomowoc to a farm north of Ashippun, so Scott could enjoy nature. The change in scenery did something for Norman also—he corked the bottle and sought professional help!.

Shortly afterwards, Willa Dorsey, a gospel singer in the style of Mahalia Jackson, came to our home. After Mary raved about Willa, Norman came to talk to her and was struck with her spirituality and compassion for people. Willa was the bridge to bringing this robust railroad man across the Lord's trestle. His job still required riding in the caboose, but Norman had a new engineer! He always refers to Willa as "God's open heart surgeon."

This ex-Korean war pilot not only won his war against alcoholism, he also nixed the nicotine habit. When Norman was hospitalized with bleeding ulcers, Margaret Buehler, who lived with us, went to pray for him with Karen. After attacking the ulcer she took on the spirit of nicotine. Norman testified that it immediately left his lungs and fled out his feet! Smoke has never again darkened the chimney of Norman's nose.

Scott's improving health and sunny disposition dealt a death blow to his depression. He participated in all parts of the Living Waters ministry including praying for others.

However, by the summer of 1975 noticeable changes took place—Scott's symptoms suggested the tumor might have returned. One Sunday night, with his head visibly puffy, he stood up and said he wasn't sure how long he was going to live. Dad Zieman led the fellowship in a powerful prayer of healing for Scott. Shortly afterward he was examined by Dr. Levin in Milwaukee who concluded that the edema causing the swelling disappeared!

It is traditional for the Soergels to join us for Christmas Eve, in addition to Karen's aunt and uncle, Erica and Harry John and their eight children. The Johns operated DeRance, the largest religious foundation in the world. Although located in Milwaukee, DeRance had such close connections with the Pope it was dubbed "Vatican West." The guests visiting "Vatican West" from all over the world were as varied as the visible shapes at Vic Tanny's. They ranged from Cardinals to the destitute. Many of these fascinating people were brought out to our home by Erica and Harry.

One cool July 4th the Cardinal of Uganda came and was fascinated by the motor boats on the lake. I gave him a speedy ride in our Chris-Craft, providing him with a red Wisconsin Badger ski cap to keep his head warm. He was the first African Cardinal to become a "Bucky Badger Booster!"

Christmas Eve of 1975 was no exception, as Brother Alphonso D'Ortega, a former conductor of the Rome Symphony, accompanied the Johns to our celebration. Brother Alphonso had recently been called to religious life with the order of the Holy Apostles in Cromwell, Connecticut.

After dinner he filled the music room with dramatic scores from his original compositions. Upon striking a note hard his hand sailed through the air as if he was conducting an entire orchestra. Brother Alphonso's baby grand grandeur reminded me of Brother Andrew's showmanship. However, this was definitely not prayer meeting material!

As I put more wood on the crackling fire, Malcolm Quay, Mary Soergel's father, reached for his sheet music. Mr. Quay, a cornerstone of the Congregational Church, wrote many hymns he could belt out at a moment's notice. Brother Alphonso accompanied him on his favorite selections which reflected his relationship with the Lord. Scott drifted off to sleep as his grandfather was singing.

Suddenly the sound of sleigh bells preempted the concert. The kids bolted like bunnies chased from Mr. McGregor's garden. They ushered in the night rider from the North Pole and steered him towards an upholstered chair. Santa's black belt went belly up under a fold of fat as he leaned forward to distribute a gift. If he didn't get in touch with Weight Watchers soon this could be his last trip south!

Every child was given a turn to sit on Santa's lap. Uncle Harry John, an avid amateur photographer possessed with professional equipment, took tons of time snapping each picture. Kids grimaced for the camera as they grabbed their gift hoping someday they would get to open it. Meanwhile, positioning his black box, Uncle Harry put his subjects through painstaking contortions in his search for the perfect pose. "Hold still," he shouted with Prussian persuasion. Then he backed off two paces to ponder his next attack as if he was photographing an apparition. Attired in long black baggy pants supported by suspenders, Uncle Harry looked more in tune with tintypes than Kodak.

Santa's knees numbed from holding the kids so long. Norman Soergel received an extra gift because he has the honor of being born on Jesus' birthday, albeit a few years later. Fortunately for Santa, Norman didn't sit on his lap. He had seen what it had done for others!

Scott woke up in time to accept his gift—a scarf which he placed around his neck to head off the draft from the windows.

Brother Alphonso, who befriended Scott earlier in the evening, was seated next to him relating the reasons he became a Catholic brother. Part of it had to do with his long battle with cancer. When Brother asked Scott to pray for his healing, Scott offered a short petition followed by a profound prophetic word—"I will see Jesus in a few days and will talk to Him about you!"

Scott died at home thirty-six hours later. As his temperature rose he silently slipped away to join Jesus at the age of twenty-four years. Scott lived six more than any mortal originally envisioned. The pathologist who performed the autopsy said, "There were no signs of tumor cells or any other medical explanation for Scott's death."

Scott's journey to Jesus was smooth because he lived on the same spiritual plane while planted on Earth. However, the physical separation was difficult for all of us to deal with.

Scott's newest friend came to his memorial service at the white-spired Congregational church in town. Brother Alphonso, who conducted orchestras all over the world, composed a poem in honor of Scott and played the organ as Harry John distributed copies to the congregation. Brother's ultimate tribute was when he proclaimed, "This is my finest hour!" If there were any dry eyes they were made out of glass.

Scott successfully conveyed Brother's message to the Great Physician—his cancer went into remission so he could continue his spiritual call.

When Scott joined the "cloud of witnesses" who are constantly praying for us, we placed his picture high up on the east wall of the family room as a symbol of his elevated status. When anyone needs a spiritual lift we point to Scott and tell his story.

The Soergel family members were more than survivors. They turned tribulations into triumph by getting treatment and becoming a tower of strength for others. Norman joined Alcoholics Anonymous and obtained spiritual heights that complement his hobby as a pilot. He retired from the Milwaukee Railroad, but still passes out tracts.

Mary wrote a moving book about her family entitled "Sing A Gentle Breeze" in which she weaves her talent for writing poetry in with prose. Working as a chemical dependency counselor she has helped hundreds get treatment. As Mary speaks throughout the Midwest she blends her Christian witness with a no-holds-barred approach to urging the hurting to seek help.

Meanwhile Scott is rooting the family on. He no longer needs the foreign intrigue of a Full Gospel convention to get prayer. He has free access to the greatest Healer in history!

# 12

# Crossfire at Cross Acres Camp

Working for Reilly, Penner and Benton gave me a wide range of accounting experience. I conducted a two-week audit of the Greater Galilee Baptist Church on Milwaukee's northside, where I met Rev. E. B. Phillips and some of his parishioners. Rev. Phillips' bubbling affirming personality convinced me I was God's miracle man of debits and credits sent on a special mission to teach bookkeeping to his people.

For the next few months I taught basic bookkeeping to twenty people in their church basement. I lost a few when we veered off into balancing budgets, but those who finished improved their job possibilities.

Another plus was getting to know the people personally. We invited families to our home on Saturdays to have fun in a rural setting. One couple who came out often were Jo and Charles Ponder and their children.

Elijah Toney, an elder at Greater Galilee, brought kids out for recreation once a month. One Saturday two of the boys paddled our canoe to the east end of the lake and couldn't make it back due to a sudden windstorm. Our neighbor, Mrs. George Markham, sizing up the situation from her picture window, ventured out into the lake in her inboard to rescue them. She graciously invited the lads in for cookies and helped calm their fears.

Mary and Norm Soergel took the Greater Galilee people one step further by introducing them to an authentic farm experience at their place near Ashippun.

About the same time, Don Sandeen asked if his Cross Acres camp kids could use our beach every afternoon. With some apprehension we agreed as long as they were supervised properly— eighty per cent of the campers couldn't swim any better than a Siamese cat in a raging river! Fortunately our shallow shore was surrounded by a sizable sand bar.

Daily at 3:00 p.m. two packed gear-grinding school buses chugged down the drive to deposit their cargo in our parking lot. Those who had no fear of water raced down the hill to see who could reach the beach first.

Brian Steinke performed triple duty as a bus driver, swimming instructor and beach bouncer. Other Living Waters people provided help in many ways. The Lord was our senior lifeguard— the Cross Acres crew swam for two summers without any catastrophic occurrences. There was nerve-racking noise, nasty nosebleeds and severe stress on the septic system, but no permanent damage to limb, life, property or the pursuit of happiness.

Don Sandeen, a man of voluminous visions, suggested more original projects than the U.S. Patent Office passed. We formed an advisory board to season his proposals with a pinch of practicality. Its members were Mary Soergel, Ken Chandler, Art Reimer, Karen and myself. Art, as President of the Milwaukee Bridge and Steel, brought badly needed business sense to the Cross Acres program.

The board meetings followed a persistent pattern. Don, arriving with a giant grin, eagerly gave graphic accounts of the great goings-on at the camp. Then in grandiose terms he talked about expanding the operation.

Don ignored the fact that the board was grafted into a sour grapevine that was grappling with grievances. The picture of perfection he was painting with his smooth sweeping strokes was as palatable as swallowing a palette of putty. Not everyone associated with Cross Acres was a happy camper!

The camp had survived two summers on Don's salesmanship and a dedicated staff. Now the faithful were forced to sandbag the operation to save it from floodwaters. As the waters arose, new revelations floated out from the camp—the devil was drowning Cross Acres in doctrines of demonology. Spirit-shouting, gagbagging deliverance sessions became the most visible camp activity. "House cleaning is more pressing than handicrafts," was how one self-styled exorcist explained the program.

We interrogated two teenage counselors to get a clearer picture. They described armies of demons invading the camp with cartoon characters in top hats disappearing down manholes. Cross Acres had deteriorated into a demonized Disneyland!

The board tried to talk truth to Don, but he stubbornly stuck to his erratic approach to conducting a kids camp. Meanwhile, defections were at the danger level! Don's own kids came to us with sad stories of how these activities were affecting their family. Their mother, Erna, a small gentle soul, was searching for spiritual help to preserve her sanity.

The time for talk was over—action was in order. One of our speakers, Rev. Jack Stanley, told us about Daystar, a Minneapolis ministry which was deep into spiritual discernment. Desperate, we decided to seek Daystar's help.

Using Christian karate tactics, we convinced Don to travel to the Twin Cities with us by train. However, we neglected to tell him he was the main event on this mission! Ken Chandler, our fearless leader, and Bill Flint, a troubled teen we took in, rounded out the fivesome forging forth into new frontiers.

## Nightmares at Daystar

We boarded the "Hiawatha" on Friday afternoon for this seven-hour scenic trip to St. Paul. My appreciation of the countryside was restrained by the uncertainties that lay ahead. If only the Lord would assure us we were on the right track. Cross Acres was so close to derailment the downside to this Daystar trip seemed non-existent. As long as the conductor wasn't a cartoon character there was hope!

We were met at the St. Paul station by Jack Winter, the head honcho at Daystar Ministries. Jack was a short, middle-aged man with clouds of CIA-type mystery surrounding him.

As he drove us to Daystar, he informed us about its history. It was formed many years before by people at one time associated with Bethany Fellowship. Daystar emphasized teaching, discipleship, discernment and deliverance. Their summer camp in Federal Dam, Minnesota, was called Zion Harbor and they had many other satellite ministries projected for other places.

After coffee and cake in the kitchen, we were all shown to our rooms. Dorothy and Jack Winter graciously gave up their bedroom for us. Before disappearing down the dark hallway, Jack said there would be a special worship service in the morning at which Don Sandeen would receive ministry. As restless as rattlesnakes at a masquerade for mongeese, sleep was out, intrigue was in. So were fly swatters—there was a fifty per cent chance the room was bugged! Wayfarers beware was the watchword.

After breakfast the next morning we gathered in their meeting room. Peaceful privacy passed by as a pipe dream—there were already one hundred people present. Don appeared more wide-eyed than usual but didn't look as if he would bolt. I was still keeping that option open for myself!

When the worship ended, Jack Winter announced there were special guests present who had come from Wisconsin seeking ministry. All five of us were marched up front like suspects in a lineup. There must be a mistake! We brought Don here for help and now we all had a problem—how do we protest in front of a hundred plus people after it's been blabbed that we migrated three hundred miles for ministry?

We were outnumbered three to one as Daystar elders descended on us like ravens after roadkill. There was no escape! Ken Chandler, the first martyr, appeared ashen as six men suddenly laid hands on him. After discerning his past they decided he had no future, outside of the Lord—his spiritual anointing for leadership would lift faster than a halo in a hurricane if he tried to do it on his own.

Bill Flint, the fifteen-year-old who moved in with us the year before, was next. Ministering to the spiritual warfare waging within, the elders discerning he was an open door to demons, and started deliverance. At a certain point they stopped when it became evident that more than a mop would be needed for clean up.

One of the visionaries saw Bill thrashing around in a turbulent sea with a thick rope tied around his waist. The other end was secured to a dock. A creepy character came along and cut the cords, sinking Bill to the bottom. The interpretation was if Bill severed his ties with the Lord, nothing could save him and Satan would do him in.

Karen's fingernails dug into my hands as the elders approached her. However, in her case there was no cause for fear—they treated her kindly. One of the men prophesied she would be a "Mother in Israel" as hundreds of hungry souls would seek her for spiritual help. Her strength in setting the captives free would come from her close relationship with Jesus. Another foretold of her teaching ministry. These words were confirmed convincingly in the years ahead.

As they laid hands on me, a vision of Jack Stanley flashed across my mind. Fortunately for him, he wasn't present, because it wasn't pleasant! My pores pumped sweat so profusely I almost slipped from their clutches. By the time they finished the ministry my mind was paralyzed by full-blown amnesia.

They finally abandoned me and moved in front of the main event. Jack Winter wedged his way into the inner circle to take charge. Don swallowed his smile as Jack grabbed his head, stared him straight in the eyes and commanded the foul demons to depart in Jesus' name. As each demon identified itself he cast it into outer darkness. Other elders pleaded the blood of Jesus and prayed in tongues. One determined demon called "Defiance" engaged Jack in a shouting match. It was an even exchange until finally "Defiance" was forced to flee to preserve his voice for his next victim. A hoarse demon is as useless as a politician with a plugged larynx!

Daystar was deja vu. We brought Don there for deliverance from his obsession with demons and now he was immersed in many more legions! At least there were no cartoon characters yet.

By the time Jack was done, Don was as limp as a lion sedated by sleeping pills. We helped him to his room where he slept all afternoon. If he didn't revive by tomorrow he was luggage rack material on the way home.

Later we asked Jack Winter how Daystar developed their deep individual discernment. Still CIA all the way, he ducked the answer.

Higher on histories than revealing deep mysteries, he told us Daystar was a haven for Lutherans and other denominationals who desired to exercise their faith on a deeper dimension. Joining the ministry was a full-time commitment of time and finances as resources were pooled for the purpose of building the king-dom.

We related about our origins and our search for seasoned spiritual help for the thirsty flock flooding Living Waters. Pres-ently we were barely meeting the needs of the long-hairs, short-hairs and no-hairs parading to our doorstep.

Jack offered to furnish our fellowship with Holy Ghost fire-power. We could select a teacher, preacher, leader, exorcist or all of the above. On edge after the Elk Grove experience we coun-tered by requesting a cook—a gentle soul who would lend spiri-tual support without spoiling the soup. Jack replied, "I have an ex-missionary in mind, Verna Dunrud. Would you like to meet her?"

Things happened so fast I almost forgot our original mission. Daystar operated like an instant employment agency called "God Power." We arrived with a wounded warrior and were about to return with a prayer warrior who could feed an army. On previ-ous hunts for a cook all the candidates wanted the kitchen sink or acted as if they received their training in Madame Curie's Salmo-nella School of Culinary Concoctions! We met Verna briefly be-fore we departed and were impressed with her qualifications.

Upon returning Don to Cross Acres signed, sealed and deliv-ered, we hoped for a total turnaround but our expectations were short-lived. Don pulled the plug on the light and left for Las Ve-gas.

The camp collapsed, his family was crushed, but they didn't stay down for the count. The Lord opened new paths of ministry. Erna and her youngest son Paul served as missionaries in South America for many years.

We pray that one day Don will break free from his bondage and re-experience the joy only Jesus can bring.

## Commies Invade Kewaunee

1968 was a rude awakening for anyone settling in for a long winter's nap. Every day produced fireworks without any cause for celebration. 1968 was about doubt, dissent, defiance, draft evasion, Dick Daley's dirty works, the death of heroes, the loss of dreams and the dawning of a new age—the age of Aquarius.

Tiny Tim tiptoed through the tulips on "Laugh In" shortly before the Viet Cong launched their Tet offensive, which proved to be no laughing matter. Aided by the North Vietnamese, the sweep through the south sent shock waves all the way to the Oval Office. LBJ's soothsayers, who lulled us to sleep with lies that we were winning, were shot with truth serum! Realizing losses of 40,000 men, the Yankees left the lost cause and returned home to face the protesters.

Tet turned the tide of public opinion against the war and unleashed the "baby boomers" who operated under the illusion they were leading a revolution destined to bring the bastions of power to their knees.

Enter George Wallace, the former Governor of Alabama, into the foray as a third party right wing law and order candidate. The "Great Southern Hope" marched across our border to blitz "The Badger State" in an early April primary. However, George was grounded by a "Golden Gopher"—Senator Eugene McCarthy. The aftershock was felt as far north as Kewaunee, Wisconsin!

Employed as an auditor for the Wisconsin Compensation Rating Bureau, I inspected manufacturing plants and performed payroll audits to ensure that workers were classified correctly for workmen's compensation premium purposes. I averaged ten audits a week, ranging from the car jockeys of Kenosha to the lumbering legends of the North woods. The auto barons always had their accounts in order, but the loggers, who I had to flush out of the forest, would forgo those formalities. They believed that books were for burning, records were for breaking and the only figures worth pursuing were perched on bar stools! Their bookkeeping systems were patterned after the Cosa Nostra's cash-'n'-carry operation.

A letter was always sent two weeks prior to an audit explaining the nature of my visit and the records I required.

The morning after George Wallace lost the Wisconsin primary I arrived at the Swinging Door Church Furniture Company in Kewaunee for an audit. After identifying myself, I was referred to a plant foreman for an explanation of the operation. Minutes later, we were rudely interrupted by a corporate officer who demanded my credentials. With lightning in his eyes, he peered at my I.D. and slapped it back in my palm with the power of an impassioned punch press. He roared like thunder throughout his interrogation.

Under extreme stress I attempted to address his questions, but was cut off by his tart tongue tirading about bureaucrats. "If Wallace had won he would have wiped you guys out," he shouted! His parting shot, as he threw me out, was to call me a "Commie!" I informed him his company couldn't operate without workmen's compensation insurance and theirs was headed in the same direction as Old Dixie! This news didn't put a dent in his demeanor— he was as nasty as a rusty nail, all the way to the parking lot.

Thank God this guy only supplied churches with furniture— if he put preachers in the pulpit there would be more fire and brimstone than Puritan days!

The only other time I was forced to flee an audit was at Afram Brothers salvage operation on the south side of Milwaukee. After head-to-head combat with the owner, I was ordered to join the junk in the yard!

In both cases, my boss, Chuck McDermott, had me back at the scene of screams in a matter of days. The second time around I was treated like a long-lost brother. It's amazing how mellow the macho can be when you serve their eviction notice!

Ultimately, I didn't blame George for the calamity in Kewaunee—his presence pumped up the "Good Ole Boys," but he didn't light the fire.

## America's Original Sin

Events on the national scene proliferated to the point that even Walter Cronkite couldn't keep pace. Burned by the Vietnam conflict, LBJ bailed out and gave Hubert Humphrey his hurrah at the Democratic Convention in Chicago.

Four days after LBJ's decision, the dreams of millions were shattered by the assassination of Martin Luther King, Jr. His Civil Rights Movement marched from Montgomery to Memphis where he met the ultimate resistance—a sniper snuffed out his life at the age of thirty-nine. The night before, Dr. King shared his "dream," but the next day James Earl Ray turned it into a nightmare!

More than a dream died with Dr. King's death. New leaders of the Left wanted no part of the Nobel Peace Prize he won in 1964, as peaceful demonstrations with moral persuasion became passé. Non-violence gave way to rioting, arson and looting as the demons of destruction decimated the cities. The Black Panthers traded firepower with the Oakland police, while out east, Washington, D.C. was a war zone.

On April 11th, President Johnson signed the 1968 Civil Rights Act which made housing discrimination illegal. At the rate the cities were being ruined the next question was how much housing would remain?

Thanks to Dr. King and his clan, blacks can sit in the front of the bus. However, very few are seen in the front of the airplane! The cash crisis facing them today is as bitter to swallow as force-fed crow during the Civil Rights days.

America's "original sin" is only forgiven through an aroused Christian conscience.


## Baby Boomers Birthday Bash

Before April ended, the Students for a Democratic Society succeeded in closing down Columbia University. Propelled by the atom bomb explosion in 1945, these post-beatniks, masquerading as peaceniks, occupied five buildings on campus for a week. With Mark Rudd as their rebel leader, the "action faction" of the

SOS seized President Grayson Kirk's office and trashed it. The supreme insult of these brazen baby boomers turning disrespect into desecration was smoking his sizable supply of vintage cigars!

Rudd's rapid rise to the presidency proved costly to the University—Columbia, the gem of the Ivy League, remained closed until fall, when it finally recovered its faculties!

The antics of Rudd's Raiders spread throughout the world—Berkeley, Mexico City, Tokyo and Paris were all challenged by spasms of student unrest.

As "Hair" let it all hang out on Broadway, evil was lurking in Los Angeles. Senator Robert Kennedy's June 4th primary victory was permanently preempted when Sirhan Sirhan slithered out of the shadows of the Ambassador Hotel and shot him full of lead. Kennedy's last words from the rostrum were, "I believe we can end the divisions within the United States, the violence,"—he never arrived in the press room.

Many wept openly as his funeral train left the City of Angels. After touching the heartland of America, it tracked up the East Coast to New York, where Kennedy's casket was transferred to St. Patrick's Cathedral in full view of television for the funeral mass and final farewells.

Public officials were added to the endangered species list. Bodyguard academies were bulging with new applicants. Dreams faded with the fallen, and the demise of heroes dealt a death blow to American Youth. The disenfranchised, feeling abandoned, despaired and dropped out—then rebellion and retaliation became the rule.

## Seeking A Second Opinion

While turmoil took over the land, Karen's timing was tested by tiny feet trying to find an escape hatch. Our second child was due the middle of June.

Coordinating this exciting event around Uncle Sam's summer camp at Ford Leonard Wood was like lengthy labor negotiations. I was due to board the bus in Pewaukee on June 14th. If

166

delivery day was delayed, I would be laboring at the "Outhouse of the Ozarks" when the kid emerged.

We kept our television low so the embryo would grow without hearing about those horrible events.

On June 9th the feet put up such a fuss I drove Karen to Milwaukee Lutheran Hospital. The kid kicked for twenty-seven hours before Dr. Verch decided to do something about it. Having arranged for a ringside seat, I put my mask in place and paraded into the delivery room.

After much pain with no apparent gain, a head suddenly appeared with a huge mop of black hair. Dr. Verch guessed it was a girl, but before I could seek a second opinion he conceded that our baby was a boy—the evidence became overwhelming! His male hormones were so hardy his voice was changing. We named our son David even though he looked more like a lady killer than a giant killer.

Dr. Verch allowed mother and son to go home on June 13th as a reward for good behavior. This time there was no competition for the kid—Granny Sutter's agency enforced retirement at the age of ninety.

My happiness was hampered by constant reminders. I had to board the bus in the morning. Separation was sad, but summer camp was a snap. My First Sergeant, Vern Kuzyinski, took sick and couldn't make the trip. My brother Jim became acting NCO in charge of clerks and ordered me to play golf every afternoon. This was a command I couldn't refuse!

'When I returned home, David gravitated to me as if I had never been gone. He wasn't playing football yet but he took giant steps in growth. Karen must have been stuffing him with her old-fashioned five-pound pancakes! Krista didn't mind sharing our attention as long as she could boss David around.

## The Second Civil War

While the summer scene was serene on the home front, battles were brewing throughout the nation. Political Armageddon was shaping up on Al Capone's home turf in August as people of all persuasions blew into the Windy City for the "Mother of All Conventions."

Mr. Democrat, Dick Daley, tried to batten down the hatches but his efforts were torn asunder by anti-everythings unleashing their full fury of discontent on Daley's streets. Baby boomers came of age with a rage usually displayed at race riots! With death-defying bravado they battled the Big Boss's beefy bobbies all over the city. Grant Park, Lincoln Park, State Street and the Chicago Stockyards rivaled Gettysburg, Vicksburg and Bull Run as the nation's most bloody battlefields.

Meanwhile, there were no halos inside Convention Hall. Politicians saturated with stockyard stench raised cain through unclenched teeth. Senator Abraham Ribicoff, a bleeding heart liberal from Connecticut, voiced his venom at Mayor Daley for ordering his bullies to beat on the baby boomers. "His Honor" returned the vehemence with a volley of obscenities aimed at the eastern establishment.

T.V. floor fighters knocked delegates over to get at the generals of the guerilla warfare. Microphones were mashed into furious faces as fast as they were retrieved off the floor. Everybody acted like donkeys headed for the slaughterhouse!

Dick Daley didn't budge. His cloned brand of Beatniks belted Yippies with billies in the stink-bomb infested night air. Abbie Hoffman and Jerry Rubin's forces were no match for Daley's distempered disciples. Outwhacked on all physical fronts, the Yippies switched to psychological warfare.

Hoffman and Rubin devised devilish plans that authorities took seriously. With malice towards all they threatened to pollute the city water supply with LSD, drug delegates' food, turn Yippies loose on their wives and camouflage cars as cabs for hijackings across the border to the Badger state. When delegates were interviewed about these possibilities, the thing they feared the most was being abandoned in Wisconsin!

The Minnesota twins, Humphrey and McCarthy, tested each other's tenacity to the final gavel. Hit with the humiliation of being LBJ's V.P. in the heat of a hated war, Hubert Horatio Humphrey was handed a hollow victory. Senator Eugene McCarthy conceded and faded into the sunset to pursue his poetic genius. There were no winners in the Windy City, only wounded warriors wanting to take flight.

Meanwhile, Richard Nixon, still saddled with a used car image, mooned and swooned delegates in Miami. Taking on renowned Republican heavyweights, Ronald Reagan and Nelson Rockefeller, he won the Grand Old Party's prize by a knockout.

Richard Milhous Nixon entered the race for the Rose Garden buoyed by the millstones around Humphrey's neck. Driven by an insatiable desire to self-destruct, tricky Dick committed his first-boo boo by selecting "Spiro who?" as a running mate. He then launched his comedy career on "Laugh In" where he shouted, "Sock it to me!" Despite Nixon's blunders, Humphrey went down with LBJ's ship.

George Wallace, "the Great Southern Hope," waged a fierce fear campaign and gained an immoral victory along with forty-five electoral votes.

As 1968 faded there were a few rays of hope on the horizon. The U.S.S. Pueblo crew, captured by North Korea, was set free for Christmas. On Christmas Eve three American astronauts circled the moon on a mission to locate Santa's workshop. They returned with clearer pictures of the moon than Nixon got in Miami with his Minolta. James Lovell, returning moonstruck, said, "It was the bright star in the last gasp of 1968." He was referring to the mission, not Nixon! Nixon's bright star was Henry Kissinger, who conducted foreign affairs like a smooth sphinx. Meanwhile, Spiro was sparring with war protestors. His main claim to maim was battering the "nattering nabobs of negativism."

By the time Father Time did his thing in Times Square on New Year's Eve, Woodstock was waiting in the wings. The counterculture wasn't ready to roll into their cocoons yet! They herded a half-million flower children into a farmer's field in upstate New York for sixty hours of nonstop "rock 'n ribald" music. The hippies said it was heavenly but many mid-lifers claimed it sounded more like hell.

Acid was still high on the hit list, and the "Cold War" wasn't ready for a hot shower, but a rite of passage took place in 1968 which saw the past fit to face the future and fathers willing to welcome back their prodigal sons.

## The Stone Bank Boozenik is Born Again

While the Devil's deeds of destruction engrossed the nation, God's army prepared for spiritual warfare with a still small voice. Flower children were a few fortnights from breaking free of Satan-seducing devices.

A forerunner who answered the call in 1961 was Jim Palossari, a big boozenik from Stone Bank, Wisconsin. After high school he escaped to see the world through the bottom of a bottle. His first stop was San Francisco. Leaving no stone unturned, Jim dabbled in drugs, drama and did time as a bartender.

This fuzzy Finn almost finished himself off before he was spiritually revived in a tent at the tender age of twenty-nine. When a revivalist slipped Jim a copy of David Wilkerson's "Cross and the Switchblade," he came under conviction when the invitation was given to accept Christ.

Jim joined Christian communes in California and a couple of years later reemerged in the Milwaukee area as a bearded father figure for the flower children. Brian and Mary Steinke knew Jim from the bad old days in Stone Bank and were amazed when he and his wife Sue pulled up in front of their home in a van with a jumbo Jesus sign on the side. They stayed in the Steinke home for four months before becoming spiritual mentors for the Milwaukee Jesus People during the early 1970's.

Spring and Summer passed with platonic pleasantries—harvest time was approaching with haste. The Lord of the Harvest worked three shifts training legions of laborers to gather in the grain.

Going with the flow of this spiritual awakening, we continued to be sponsors for Luther League and Karen taught junior Lutherans. Living Waters added a Sunday night service to accommodate the influx of teenagers.

# 13

# Fire Hydrants Only Fly on Friday Nights

Shortly after Rich and Jane Ritzenthaler moved to Oconomowoc, they attended our meetings. Rich was a handsome young entrepreneur whose get-rich inventions included developing a single-control faucet system. Jane, an attractive redhead, modeled and was involved in theatre.

Their Christian commitment led them into part-time prison ministry at Fox Lake Correctional Institution. There they met Butch, a young man who paid his debt to society. Before being released he needed help with his reentry phase. Impacted by New Testament teachings, Rich and Jane invited him to live with them until he could get connected.

Butch's friend Franky from Milwaukee moved in with the Ritzenthalers, also. The boys had a crush on cars so we let them work on their wrecks in our big garage which has a grease pit.

Art Reimer hired Butch as a welder at Milwaukee Bridge and Steel Co. Butch gravitated to the green stuff the old-fashioned way and kept his nose out of the nether world.

The boys experienced only one slight setback. One Friday night Rich loaned them his white Eldorado because their cars were kaput. While heading east on Capitol Drive in Milwaukee a red fire hydrant unexplainably leaped off the curb and landed in front of the Cadillac! The high-flying hydrant was pounded to the pavement with a pulverizing thud, resulting in considerable damage to Rich's dream car—Eldorados weren't made to endure this type of temporal trauma.

When the police arrived, Franky and Butch were sprawled out on the curb trying to recall which wacko had been behind the wheel. Feeling no pain, they continued to rack their brains as Rich and Jane's junker was hauled away.

The "fuzz" ruffled the boys' feathers but Rich remained cool as the contingent came to debrief him on his butchered beater. Jane expressed more grief but the long-suffering saints decided to take the twosome back.

## Strangers in the Night

A month later Franky and Butch spent a weekend at our home when Ritzenthalers were away. They stayed in our number one guest room at the end of the second floor hallway.

Saturday at 2:00 a.m. we were awakened from a deep sleep by the sound of a car trunk closing below our window. Limited by mega-myopia I saw two shadows lugging something heavy in their hands. I grabbed my glasses and bolted down the back stairs.

From the dining room window I determined it was Franky and Butch carrying some mysterious object wrapped in a black sack. The booty was too big for a Saturday night special and too small for a stiff. Hopefully it wasn't a bazooka!

As they approached the west end of the house they laid their loot on the porch floor. Maybe Victorian architecture turned them off and they were going to bomb the place! The possibility of a heist also played havoc in my head—harboring fugitives would go over great with the neighbors.

After Franky helped Butch onto the porch roof, he fetched a rope out of his car and tied it to the cargo. As they wrestled the weight to the roof I searched for a better vantage point—there wasn't any.

A few minutes later there were rumblings in their room. Fighting fear I put my right ear flush with the door to hear their heated debate over this forbidden treasure they had forced through the window. I detected the word "tools" as heavy metal punished the pine wood floor. From the sound of things they were either dealing in farm implements or practicing wood carving.

Wagering I wouldn't be wasted, I knocked on the door. Momentary silence was followed by a loud "Yea." I yelled, "Hey man! What's happening in there?" Butch answered, "We couldn't sleep, so we decided to bring some crap in from the car." This really put

172

my mind at ease! So, insomnia was the culprit. I was ready to shout, "What kind of crap?" when I was checked in my spirit.

At this point the only thing I wanted to know was when Jane and Rich were returning home! Never mind why a window was superior to a door or why tools were toted into a bedroom before breakfast. Who cares who they belonged to or whether they were used for working on tie rods, tumblers or some other twisted task. Only a ghoulish gossip would want to know the contents of the mysterious black bag that looked like a beheader's hand-me-down from the French Revolution!

Will-Kill wasn't the answer and the cops might start a shootout. My parting shot was, "I will see you guys at breakfast," as I barreled back to our bedroom to fill Karen in on the crisis. She registered a 9.5 on the Richter scale, but being a social worker she wanted to give these strangers in the night a second chance.

Breakfast was brief but friendly—there was no mention of the early morning madness. Saturday night proved to be as peaceful as a prayer tower in paradise. Sunday night was a preview of the Rapture—Ritzenthalers came to reclaim their roomers!

When we talked to Rich and Jane about our weekend who-dunit they agreed it was strange but had no clues to close the case—it's still gathering dust. After thirty years it appears in the top ten "unsolved mysteries" of the Victorian House on the Hill. The Rabbi Samuel Perlstein saga heads the list.

The boys moved back to Milwaukee a month later. Butch kept contact and often came out when I was working in the woods. Taking advantage of his natural talent with tools, I had him cutting brush while we caught up on the latest. Butch kept his job as a welder and curbed his compulsion for fire hydrants—leaving their fate to the canine contingent. I still work in the woods but haven't seen my bushwhacker for over twenty years.

## Flunking as a Family Counselor

Karen taught Junior Lutherans but not all the kids acted like Junior Christians! A specialty of Bill, a freckle-faced twelve year old, was spit balls. After many mischievous episodes, Karen concluded that his aim, which was quite accurate, was mainly for attention. Reaching beyond his behavior, Karen befriended Bill.

Bill was adopted as an infant by a wealthy couple attempting to save their marriage. After the experiment failed, Bill floundered when forced to live with his emasculating mother, Florence. His sister Sally, insecure and full of fear, managed to survive, but Bill, bearing the brunt of the rejection, was about to hit bottom.

Karen elicited positive responses in Bill through attention and affirmation. When the group crafted puppets, Karen helped him collect materials to make the largest puppet. He developed pride in his creative abilities.

One night Pastor Holland called me concerning a crisis in Bill's home. Pastor had just returned from a heated family counseling session and was burned out. Talking in terms of a tag team he asked me to take over for a time. Lacking any training, I was reluctant to tiptoe on this tightrope—I had seen what it had done for others! However, Karen, who promotes me as the Jack of all trades, urged me to launch out and be a big brother to Bill.

It was dark by the time I arrived at their apartment. Florence, a bleached blonde with icy blue eyes, offered me a front row seat for the fireworks. Stern as a riverboat run aground, she blasted Bill about his bad behavior. I interrupted her ten-minute tirade to seek a second opinion. Bill's face reddened as he responded with a forced politeness, "Yes sir, I am bad."

Bill was either brainwashed or too fearful to talk in his mother's presence. When I offered suggestions, Florence snapped, "That's fruitless-they have been tried before and Bill has failed!"

It would take more than heated hostilities to melt this iceberg. However, Florence did agree to let Bill come to our home after school a few times. She made it plain that he had to earn the privilege by practicing "sinless perfection" at home.

Bill blossomed like a flower freed from a weed-infested garden. Karen kept him captivated by crafts and I took him waterskiing. Of course we always saved time to pass the pigskin around. Most of all, Bill enjoyed relating—he possessed a good sense of humor and expressed himself positively.

A year later Bill and his family moved to Fort Wayne, Indiana. We offered to provide a home for Bill, but Florence, still branding him "bad," didn't believe a scenery change was the solution. Florence and Fort Wayne weren't the answer either—a classic underachiever, he earned straight "F's"! High on drugs and other degradations, he joined a gang called "Satan's Sons" and lived up to its name.

Finally, at fifteen, Bill ran away and beat the police to our place—they had been searching for him in a five-state area. At first, Florence insisted Bill be put in a home for delinquents. After nightmare negotiations, she agreed to let him live here if we would take punitive action. His sentence was to be an off-campus student at a residential treatment center called Lad Lake. Our friend Ralph Magnus, who was the director, made it possible.

Encouraged by Bill's progress, we took another bold step the next fall and enrolled him at University Lake School in Hartland. Dr. DePeyster, the headmaster of this prep school, reminded us the route from Lad Lake to U.L.S. is a road never traveled. However, he gave Bill a chance and nobody was disappointed—he maintained a "B" average and played on the soccer team.

By spring, Bill's grades slid and other symptoms surfaced. He was sullen and spacey at times and hung out with suspected druggies from town. One kid named Steve, who had long blond hair, wire-rimmed glasses and a weak male ego, put pressure on peers to purchase pot. Once he had kids hooked he steered them towards exotic drugs such as elephant dust.

Bill was forbidden to associate with Steve, but that was like trying to separate Mona from Lisa! By the age of sixteen, Bill was an accomplished con artist who could manipulate a monkey out of his last banana.

He had ten excuses ready for each accusation. Occasionally he still flashed a smile, but his freckles were fading fast behind his long scraggly hair hanging on all fronts.

Bill blasted our ears and his mind with heavy metal. The only Sabbath he observed was Black. When we told him Satan's music didn't mix with God's house, he turned his "acid rock" into a road show. He still came to our Sunday night meetings, but only because it was a condition for staying in our house.

## Rocky, We Hardly Knew You

A month later, Bill was caught with a pocket full of pot and escorted to the Waukesha County Court House. Rocky Atkins, a county social worker, possessing a big heart for troubled teens, tore up Bill's file. We warned Bill this was his one chance for a changed life and not to expect more.

Bill was on better behavior for a while, but justice wasn't served in Rocky Atkins' case. Rocky joined the Town of Summit police force and stopped at our house occasionally to see how our work with kids was progressing.

Meanwhile, Alan Randall, a young man from Middle Genesee Lake, stole his neighbor's car and gunned him down in cold blood when he tried to reclaim it. The chilling killing numbed the Oconomowoc area. People, petrified of venturing out, put pressure on the police to apprehend the unknown assailant promptly.

A few days later, Rocky and his partner, Wayne Olson, while making a routine return to the Summit police station, were blasted into the next life at point-blank range by a sniper hiding in the brush.

He swiped their bullet-riddled squad car to commit a burglary. Upon returning the vehicle, he hopped on his bike to pedal home in the new fallen snow. Tracks tripped up this 16-year old killer.

Rocky spent most of his adult life helping kids. His life was snuffed out by a crazy one who hadn't been reached in time. Was Alan Randall crying out for help or was he too cold-hearted? I don't know the answer. However, one thing is certain—Rocky deserved a richer reward on Earth! Rocky, we hardly knew you, but the Lord sure does!

## Jesus is Real!

Rocky wasn't around to bail Bill out anymore, but that didn't stop Bill from treading troubled waters. One day he left a note on his pillow saying he was on his way to a rock concert—three days later he returned glassy-eyed with a grimy knapsack on his back. He apologized, but his perception of repentance was more empty promises.

Despite Bill's eerie escapades he was a likable kid—that was the maddening part. Among those who befriended Bill and tried to help him were Mom and Dad Ziemann, Gordon James, Andrew Culverwell and Willa Dorsey. At times he struggled to be free, but was unwilling to cut the cords of bondage.

Jesus People from Phoenix lived with us for a few months and Bill took a liking to their leader, Jimmy Sutherland. When Jimmy returned to Phoenix, Bill joined his crash pad of Jesus Freaks. Bill even sounded excited about Bible studies!

However, his enthusiasm for the spiritual was short-lived—he abandoned the clan for chemicals. I was awakened one morning at two o'clock to be told, "Jesus is real!" It was Bill calling from some dive in Phoenix where he had taken the plunge. Three times he shouted, "Jesus is real!" The message was true, but the spirit behind it was soused with "the sauce." I told him to sober up and call me later.

Bill, still in his teens, was a high school flop out. We talked seriously about the Army as an alternative lifestyle. Maybe "Uncle Sam's Billion Dollar Band" could beat some sense into him!

Desperate, we didn't envision any downside to this decision. Florence was for it. Bill was willing, but his flesh got weak over parting with his long locks. After we exorcised his "Samson spirit" he became gung-ho Army all the way to basic training at Fort Knox.

## The Las Vegas of the Great Lakes

After basic, Bill came home to fight another battle—marriage! Denise Goetzke, a quiet, attractive brunette, was his intended. He met her at a drug culture hideaway in Oconomowoc where long-hairs hung out.

Both were too young, age-wise and otherwise, to live in wedded bliss. Karen and I, Florence and the State of Wisconsin all agreed, but Bill and Denise vehemently dissented. Talking this gluesome twosome out of unholy matrimony was like trying to take LBJ's Texas ranch away from him—we couldn't get past the bull!

Bill couldn't legally get married in Wisconsin without his mother's permission. However, Michigan was another matter. They plotted an Upper Peninsula pilgrimage to pay homage to the Justice of the Peace.

Coming to grips with the graffiti ground in the wall, I offered to drive them to Menominee, Michigan. For the first time in weeks there was no argument—neither one was a walking wonder!

The heavy-duty drug counselors of today would label me an "enabler," but in the early 70's the most serious indictment for this offense was a "do-gooder."

Menominee, the Las Vegas of the Great Lakes, located fifty miles north of Green Bay, is the closest point for those on the loose to tie the noose before coming of age. Bill was decked out in Uncle Sam's finest, while Denise wore burgundy velvet as they crawled into the rear of my 1969 red Riviera.

The three-hour trip was a drag for the driver—all the action was in the back seat! I felt like I was running a taxi service for draft dodgers destined for Canada. As we crossed the Michigan border we were greeted by a blizzard. I could still see the road, but my passengers were blinded by everything except each other.

When we entered the County Courthouse chambers we realized we weren't alone. The room was packed with nervous couples who beat the same path across the border. I always thought the traffic on Highway 41 was the mad dash of deer hunters, Packer backers and fighting Illini escaping the congested continent of Chicago. Now I was pleased to find out that at least some of our tax money was poured into perpetuating the human race!

The Justice of the Peace linked the couples in short order and sent them on their way. It was like getting married at McDonald's!

The Menominee Mothers of the American Revolution, known locally as M.M.A.R., provided goodies on paper napkins for couples unconcerned about their curfew.

Bill and Denise posed for pictures on the courthouse steps, proving they were there in case their papers were confiscated at the border.

We drove straight to the reception at the Fox and Hounds restaurant in Hubertus, Wisconsin. The newlyweds were puzzled when I pulled up to the parking lot and a valet pulled them out of the back seat. Apparently I forgot to inform them about this post celebration. They recovered when they discovered the reception was restricted to the three of us, plus Karen who joined the party. Cake was served but the gourmets at the other tables were too busy downing their dinners to bother with the bouquet or go after the garter.

Upon arriving home there were a few well-wishers waiting. Feeling bad there weren't more, Karen arranged a second wedding the following week. This time there was only one couple with fifty guests rather than vice-versa. We had a full fledged preacher who vouched for Bill and Denise's vows by candlelight in our family room. Minnie Main made a massive two-tiered cake for the reception.

Their honeymoon was put on hold when Bill left for advanced infantry training at Fort Eustis, Virginia. Upon completion, Uncle Sam sent him to Nuremberg, West Germany, where Denise joined him.

# 14

# European Vacation

Having traveled extensively in the states we decided to take a trip to Europe that spring. American Express helped us map out a seven-week eight-country itinerary. What excited me the most was intercontinental carriers limited the luggage allowed and Europe was further from the madding crowd descending on our domicile!

We launched our 1972 tour on a large Lufthansa plane with two hundred extra pounds of luggage. Karen stuck to her "scale story" as I stood arguing with the airline official. We not only paid the price in the airport, we paid for the next seven weeks! As I boarded the plane I had visions of being rushed to a Heidelberg hospital for emergency hernia surgery.

The next morning, after a sleepless night, we landed in Frankfurt in a driving rainstorm. Gretchen Soergel, the kids' nanny on the trip, took care of David and Krista while Karen claimed the baggage. I hunted for the Hertz desk to rent an Opel Ascona.

When the luggage met the Opel it was a mismatch. We crammed the cases in the car but there was no room for people! Samsonite guarantees to perform under all circumstances but I never witnessed one drive a vehicle. I informed the family our choice was between five beat people on a baggageless journey or ten sizable suitcases ill-suited to find their way out of the parking lot.

We were miraculously spared from making this agonizing decision when Karen came up with a down home remedy—find a larger vehicle, pronto! The only alternative was to cut our vacation short seven weeks.

Not desiring to limit my sightseeing to the Frankfurt airport, I backtracked past all these foreign signs ending in "fahrt" and found the Hertz desk. Knowing Karen had Volkswagen Bus on her brain, I exchanged for one straight away. Hopefully this stick shift monster would maneuver over mountain roads and narrow streets.

After loading the bus in relentless rain, I ground the gears through the parking lot and headed south on the Autobahn. The bus, which we named Baby Blue because of its color, was big on room and poor on power. BMWs and Mercedes passed us like we were running on our rims.

Heidelberg was our first destination. After driving down numerous narrow one-way streets, I abandoned Baby Blue to seek directions. If we ever located the hotel we would never leave. Bavarian hand language paved the way to finally finding the Europaischer Höf.

We slept the good part of forty-eight hours. Our only diversion was a daily excursion to the dining room to feast on Wiener schnitzel and apfel strudel. On the third day a Student Prince showed us the sights of his home town. I didn't sleep well that night as I had nightmares about navigating the bus to Baden Baden the next morning.

## Leaning Over the Ledge at L'Abri

After Baden Baden Baby Blue started behaving better. The brash kid mellowed out by the time we hit Switzerland. It still balked at steep grades, but it was through throwing tantrums.

We spent a weekend in Montreux at the east end of Lake Geneva. We took a cog railroad train up the mountain to view quaint villages and alpine wildflowers. The lake looked like a bathtub below.

On Sunday we visited L'Abri, a religious retreat in the mountains thirty minutes from Montreux. Dr. Francis Schaeffer and his wife Edith founded this Swiss bliss for believers from all over the world, who come for Bible studies and communion with their God.

I forced the accelerator to the floor for the entire climb up the steep, narrow mountain road. I parked Baby Blue in back of the chapel which was built on the side of a cliff. If skeptics didn't find the Lord in these surroundings there wasn't much hope.

After the ledge scares the Hades out of them, God's creation quickens their spirits!

Karen was so eager to get a good seat we saved the sights until after the service. We were the first of the flock to arrive. I hummed "Only the Lonely" and kidded Karen about earthquake warnings. She was not amused. It wasn't her fault—we were all victims of a pre-dawn wake-up call that was wearing thin.

Ten minutes later the congregation trickled in, but the big barrage didn't hit until right before the service started. Usually evangelicals arrive early to stake out their space—these people were probably sent by the Pope for an ecumenical pilgrimage!

Stringed instruments played when Dr. Schaeffer walked in. He resembled a composer from a previous century. His preaching was polished to the point that anyone dozing would miss the message and wake up lost, but still redeemed.

Towards the end of the service a young man stepped forward for water baptism. After grilling him on his faith, Dr. Schaeffer picked up a gray metallic wash basin and poured all the water over the man's head. This method was a watered-down vertical version of total immersion. Jesus' disciple was drenched while people seated up front experienced part of the overflow. The baptizer was blessed also, as he had a twinkle in his eyes when he announced the benediction.

After church we met Edith Schaeffer and a few staff members. A bubbly blonde named Jane asked about our religious background. When Karen mentioned attending Wheaton College, Jane responded warmly. However, when I related our involvement in Charismatic Renewal, she cooled off a few degrees. She said, "The only person I know who was baptized in the Holy Spirit committed suicide shortly afterward!"

I replied, "According to Acts 2:4 it isn't supposed to happen that way—speaking in tongues should be the initial sign! We have prayed with hundreds for the baptism in the Spirit and haven't lost one yet! I understand why you're gun-shy but give it a larger sample. Your friend must have possessed a self-destructive spirit." Jane thanked us for our insight.

After a brief tour of L'Abri it was back to the bus. I secured my seat belt in case Baby Blue careened off the cliff while I was turning it around. Karen, Gretchen and the kids directed me from ground level. As I inched the bus back and forth I got clumsy with the clutch and it lunged towards the ledge. Karen screamed and the kids cried. Jane would never seek the baptism of the Spirit at this rate! I hit the brakes just in time and after taking out a bush, I maneuvered Baby Blue in the right direction. With the trauma passed, I ordered my fellow travelers back on the bus for our return trip to Montreux.

## Overdosing on Salzburg Nockerl

The next day we followed the Sound of Music trail all the way to Salzburg, Austria. That evening we indulged in a scrumptious raspberry soufflé called Salzburg Nockerl, which was served piping hot in a large oval dish. One dessert order was sufficient to finish off four people, especially after feasting on Wiener schnitzel.

The following night we attended the famous Marionette Theatre next to the palace. The show started at 7:00 p.m., which created an eating disorder—Salzburg Nockerl isn't served at fast food joints and gourmet places didn't open until later. My taste buds told me to have Gretchen try room service. We were all pleasantly surprised when she was able to place an order.

Forty-five minutes later three waiters arrived with enough food to feed an NFL football camp. Besides appetizers and entrees, they paraded in five portly platters of Salzberg Nockerl. We were facing an order apiece instead of one order for five people! The dessert had either multiplied due to a language disorder or the waiters were playing dumb! We pleaded with them to take some soufflé back but all they did was display English anguish, acting like three stooges on a silent retreat.

It was already 6:00 p.m. and we had less than an hour to wolf the Wiener schnitzels and knock off the Nockerls. The soufflés started to sink as we entered this race against time and tummy. Karen and the kids tackled the desserts as a tag team tandem while Gretchen and I polished off an order apiece. There were only two to go when I took pity and called a halt to this Nockerl nonsense—they were in danger of overdosing! Raspberry soufflé was squeezing through the whites of their eyes! At this rate we were a few spoons away from eating the tickets also.

Miraculously we arrived at the theatre in time for the opening curtain. David and Krista fell asleep shortly after. I heard Gretchen snoring during the second act but later she claimed it was just her stomach settling. We never ordered Salzburg Nockerl again—I can still taste it!

## Losing Our Lunch to the Lions

We arrived in Vienna on June 9th still filled to the gills. The next day was David's fourth birthday. We made him a glittering gold paper crown and proclaimed him "King for a day." He wore it proudly to the "Prater," a large amusement park.

Karen discovered a boat tour down the Danube to Bratislavia, Czechoslovakia. I was apprehensive about entering a communist country but Karen's insatiable appetite for adventure won out.

By 12:00 noon the next day we were eating lunch at an outdoor cafe with the other people on the tour. Nervousness curbed my appetite. Not only did they retain our passports on the boat but now we were seated in an open air arena with weather-beaten workers standing along the railings jeering at us. Others made rude, crude gestures. The Christians already lost their lunch to the lions in Rome and it looked as if our fate in Bratislavia would not be any better!

When we asked the English-speaking Czech guide if we were on the menu, he replied, "As long as you stay with me you are all right." This was as reassuring as sticking close to the captain on a sinking ship! Outside of indigestion there were no further incidents.

After lunch we boarded a bus for a tour of the city. Karen saw a man in priest's garb and inquired about religion in Czechoslovakia. The guide clammed up tighter than a cork on a champagne bottle. Looking as if he might explode any moment, I suggested we move to the back of the bus. At the next stop, on the back shelf of a store, we discovered a cornhusk figure of a young girl kneeling in prayer at an altar. Our faith was restored.

By 6:00 p.m. we were reunited with our passports. Our spirits lifted as the boat pulled away from the heaviness hovering over the city.

The tour group tore into a Hungarian dinner while serenaded by live gypsy music. The violinists, attracted to David and Krista, had them dancing before dinner was over. With no hecklers on board, finishing the food wasn't a problem.

Upon arrival at the Bristol Hotel everybody looked fatigued enough to faint. Reminding my family we were on the "American plan," I quickly moved them into the dining room. The maitre 'd appeared mystified as we paraded past.

The table talk was strained as the family claimed they were filled to the fibula and desired sleep. Undaunted, I ordered five Wiener schnitzels but skipped the Nockerls! Gretchen and I gave the food a good go but most of it was stuffed in a "hund bag" for breakfast.

## Nuremberg Trials

After leaving Vienna, I refused to stop Baby Blue for food— only to fill the tank and siphon kidneys. The family had "hund bags" to fall back on. Karen told me to clean up my act quickly— "Mom and Dad Ziemann are joining us in a few days and they can't hack this inhuman treatment!"

Nuremberg was next on our feast or famine safari. It took us almost an hour to find Bill and Denise's home after arriving in the city. Denise greeted us, as Bill was still at the army base. He was due home soon, provided he didn't stop at a pub—an hour later he was still no-show.

Bill had volunteered to secure our lodging and presently he was missing in action. Nervous about losing our room, I suggested we drive to the hotel and register. Denise agreed, but neither she nor Jane Wagner, her friend visiting from Oconomowoc, knew the name of the establishment! Acting discombobulated, both pointed fingers towards A.W.O.L. Bill. It was already 7:00 p.m.— That crunch time when desk clerks drop pen pals and rent rooms to warm live bodies armed with cold hard cash!

The seven of us boarded Baby Blue to search the city for an overnight sanctuary. Denise's leads proved as hopeless as leaving the porch light on for Adolph Hitler. No one knew Bill Flint and the hotels had been fully booked for weeks.

Bill still didn't answer at home so we decided to try the downtown area. Dark foreboding clouds hung heavy over the heart of the city. We passed bombed-out buildings that laid dormant ever since Hitler fled.

Our group kept up a brave front in spite of being turned down at three more hotels. How could this sacked, soiled city be so popular? One would have to scrape the soot to see the sights! Nuremberg was born from the bowels of the Black Forest, and the Third Reich stunted its growth.

We sought suggestions from natives and followed up on every lead. Jane, our faith-filled intuitor, told us the Lord would find us a place—it was obvious Bill hadn't! I wanted to believe, but I had a bad feeling in my belly that we were all on trial in Nuremberg.

I dropped these six starving saints off at a restaurant so I could continue the search. Before I sprung them from, "Baby Blue," they agreed that anything I could scrape up, short of a flophouse, would be acceptable. Maybe there was a rescue mission around the next corner!

I called Bill—he was finally home, but he still wasn't all there. I grilled him about the reservations and he slurred something about letting Denise handle it. Bill was no bible scholar, but he had a firm grasp of the Garden of Eden scene. He was sober enough to blame his wife even if his life was on the line when she arrived home!

A grease monkey directed me to the "Schlosshaus" on the edge of the centrum. It was instant nostalgia—possessing a regurgitating resemblance to the Wilson YMCA in Chicago.

A friendly fraulein led me to a fourth floor room. There was no elevator and the stairs creaked like a fire escape. At one juncture we went outside and walked across scaffolding to an adjacent building. Hauling our luggage to this hayloft would be the highway to a heart attack! As stark as a plucked chicken headed for the soup, the room's one redeeming feature was plenty of floor space, which we needed desperately.

I'm sure the family wouldn't mind walking through someone else's room to get to ours—the clerk was offering me the caboose of a two-room suite. I seized the moment and signed up before some other sucker salvaged the last room in town. Karen wouldn't kiss me for finding this place, but as long as she honored our agreement she couldn't kill me either!

I returned to the restaurant to spread the good news. Upon cross-examination I emphasized to Karen she would have to see the "Schlosshaus" to fully appreciate it. One of her concerns that had me wondering also was, "where is the washroom?" In my haste I forgot we needed one!

The communal commode turned out to be twenty paces down the corridor. At least it was in the same building. Karen wasn't ready to purchase the place, but under the circumstances she agreed the pad was passable.

Jane and Denise moved in also. Karen's worldwide counseling ministry was ready to roll—Denise was pregnant and having problems with Bill.

The girls helped me haul the luggage to our loft. The young couple in the adjacent room appeared puzzled by this parade of paraphernalia. They smiled as they pointed at the baggage. We tried to communicate but language became a barrier. "Achtung!" didn't' seem appropriate. They probably paid more for their room, as they had two folding chairs and a small couch.

Our troop took a final trip down the hall so we wouldn't awaken this couple during the night—there were hints they might be on their honeymoon.

Three of us hit the pad and the other four hit the floor. Karen, David and I were wedged against the wall in a twin-size bed. One fraulein on the floor snored all night, which helped muffle the noise from the street. I don't know if her source was sausage or sauerbraten, but thank God it wasn't baked beans!

The cute couple split before sunrise—either the snoring got them or they feared we would conscript them to be bellhops.

We saw Bill before he left for the base—he looked bad. Friends who worked in the hospital supplied him with drugs which he downed with drinks. He didn't want to talk about it. Nuremberg was no Nirvana—we left with heavy hearts knowing Bill was speeding down a dead-end street.

## A Rumble in the Rathskeller

Our spirits were lifted in Darmstedt, Germany, by the Sisters of Mary, a Lutheran order started by Mother Basilea Schlink after WWII. Their universal ministry of evangelization shares spiritual joy with a hurting world.

Previously we had fellowshipped with the Sisters at their Canaan in the Desert location near Phoenix, Arizona. Their oasis overwhelmed us with warm welcomes, inspired singing and time-tested teachings. Sr. Lucia and Sr. Josepha have spoken at Living Waters many times.

Mom and Dad Ziemann, on furlough from their African mission, joined us for this special weekend at the Motherhouse in Darmstedt. The Sisters exhibited the same heavenly spirit we experienced at Canaan in the Desert. Mother Marteria, the co-founder of the order, gave one of the messages.

On Monday all of us boarded Baby Blue and drove towards Wiesbaden to a large castle surrounded by vineyards high above the Rhine River.

Our room rates included three meals a day so we pushed hard to arrive by lunch time. It was 2:00 p.m. by the time we pulled up to the castle to unload our cargo. I suggested that the others run for the Rathskeller before it ran out of food.

By the time I got there, the no-nonsense waiter was steamed about our late arrival. Karen came close to tangling with him while ordering for the children—I was next. When I ordered Wiener schnitzel he reacted as if I had set off a cherry bomb in his shorts! He shouted, "Wad da ya mean Wiener schnitzel?" Pointing at the menu I replied, "This Wiener schnitzel, right here!" He erupted into an unintelligible tirade. We were nose-to-nose, which gave him an unfair advantage, as his outdid Jimmy Durante's.

While Dad Ziemann, who understood some German, tried to calm him down, he kept yelling "Wiener schnitzel" as if it were a swear word. Whatever possessed this guy wanted to get out bad—an exorcism was in order! For all I knew maybe he was trying to tell us the veal was crawling with vermin! The waiter left such a bitter taste I asked Dad to cancel my Wiener schnitzel and tell him I would take anything! Everyone else was too petrified to order.

The waiter was out of sight but not out of sound—he had another round with the chef in the kitchen. If it ended in a knock-out there would be no lunch.

I don't know what I ate but at least it didn't move. Two more days of dining under these conditions and our next stop would be the psycho ward. Travel books warn that camping in castles can be uneven at times, but this guy was a basement case!

After informing the front desk about our rumble in the Rathskellar, we demanded a different waiter for dinner. I don't know where they stashed him, but we never saw him again. He was too tough to put on the menu—the guests would have choked to death! The Heimlich maneuver was forbidden in this region—there were rumors it had been developed by Nazi war criminals!

## Land of the Midnight Sun

After saying good riddance to the Rhine we traveled north to the land of the midnight sun. Tracking lost relatives in the dense forests of Småland, Sweden, was difficult.

When we finally found Nils-Eric and Güllan Noryd's "stuga" near Norrhult we stayed for a week. They treated us like Swedish Royalty even though we were only second cousins. Every day they guided us on a pleasurable tour without asking us for our passports. On the way to a Swedish glass works, we visited the birthplace of my maternal grandfather on a remote lake in the woods. His one-room "stuga" had a yellow enamel tile stove in the center and a small bed in the corner. We also spent a day on the ancient island of Öland in the Baltic sea.

190

Nils-Eric and Güllan rounded up relatives from miles around for us to meet. I never questioned their allegiance, but I am sure many of them were Viking fans.

One day in Växjo, after seeing the Immigrants' Museum, we visited Paul and Mary Thorne. When Karen and Dad Ziemann were told that the Thorne's teenage daughter had measles, they went into her bedroom to pray for her recovery.

Every night at the Noryd's farm house we toasted our feet by the fireplace as the windows were warmed by the gentle glow of candlelight. Vikings didn't seem so fierce in this setting. My mind meditated on the courage it took for my ancestors to leave this lovely land to set sail for the unknown of the new world seventy years before.

We arrived in Stockholm the third weekend in June for their "midsummer" celebration. The boats in the harbor, bound for the Baltic Sea Islands, were decorated from stem to stern with garlands of flowers for the festivities.

Leif and Lottie Sandström, took us to Skansen, a public park in Stockholm, where Swedes in native costumes danced around the maypole. They weren't about to be outdone by the "Midsummer" merrymaking at Al Johnson's Restaurant in Door County, Wisconsin. The Stockholm Swedes don't have to answer to the "square heads" from Chicago, either!

Leif Sandström, a second cousin, is my most visible Swedish relative. As head of Advertising for Marabou Chocolate Co. he made many trips to the United States in the 1950's, during which he visited our family. Later on, when he started his own company, he gave future screen star Joan Collins her first major role—in an advertising film!

Leif is also a church leader, historian, musician and would make a great politician. In 1993, at the age of 78, he was given the "Swede of the Year" award as a guardian of the Swedish culture on the Costa del Sol in Spain, where he maintains one of his homes.

During our Stockholm stay, Leif played his favorite Swedish hymns on his grand piano in the evenings. His touch would even tickle Lina Sandell, the famous hymn writer from Smaland, whose childhood home we visited.

Sleep was scarce in Stockholm. The midnight sun activated our minds towards nocturnal nuances such as reading the paper outside at 1:00 a.m. Any pleasure the Swedes reaped from summer solstice was paid back during the short dark days of winter.

Norway was next. On our way north we were almost wiped out by a humongous rat that raced in front of Baby Blue near the border. After the hysterics ceased, we agreed the Swedes should saddle up these ravenous roving rodents! Dad Ziemann longed for his big game gun.

Instead, we hunted down a restaurant and painted a vivid picture of "the beast" to the waitress. She laughed and claimed it wasn't a rat, but a protected wild pet that brought pleasure to the people of the north. Still concerned this imposter might be a Harlem hit artist, we made sure it wasn't on the menu!

We quit splitting hairs over rodents and shifted our attention to Krista who was as pale as an albino puppy about to puke pablum. Karen felt Krista's forehead and suffered second degree burns. Dad prayed, Krista improved, but suddenly relapsed! Using his plate as a mitt, Dad's quick reflexes caught it in midair as if he was chasing a foul ball. Dad casually passed the plate to a busboy and said, "Sorry, sir, but I had an accident." It's heartwarming what a true shepherd will do for his sheep—from then on we called him Sir Walter Raleigh!

## Nordic Ski Bums Invade the Streets of Oslo

The moment we crossed the Norwegian border Karen longed for Lapland. Her romanticized picture of the Nomads of the North was 1,000 miles away from reality. I had nothing against the North Pole but felt like a wounded wombat after battling Baby Blue for the last six weeks.

Norway isn't known for its interstate system. Presently we were driving in a barren wasteland where the roads provided more bounce to the ounce than incarcerated coke. Volkswagen victims were putting on the pathos of prisoners pressuring for parole.

Suddenly we were rescued by a reindeer posing for pictures in front of the "last outpost." The smattering of snow remaining on the rocks from the robust winter enhanced the authenticity. Bright multi-colored Lap hats were in order for everyone.

Karen was clear about her disappointment, but down deep she agreed that a thousand-mile trek through the tundra of Lapland would result in losing more than our lunch. Baby Blue would be black by the time we got back.

After two days in Trondheim we traveled south towards the fairyland fjord country. We scheduled a stopover at a hotel on the rim of a glacier. What looked like a snap on the map turned out to be a two hundred mile grueling grind over teeth-shattering terrain. Pressing all day to average twenty-five miles per hour, we were still far afield by early evening.

Finally a vintage Viking told us to veer left on a road that resembled a bridle path. There were no signs present except fatigue. A half hour later there wasn't even a sign of civilization!

Meanwhile the natives of the rear seat remained restless and it was too narrow to turn Baby Blue around. Rarefied air and rocky roads rarely bring out the best in people. Karen was already cured of Lapland fever. At 28 kilometers we were saved by a Saab that almost sideswiped us from the opposite direction—the driver confirmed there was a hotel behind him.

The midnight sun allowed ample light to admire the snow-framed glacier lake. However, the hotel looked like a worn-out Wisconsin feed mill. The reviewer must have been run over by reindeer before he recommended this hostelry! He was right on the rustic but wrong on the charm, unless one considers saunas substituting as outhouses cute! We hit the hay by eleven and bailed out by seven the next morning.

On this day our only delay was waiting for a car ferry to carry us across the Sagna fjord leading to Ulvik.

The Brakanes Hotel was a palace compared to the granary at the glacier—it even had indoor plumbing. The only downer was the elevator—Krista and Gretchen got stuck inside for forty-five minutes. They remained calm but the rest of us panicked!

I thought they went for a walk when suddenly I heard a disturbance in the hallway. Assuming it was the bellman bemoaning the bulkiness of our bags, I paid no attention. It turned out to be the manager trying to contact the girls trapped in the elevator!

By the time we arrived it didn't sound as if they needed much comforting—they were still giggling. However, Karen was close to cashing it in! Despite assurances that a repairman was on the way, she sent a search party after our official prayer warrior, Dad Ziemann.

A half hour later the giggling gave way to genuine fears—it seemed as if the repairman was coming from Lapland. Keeping Krista and Gretchen engaged in conversation, I shouted down the shaft, "The chef is sending down two Salzburg Nockerls." The girls started giggling again.

Finally the man arrived and freed the prisoners in a matter of minutes. Peeling off their macho mask we sat them down and prayed that the Lord would touch any trauma they experienced. After the elevator episode, the stairs became the popular choice.

Bergen, Norway, was our next stop. It is a beautiful coastal city with a harbor on the Atlantic Ocean. The first night we noticed a street evangelist preaching at the port. As we gathered closer to hear the "Good News" in Norwegian, we witnessed that the same "Spirit" was present. The next day we visited the famous composer Edward Grieg's home and toured a stave church over a thousand years old.

Saving Oslo to last, we checked into a fashionable downtown hotel. While walking down the main drag, we encountered wasted wipeouts overdosed on drugs and alcohol. Some, too stoned to solicit coins, were sleeping on the sidewalks. A bearded sea captain was perched on a wooden stool with his head propped against the door. If someone opened it he would go down with the ship!

That night it wasn't the midnight sun that kept us awake, but three nocturnal Nordic nomads skiing down the boulevard. The frenzied crowd cheered as wood and metal met the dry pavement at a feverish pace. Poling past our window, outfitted in full regalia, they turned right through the lobby with their fans in hot pursuit. Two hours of belting down brews in the bar fortified them for more raucous revelry. I bolted our door in case they used the third floor for a jump!

The next night was noiseless—Nordic ski bums never hit the same hotel two nights in a row.

We traveled south along the western coast of Sweden to visit my cousin Carl Hägert and his family at their island home near Göteburg. The people of this region were still reminiscing about the night their native son, Ingemar Johannson, knocked out Floyd Patterson in Yankee Stadium for the heavyweight championship of the world.

Mom and Dad Ziemann said good-bye in Copenhagen and flew back to Ghana. It was more peaceful for them there—crashing with kids in the back of a bus takes its toll! Abandoning Baby Blue in Frankfurt, we flew to London.

## Stricken at the Savoy

Andrew Culverwell met us at the Taunton train station to drive us to South Chard where we spent a week at Harry Greenwood's home. Uncle Harry was on one of his "worldwide win them for Jesus tours," but his wife Pam was a most pleasant hostess.

South Chard is a charming village of hedges, petite gardens and humble homes a few miles from the sea. Andrew took us on his boat to see the site where "The French Lieutenant's Woman" was filmed in Lyme Regis.

The South Chard church is known for its spiritual fervor. Its founders, Rev. Sid Purse and his wife Auntie Mil, held enough services that week to save every sinner for several counties. Glorious praise and crescendo-climbing choruses combined with powerful preaching and impromptu testimonies. Every age was actively engaged—ten year-olds gave teachings and toddlers prayed for healing.

Tambourines teased the timbers as waves of anointed dancers glided around the room in rapture. They made Arthur Murray look like a misfit! Karen coaxed me to join but I replied, "No thanks, I have seen what it's done for others!"

Jim and Sue Polossari, the leaders of the Milwaukee Jesus People, arrived in South Chard the last night we were there. We conversed in Harry and Pam's kitchen until the wee hours of the morning.

The following day we boarded the train for London. We stayed at the Savoy but skipped the stompin'.

Karen and Krista saw Rudolph Nureyev dance in Swan Lake at Covent Garden. By the third act he was so weary they threw him water wings! Karen came back raving but Krista was disappointed—there was no red-nosed reindeer. When I asked Karen if Nureyev was as graceful as the spirit-filled South Chard dancers, she replied, "Yes, considering Rudolph had to rely on the flesh!"

That night Karen became seriously ill with a high fever. By morning her body was bloated and full of a red rash. This angel of mercy was grounded by measles! We were trusting that her prayer partner, Dad Ziemann, wasn't stricken by the same fate. Sweden was supposed to be the Welfare State, not the center for communicable diseases!

As Karen lay listless, the kids and I prayed that the Lord would release her from this infirmity. Later that morning the hotel doctor arrived. We knew the Savoy was first class, but this guy was a gas. Decked out in a dark gray tux with tails, he looked as if he came directly from the Queen's coronation. The concierge must have told him Karen was related to royalty! My mind revolved like a cash register. I desired top care for Karen, but didn't want to be taxed by the tux treatment—Time Insurance would never pay for this!

Karen's head had puffed up to pumpkin size and her body looked ravaged by killer bee sorties! When I informed the doctor she didn't always look like this, he snapped back, "I should hope not!"

He performed a precise exam with a variety of instruments extracted from his long black bag. If he pulled out a proctoscope, I was going to accuse the concierge of hiring a handyman and splitting the fee. He eventually diagnosed a severe case of measles and gave her a shot.

Karen had the choice of staying at the Savoy or shipping out to a contagious disease sanitarium. This was like choosing between Buckingham Palace and Alcatraz! We opted for the Savoy even if it meant digging ditches when we arrived home.

Gretchen and I alternated as nurse, nanny and maid. No one else was allowed in the room except the doctor who came daily. On the seventh day, when Karen's temperature hit 105°, Uncle Sid came from South Chard to intercede for her the entire afternoon.

That evening, when Karen thought she was dying, Mary Soergel in Oconomowoc and Willa Dorsey in Portland Oregon, both discerned she desperately needed prayer. Willa, the most powerful prayer warrior I know, kept up her all-night vigil, rebuking the spirit of death!

On the eighth day there were visual signs of improvement and by the ninth day Karen was talking about food and clothes. I was rejoicing that she was well, but fearful a shopping spree was only a day away.

On the tenth day the doctor gave us the okay to travel home. Fortunately it was a Sunday and the stores were closed.

After attending church to give thanks, we took a taxi to Speakers Corner in Hyde Park. All the problems of the world are solved in one afternoon by self-styled orators running off at the mouth.

On the way back to the Savoy we stopped at a street market called Petticoat Lane. It wasn't Harrod's but it was higher class than Maxwell Street. However, I missed the pigs knuckle paperweights and the filthy five-dollar fur coats!

The next morning my breakfast turned distasteful after perusing the bill. It had more entries than a multi-million dollar lottery which I needed desperately to win. The doctor didn't charge for renting the tux—it appeared as if we bought the bloody thing! There were enough extra room charges to blow up the entire block!

We boarded two black London cabs and headed for Heathrow Airport before the Savoy added a departure tax for our luggage loitering in the lobby.

# 15

# Matchmakers, Motorcycles and Mothers-in-Law

Bill, delving deeper into drugs, separated from Uncle Sam on a medical discharge. Andrew Culverwell escorted him back to the states where Bill entered a VA hospital in Tennessee for treatment. Upon release he set up house with a border state babe named Janice.

While Bill was two-timing in Tennessee, Denise moved in with us and took over our kitchen. Her special culinary concoction was cherry cheese blintzes for breakfast which were as sinful as Salzburger Nockerls. I added an extra day a week of jogging to blitz my "blintz - belly!"

New Years passed with Denise's baby due any day. If the kid could hold out until January 20th, it would be born on Karen's birthday. Her birthday came and so did a blue-eyed, blond-haired baby boy named Jeremy James Flint. Karen was in the labor room so they could celebrate together.

Bill, acting more like Jesse James, came to see his son shortly after his birth. He stayed two days and told Denise he wanted a divorce. Three months later he moved Janice up here and rented a broken-down farm house near Sullivan.

One night we were awakened by one of Bill's S.O.S. calls. A devilish drug-dealing dude named Ray shot up Bill's van at the farm. Ray was so rotten he stashed his wife in a nursing home when she was nineteen! Bill's vehicle looked like Swiss cheese and he feared he might be the next victim in this cat and mouse game.

Believing God delivered him a doomsday message, Bill desired prayer. We weren't fired up by his foxhole faith, but we couldn't say no.

After revving up the red Riviera, we headed west towards Sullivan. If Ray was still on the prowl our Riviera could run into a similar fate!

Locating the farm in the dark proved difficult, but Bill's van gave it away—illuminated by porch light it looked like a war relic from Nuremberg! Scanning the shadows for movement, we stepped out of our car to the sound of silence. Bill must really be freaked—there is no "acid rock" rocking his house! As we crept closer the silence was broken by Bill's Doberman. He called off the dog and let us in. Grimy green bulbs cast a spell on a sickening Satan's poster of a rams head laying in a large pool of blood.

Bill's speech was so muddled he couldn't relate much about his run-in with Ray. Karen lost her cool when a rat ran under her chair. He was not alone—there were more unsettling sounds in the dark corners. Bill better trade his Doberman for a six-pack of cats!

We talked to Bill straight and told him no miracles would take place until he abandoned his life style. He was in no condition to make choices that night.

Ray's Swiss cheese operation apparently shut down for third shift—our Riviera appeared unscathed as we approached it in the wee hours of the morning.

Once the panic passed we didn't see much of Bill—occasionally he would call but he was too ashamed to come over.

We escaped Bill's next trauma, as it hit over the holidays when we were in Phoenix. Dad Ziemann, who was home on missionary furlough, wasn't as fortunate!

One cold night when Bill was cleaning his rifle, it accidentally fired a round into Janice's right leg. After hustling her to the hospital in his air-conditioned van, Bill called Dad. Dad prayed for her splintered leg until the danger period was passed. Janice eventually recovered but Bill didn't. He couldn't lay off the primary love object of his life—the chemicals that controlled him!

Janice, tired of being the target of afflictions and addictions, moved back to Tennessee. Bill fled to Phoenix and Denise and Jeremy remained with us.

Phoenix proved to be fertile ground for finding chicks. Three months later Bill got married to one named Jessie—the matchmaker was Harley-Davidson. Motorcycle mania reigned for two years as they tore up the terrain until finally they ran out of gas and got divorced. Bill got along better with his mother-in-law Nan—so he moved in with her. She had a crush on Harleys also!

The following Christmas when we were staying at the Arizona Biltmore, Bill bombed over with his latest roommate. We had met all his others, so why break the cycle.

The two in-laws, appearing more like outlaws, roared up to the entrance on one bike. Their helmets hid their huge age difference. Behind black leather emerged a pleasant middle-aged lady from New England. Nan wouldn't pass for a pastor's wife, but she wasn't as hard as her helmet, either. Bill claimed their relationship was purely platonic and we weren't about to argue with him. Mothers-in-law have always been given bum raps— maybe this would improve their image!

Bill bounced back and forth between Nan's place and various V.A. hospitals. For variety he visited jails and halfway houses. Some trips were associated with physical ailments, but the majority were chemical related.

We continued to get early morning wake-up calls from Phoenix pubs. Bill gave us blow-by-blow accounts of his latest battle with the bar's "behemoth of the month!" He always left his forwarding address.

Nan finally got fed up with Bill and evicted him. He crashed in a pad near Cave Creek where he could wheel and deal in the natural decor of the desert.

## The Case of the Cave Creek Creep

A month later we received a collect call from Bill's one-man Cave Creek commune. A mean midnight marauder had just plastered his picture window to smithereens with an elephant gun! Bill wasn't hit but was having trouble sleeping. I shouted into the phone, "hot lead isn't a heaven-sent cure for insomnia but neither are early morning phone calls!"

I should have told him to get the lead out and go back to bed, but my Christian conscience called "Karen" wouldn't let me. Instead, I said "Your hit man was either Ray trying out new turf or the landlord trying to collect his rent." Bill, in no mood for mirth, spit out the grisly details again. Remembering that the call was collect, I cut him off and told him to inform us if there were further fireworks. That proved to be a mistake—there were!

The next night the madman returned on his cycle to cave in Bill's cactus and pump twenty rounds into his living room. Bill was in excruciating pain from a ricochet to his right ankle. We told him to call the cops.

Meanwhile Minnie Main, who had cooked for Bill at our home and treated him like a son, called on our other line. Bill, having phoned Minnie many times with all the gory details, had this 70-year old so upset she was ready to fly to Phoenix to take on the kamikaze character by herself!

The following day we received Bill's CNN update—the motorcycle maniac hit again. He was getting bolder—the latest attack was in broad daylight. This time the black-hooded hothead leaped off his cycle like a crazed Superman and propelled himself through the patched-up picture window! He picked off Bill's Doberman before going on a search and destroy mission. Moving through the house like the head honcho from Wil-Kill, his big bazooka blew gaping holes in the walls. If he was after rodents, why did he shoot the dog?

After plastering the crockery in the kitchen the hit man turned his attention towards Bill cowering in the corner. He shattered Bill's right kneecap and came close to piercing Bill's ears with parting shots before hopping on his Harley.

Racked by pain in a pool of blood, Bill managed to crawl to his phone to call the cops. I pleaded with him to hang on until help arrived, but after a few moans and groans the receiver went dead. Hopefully Bill didn't follow suit!

Wavering between horror, confusion and suspicion, we called Minnie. Having already received her daily "due diligence" report from Cave Creek, she was too distraught to talk.

We contacted Dot and Gordon James who moved to Phoenix to become directors of a home for emotionally disturbed girls. A former staff member resigned under extreme stress after a girl tried to drown her in the pool.

We helped Dot and Gordon adjust to their new surroundings—it reminded us of home. Providing them with a pipeline of talent and trauma we sent a girl by the name of Angel down there who acted like the devil. After five murderous months of thrill and chill treatment, Angel was shipped back to Milwaukee in a straitjacket! Albeit unorthodox, this wasn't cruel—it was the only way to keep her out of the cockpit!

To make amends we arranged for Ken and Ann Chandler's daughter Lynn to cook at the Encanto Girls' Residence. She lasted a year without winding up in the soup.

We even provided clergy for retreats and seminars. However, when Father Sy Svoboda from the Columbian Seminary flew southwest his stay was short-lived. In Roman circles his collar was his calling card, but in the fertile fields of fundamentalism it cut his throat. The Bible Belt Board didn't see eye to eye with Father Sy. Gordon was grieved, we were peeved, but Father Sy was relieved—he wasn't ready to receive the same reward as St. Joan of Arc!

After two years of this run-around, Gordon resigned and set up private practice. He also taught sociology at community colleges and worked with senior citizens in Sun City.

Gordon, the Sherlock Holmes of the evangelical jet set, was well-qualified to ferret out what happened to Bill. He could smell a rat days before it died in the wall.

Gordon couldn't locate Bill at any hospital so he gathered his gear and headed for Cave Creek.

Puzzled by Bill's picture window being intact, he combed the backyard for clues. Closing in from the rear he peered at Bill lying motionless on a floor mattress—there was no sign of blood. He rapped repeatedly until Bill limped to the door with an Ace bandage around his right knee. Shocked to see Gordon, Bill blocked the entrance pleading the place was a shambles.

They hashed this out in the front yard—Bill did most of the talking. Sticking to his story like a damp stamp, he claimed he replaced the window and was released from the hospital this morning after emergency surgery. However, when Gordon pressed Bill's flesh as to which hospital, he came down with a convenient case of amnesia!

Bill was hanging himself under the scrutiny of this seasoned super-sleuth. Gordon was never one to rush to judgment but in this case he had heard enough. He bid Bill adieu and drove to his office.

Gordon reported his findings but craftily let us draw our own conclusions. There was no evidence of gunfire and no police record of any recent rumble. Bill had been to all the hospitals in the Phoenix area, but not lately.

We deduced that the Ace bandage was designed to cover up an old knee injury. Bill was known for bad trips, but this three day deluge almost did all of us in! What kind of chemical concoctions produced this delusion? The prime candidates were coke, angel dust, alcohol and aspirin. This mixture was potent enough to make anyone see midnight marauders with elephant guns!

Gordon was the calming influence in cracking the incredulous case of the "Cave Creek Creep." Our sleep was restored and collect calls were curtailed. Gordon followed up on Bill and has been his faithful friend through the years.

When Bill's dad died a year later he left him a sizable inheritance. Bill blew it all by living the high life. One Christmas after trading his cycle for "Town and Country" toys, Bill pulled up in front of the Arizona Biltmore in a chauffeured white stretch limousine with a bar and television in the back. He looked like a recycled rock star as he emerged in his leather vest and tattered Levis to join us for breakfast in the Gold Room. Breakfast was the only meal he could stomach before the chemical onslaught waged relentless war on his ravaged body.

By his mid-thirties Bill appeared wasted enough to have served in both World Wars in addition to suffering through the Great Depression. He checked in and out of treatment centers as if they were resorts on the Riviera!

## Jeremy James Hits Oconomowoc High

Denise made cherry blintzes for our over-extended family for six more years—her change of pace was pecan rolls. We grew so weary gaining weight we had to invest in freight scales to watch it.

Denise guarded the kitchen as if it was Fort Knox. Anyone caught snitching food was exiled to our mosquito-infested island as vulture bait. Old Testament-type therapy proved to be more effective than psychological counseling.

Jeremy was a joy to have in our house despite shrewd manipulation games which all kids learn before Monopoly. After he mastered his mother's number, he put us to the test. Parents have a built-in instinct to protect their offspring even if the kid is burning down the house!

Denise, in no mood to be outdone by Bill, got married again. Rev. Ferd Bahr performed the ceremony. Willa Dorsey provided the music and Jeremy was the ring bearer. Not even a Missouri Synod pastor, a black Baptist gospel singer and an only son could cement this relationship—it ended quicker than the Cuban crisis! Denise and Jeremy moved back in our home for another year until they relocated in Phoenix.

Denise shared Jeremy with us for summers until he was twelve. At that point she let him attend school in Oconomowoc and live with us full time.

Jeremy is a handsome six-foot blue-eyed blond who excels in sports and inherited a crock-full of culinary talents. His high IQ was wasted in high school because he was too stubborn to apply it to any effort as mundane as schoolwork. After playing tag with the truant officer he dropped out of school and joined the National Guard.

As a loyal alumnus of Oconomowoc High, he set up shop in the school hallway to recruit students for Uncle Sam's Billion Dollar Band. His pragmatic approach was preempted abruptly by the assistant principal, Mrs. Hall. She rightly discerned that a dropout's attempt to sign up students for another cause could reap damaging psychological effects on the entire school system! Jeremy's recruiting was relegated to the streets.

After six months of sidewalk psychology, Jeremy saw the educational light and passed his GED exam so he could enter college. In his first semester at the University of Wisconsin-Waukesha, he played soccer on the championship team and was two "B's" short of straight "A's".

The following February Jeremy faced one of life's stinging realities—his father faded away at the age of thirty-seven. The "Cave Creek Creep" didn't do it, but decades of doing drugs and other debilitating substances did!

Jeremy doesn't have many positive memories of his dad, but he took his death hard. He made arrangements for a military funeral and came back from Phoenix with the flag that draped Bill's casket.

Shortly after, Jeremy took a leave of absence from school to join the regular army for three years. He is stationed in Germany not far from Nuremberg. Hopefully all his trials there will be trivial! Shortly prior to leaving for Germany, Jeremy latched on to a lovely Irish lass named Linda Brannan. Linda lives near us and has visited Jeremy many times in Bavaria.

Back in 1966 we never dreamed what fourteen-year old freckle-faced Bill would drag us through. If someone had foretold his future, we might have used Uncle Harry's line, "No thanks, we have seen what it's done for others!" However, in our younger years the temptation would have vanished like a vapor in the morning sun. It's hard to say "no" to need, especially when faced with a lad who deserved a better break in life.

Bill cut the cords of his rescue rope and sunk to the bottom. Jeremy has come full circle and chosen the recovery road that leads to a full life. What the moth has eaten the Lord has restored.

Bill was the beginning—the end was many light years away. Sixty more kids would pour through our door before the scars of burn-out slowed our stamina. Reinforcements were rapidly approaching over the horizon. The Jesus People, weaned of their wasted ways, were marching ten abreast to the beat of a different drummer.

## Haighting Ashbury—Loving Jesus

Woodstock was billed by the blinded as Utopia—it ended more like the tragedy at Wounded Knee. A sea of sucking mud supported a half-million spaced-out hippies at this upstate New York hog farm. Bodies in sleeping bags, blending in with Mother Earth, were mangled by tractors hauling water.

Humanity reared its raw wounds. The river was for washing and the woods for making whoopee. A child was conceived in a canoe by a couple floating on the farm pond. Non-stop raucous acid rock drowned out all other sounds for days. Even the drugs were downers—bad brown stuff floated around producing acid rain pollution! Musicians were so stoned they didn't know whose music they were playing.

The wounds of Woodstock festered far beyond the farm— while some performers were launched, others were celebrating their last hippie hurrah!

Janis Joplin stumbled on-stage, spitting and cursing like a drunken gunslinger. Toting two whiskey bottles, she screamed and slurred a series of songs before staggering into the tent to shoot up some more. Fifteen months later she pulled the final curtain at twenty-seven years young.

Jimi Hendrix paved the way two weeks before, while it took Keith Moon, of the Who, eight years to surrender his claim for immortality. Others would have been grateful to be dead rather than endure chemical warfare day in and day out!

The angry seas of mud and drugs swallowed up souls like a shipwreck during monsoon season—thank God there were survivors. Thousands thought to be washed up were swept away by the tide turning to Jesus. Burned out beatniks were long gone and fields of flower children were finding faith by the early 1970s.

Rip Van Winkles of various religious denominations were aroused by this Great Awakening. The ecumenical enlightenment of the Jesus People Movement and Charismatic Renewal ushered in an era of love, as separate streams flowed into a roaring river of spiritual revival.

A crew cut could cuddle a longhair and a hard-nosed conservative could coddle a bleeding heart liberal. Material things didn't matter—only Jesus. Dawn made each day a joy to serve the Master.

Tie-dyed Jesus Freaks joined squares straight out of Sears & Roebuck to work the streets. John Lennon, who boasted that the Beatles were more popular than Jesus, was among the missing. Go-go joints, stripped of their fleshly facade, were turned into Christian coffee houses. The Hollywood Free Paper, barely dry off the press, was peddled by the impassioned in every precinct. The Milwaukee Jesus paper was called Street Level.

Jesus Christ portrayals were put on wanted posters, and promoted as the notorious leader of an underground liberation movement. His crimes included winemaking, food distribution, busting businessmen, challenging religious leaders, fraternizing with criminals and prostitutes, and practicing medicine without a license! His appearance was typical hippie type—long hair, beard, robe and sandals. Armed with the radical message, "Love one another," He was considered a dangerous rabble-rouser whose aim was to set the captives free!

Christian businessmen, who prayed for these waywards for years, wept as they witnessed mass baptisms along the California coast. Pat Boone baptized Jesus People in his pool faster than he could pump chlorine!

Not all converts were flower children—some were Outlaws. An entire motorcycle gang from Orange County adopted the Lord as their new leader. Not to be upstaged, celebrities cashed in also. Johnny Cash and Paul Stookey joined the ranks of the redeemed. Arthur Blessit, a self-styled street evangelist, lugged a large wooden cross across the country. His message—"Tune out to drugs and turn on to Jesus."

Jesus People clustered in Christian communes. They studied scripture in the mornings and spread the Good News all night. Redeemed rock bands rolled all over the land reveling in revamped "Rock of Ages" music. The sound was loud enough to levitate the living and raise the dead. Words weren't instrumental in relaying the message—it was written on their faces. Rejoicing over the Rapture was a far cry from spacing out on speed!

Larry Norman and other top rockers joined the Jesus People. Milwaukee gave birth to "The Sheep" and "Resurrection" bands.

The Jesus Revolution infused spiritual fervor but only a few from the pews hit the street. Rev. Robert Terwilliger of New York's Trinity Institute reported, "There is spiritual revival everywhere—except in the Church!" Pharisees, trying to stampede the fire, depicted Jesus Freaks as products of psychological lobotomy. While Sadducees snubbed these utopian upstarts assuming they would suffer a fanatic's fate—annihilation.

However, those churches with foresight flung their doors wide open to the Jesus People. Discerning that ecstasy was Godlier than apathy, the elders encouraged setting "faith fires" under the seats of the sitting saints. They prophesied that the street people of today would be the pulpit pounders of tomorrow.

Ecclesiasticals weren't the only ones struggling with schizophrenia—parents were caught in the confusion also. They didn't want their kids on drugs, but flying high on "Jesus power" presented other problems. Suddenly confronted with the salvation message, status quo seemed a safer sanctuary. Flower children didn't push their parents into psychedelic drugs, but they sure hit them hard with the gospel!

Family crises were created over conversion. In most cases Mom and Dad held firm to their form of godliness and refused to swarm the streets. What would their bridge partners think if they screamed in the local supermarket, "Repent, the Kingdom of God is at hand?"! In reality, very few Jesus Freaks resorted to John the Baptist barnstorming but the media did a number on them.

Parents possessed a genuine fear that their prodigal sons and daughters might be deceived by a cult. Some Jesus People leaders, stumbling on power and pride, dove headfirst into caldrons of the cults. Brainwashed, many of their flock blindly followed. "The Children of God" and "The Way" were two groups that veered miles off course.

From 1968 to 1977 Karen and I expended time and energy in helping young people mature as Christians. Over 60 kids lived in our home at various times from four months to four years. Whether they had been flower children or cut-up crew-cut kids, their current common denominator was their desire to follow Jesus. Most were a pleasure, others were pains, but all were sent for a purpose. Almost all carried the ball for a long gain but a few fumbled near the fifty-yard line and never recovered.

For each one who resided with us there were scores more who passed through our doors searching for fun, faith and fellowship. There were prayer and praise meetings, Bible studies, bull sessions and burn-out. The Jesus People had landed, but not lightly!

Sometimes their childlike faith was weighted down by heavy baggage—burdens were byproducts of being raised in dysfunctional families. Prayer and deliverance were available, but psychologists and treatment centers were suspect. In the Jesus People world of witnessing and weatherproofing, compulsion counselors and shrinks were portrayed as parasitic paramours pecking away at God's ordained order! It was more spiritual to stuff shadowy symptoms under religious rugs where they would gather dust and never be dealt with. Many prodigals were destroyed by this delusion of denial.

## Saint Vincent of Lombard— Patron Saint of Packerland

Milwaukee, the last bastion to bounce on any bandwagon, is considered the most conservative city west of the Vatican. In 1968 Milwaukee still sported enough flat-tops to carpet every football stadium with artificial turf. Every fall the European fashion world loads twenty barges full of last year's winners and floats them towards the Beer Capital. When the merchandise arrives two years later, it is aged in warehouses for six months more before it is displayed on boutique floors.

Milwaukeeans' bulldog tenacity goes with the territory. Impeded by a Prussian presence they are reluctant to release anything—hula-hoops are still as popular as Harleys. Fortune's Five Hundred test all their new products here—if they sell moderately in Milwaukee, they will smash records in the rest of the country.

When it comes to spiritual matters, Milwaukee is often more progressive. There are still pockets of people who envision heaven as a denominational rest home, but many, having broken free of this stiff stance, are standing tall with their spiritual siblings.

Grass roots ecumenical endeavors have found green pastures with many Protestant and Catholic leaders throwing down their pitchforks long enough to embrace each other. Bishop Richard Sklba respects other believers' religious traditions and Archbishop Rembert Weakland is known nationally for his openness.

However, the most eclectic ecumenical ecclesiastical of all times is Saint Vincent of Lombard—the Patron Saint of Packerland! He created a Green Bay brotherhood for all believers by turning a team of country bumpkins into a nationally feared football force in the twinkling of an eye. Saint Vincent's anointed annihilators emerged victorious on every crusade, while his victims limped out of Lambeau Field pleading for mercy. He swept through two straight Super Bowl wins with his eyes on the White House—the ACLU stopped him with their tenacious "separation of church and state" goal line defense.

Despite being relegated to the Washington Redskins, St. Vincent of Lombard was the first Catholic to be canonized alive! The Vatican didn't have to search for miracles. However, the Great Jehovah, who always champions the underdog, saw the mismatch and called St. Vincent home. St. Vincent went to heaven and the Packers went to hell!

The glory years faded faster than the hair on Ray Nitschke's noggin. Not even "Devine intervention" could save the team. Daffy Dan Devine traded a field full of first round draft choices for a senior citizen and the Packers haven't passed through the Promised Land since!

Meanwhile our Patron Saint is still in touch. Many years ago I met a Pentecostal pastor who made contact. As a young preacher he was worried that the "Rapture" would interrupt his ministry. After months of agony he withdrew to Lake Michigan for meditation. Somewhere in the silence he tapped into St. Vincent who gave him this comforting word—: "My Son, never fear. St. Vincent is here. The 'Rapture' remains on hold until the Packers win another Super Bowl—no man knows the time or season. What Devine did was a demonic demonstration against divine order. There are no new Starrs on the horizon. Forrest fathered a field of thugs while Infante fostered futility, when his "magic man" ran out of tricks. The "Pack" doesn't have a prayer, without a Minister of Defense! It will take Wolfman Ron, a Ragin Cajun and a Big Swede, plus speed to succeed. Eons will pass before you are drafted into eternity. Say hello to Max, Paul and Ray—they haven't kept in touch."

The pastor pleaded with me not to blow his cover. If his congregation discovered he was communicating with the Saints, his fate would be worse than John the Baptist!

# 16

# The General of the Jesus People Army

The fields were fertile for the Jesus Freaks to break ground in Milwaukee. Jim Polosaari and the Full Gospel Businessmen united forces for an outreach at the War Memorial to ignite the flickering flower children with a holy flame.

We were invited to a planning session at Nancy and Mike Kuzmic's house led by Belinda Bartolotta, who was to be the featured speaker. By the time we arrived, conservative business types were scraping shoulders with disheveled long-hairs. Belinda, a Jesus People leader from Seattle, was already revving up the troops for a combined land, sea and air assault on the Milwaukee area.

Her camouflage attire, combined with her hard demeanor, demonstrated battle scars going back to the beat generation. If Castro keeled over in Cuba, Belinda could be next in line! Her rhetoric revealed a divine call as General of the Jesus People Army. Destiny demanded that the forces sweep in from the Northwest to scatter any semblance of spiritual status quo. After God's army launched grenades, hand-to-hand combat was in order!

Bill Toll was bug-eyed as he registered seismic shock. Belinda's power of persuasion could convince lifelong GM men to throw money at corroded Edsels!

Her flashing brown eyes beamed bazookas at the men as she barked orders, "Hit the phones for Jesus while there is still time to turn the tide!" Parting like privates in boot camp competing to call home, they sounded the alarm for the full scale offensive.

When Wisconsin Bell's boys returned, the shouting shifted to hitting high schools for Jesus. Trying to line up suburbia for a quick blitz, Belinda asked us to secure Oconomowoc High School. Challenging the vigilante euphoria sweeping the room, we expressed serious concerns—storming street people with these tactics was one thing, but assailing school kids with this militant message was like torching your house at midnight and expecting a good night's sleep!

The Bartolotta battle cry was "Move them out of the hall-ways and onto the highways for Jesus." Who needs an education if the Lord is lurking around the corner to come and claim us? The "end times" are God's tempest turned loose on the land, not study time! Students will fade faster than "pet rocks" in a land-slide, while teachers will be left to educate each other.

Refusing to go with the flow found us booted back to boot camp for more brainwashing. At least we managed to escape the stockade! Oconomowoc High was temporarily removed from the hit list, but maneuvers were being mapped out for other schools in the area. Meanwhile, the War Memorial Rally was shaping up as Woodstock West!

The short-hairs and the no-hairs were outnumbered three to one by long-hairs as hundreds of enthusiasts jammed into the meeting hall. An upbeat Jesus band challenged the ears of all who entered. While the Jesus Freaks were caught up in ecstasy, the Full Gospel crowd cringed, scanning the stage as if Guy Lombardo would miraculously appear to save them from this high-powered piercing Armageddon.

Mixed in with this melting pot of humanity were a couple of canines. Thirty feet to my right was a German Shepherd who appeared as if he was attending his first Jesus People rally. A few rows in front stood a mongrel who had the same mean demeanor as his master. Belinda Bartolotta wasn't blowing smoke when she shouted, "The whole world is being won for Jesus." If dogs were answering the call, the "end times" were upon us!

As the band belted out its last number, Jim Polosaari grabbed the microphone to restore order. After giving a ten-minute testi-mony, he outlined his vision for street ministry in Milwaukee.

Jim introduced Belinda, who was instant energy. Attired in Jesus Army issue, she delivered the same militant move 'em out message the comrades received in Kuzmic's living room. Shout-ing in cadet cadence, she centered her eyes on the ceiling as if her words were straight from the Great General. The days of dreaming and drugs are down the drain—Jesus is organizing for the end battle! His army is infiltrating the streets to save every sinner who surfaces. Lay down your learning, your living, your life and even your wife, if need be, and latch onto the Lord's legions sweeping the land.

Belinda ignited the long-hairs with electrifying elocution which left little confusion about the task at hand. Even the dogs reacted! When the mongrel howled as if he had treed a possum, laughter rippled through the crowd. It took more than a mutt to muzzle Belinda. Without missing a beat she out-shouted the dog—it was a mismatch!

Jim Polossari joined her at the microphone. They took turns challenging the audience to come forward to join Jesus. After making more appeals than the March of Dimes, over one hundred long hairs responded—even a couple of chrome-domes decided for Christ. The German Shepherd's master ushered him out before he could answer the call—it was time to return to Brady Street to guard the store.

Belinda finally laid down her arms and left the following day for her next salvation sojourn. Somewhere in the heat of battle she became bewildered about the enemy's identity! Deception was her downfall, desertion was her crime. She joined forces with the Children of God, a West Coast cult which captured the minds of disenfranchised flower children.

## Brady Street Believers

Jim Polosaari's legacy was to lead the mobilized Milwaukee Jesus People to victory. John Herrin was his head honcho. Their first house near Brady Street became so crowded the walls started wailing and the neighbors followed suit. They commandeered a larger facility on Farwell for their commune and training center.

The leaders instituted a rigid schedule for the former floating flower children. Adopting the motto, "To shine for the Son, you can't rise with the moon," a typical day the Jesus People way was pray, eat, work, study the Word and hit the streets. Salvation teams swept the walks of wounded souls and steered them towards the Jesus Christ Powerhouse on Brady Street.

This Christian coffeehouse, filled to the brim with ex-beats every night, became a spiritual showcase for musical talent. The heavies of this Holy Ghost hootenanny were a gospel rock band called The Sheep. When The Sheep finished, their Shepherd took over. Jim Polosaari, tapping into the power of the Powerhouse, pleaded with druggies to ditch their crutches and march with the Jesus People on their far-out faith trip!

The Sheep grazed all over Southeastern Wisconsin in the early '70s. Jim Schwab, Bo Lohman, Reed Middlestead, Moe Barker and Mike and Mary Dammerow all banded together for this powerful outreach. Some Sunday nights the shepherd put The Sheep out to pasture so they could perform at Living Waters.

Another method of spreading the "Good News" was distributing a monthly Jesus People paper called Street Level. Sue Polosaari, the editor, saturated Street Level with testimonies of ex-hippies whose current home was "hallelujah land."

Street Level ran the story of Bill Lowry, a former salesman turned tent evangelist. Bill's former main claim to fortune was selling twenty-six mobile homes in one day, while drunk as a mortuary monk imbibing embalming fluid. Bill abandoned his mobile homes to lead the "Jesus People Traveling Tent Revival" all over the Midwest. Neither mud, nor rain nor snow could derail this religious roller coaster—rowdy renditions of "Give Me That Old Time Religion" were always followed by a "Git Right With God" message.

In 1972, while attending the Jesus People Training Center Commencement on Farwell, we discovered everyone was splitting including the shepherds! It was the largest mass exodus since the Israelites fled Egypt—even the marrow was scraped off the Pharaoh! It was as if some sanctified soothsayer predicted the "Beer Capital of the World" was about to plunge into Lake Michigan and those left behind would sulk in their suds. No shepherd ever admitted fault, but the remnant of sheep remaining wasn't enough to run a Christian coin laundry, much less a Powerhouse!

Bill Lowry revived his traveling tent revival. John Herrin herded his flock to the decadent South to retrace General Sherman's steps. John turned the Resurrection Band loose on the rebels—which made The Sheep sound like little lambs when it came to dishing out decibels. It was open season on cemeteries—the dead in Christ returned in droves!

After sweeping the South for the Savior, John Herrin and his holy hippies settled in Chicago. Some still live in Christian communes and witness in the Windy City. The Resurrection Band hasn't missed a beat in over twenty years, but some members are bearing bifocals! Their Jesus People U.S.A. publishes a monthly magazine called Cornerstone, which provides a firm foundation for Christian living for all flower children who haven't faded in with the old fogies of the faith.

## Lonesome Stone

Jim Polossari, not about to be upstaged by the upstarts, led The Sheep on a full Gospel Businessmen's airlift to Europe. The tour was to take two weeks, but two years later The Sheep were still stirring things up on the Continent. The concerts started in Scandinavia and drifted south to Germany, Holland, Belgium and England.

Jesus People's popularity was at its peak in the early '70s—thousands of floundering flower children were drawn into the fold. In a Helsinki Lutheran church the entire assembly answered the altar call.

The Jesus People were on a roll spiritually, but their earthly road was rocky. Victimized by vindictive vehicles, many times the flock was forced to be foot soldiers for the Lord. Food was in short supply. The Jesus People staple was "disciples' steak"—we call it peanut butter!

After many moons of ministry the itinerant band yearned to settle down. The original Sheep gravitated to the grazing fields back home, but they recruited revved-up replacements.

Mike and Mary Dammerow, who returned from London, asked Matt Spransy to play keyboard with them in Milwaukee. Matt, from Oconomowoc, was part of the Living Waters band called Salt of the Earth. His brief Beer Capital audition ended in an airplane trip to London to join The Sheep. Music was Matt's first love and Siv Algotsson from Sweden was his second—they were married in 1974.

The new London crew created a narrative with music entitled How Jesus People Come Alive. Kenneth Frampton, an English entrepreneur doubling as a sugar daddy, rented the Sundown Theatre for rehearsals. Months later the production was reworked into a full-scale multi-media rock musical called Lonesome Stone—a Christian Hair with appropriate vestments. Two of the London cast from Hair were allowed to link up with Lonesome Stone after they put on the full armor of the Lord.

This story of a hippie from Haight Ashbury who found his way to Jesus, sold out shows at London's Rainbow Theatre. The long Rainbow run produced enough gold for Lonesome Stone to tour Europe for eighteen months.

Jim Polosaari branched out to help organize the Greenbelt Festival—the premier Jesus Rock extravaganza attracting 30,000 fired-up European fans.

By 1974 half of the Lonesome Stone personnel were from Europe. Immigration problems erupted in England and the entire ensemble embarked to the "Colonies." Mr. Frampton chartered them a plane which landed in Toronto, Canada. From there they were bused in "Sunday School specials" to perform in Toledo, Kansas City, Sioux Falls and Duluth.

Finally, Lonesome Stone descended on the mighty metropolis of Oconomowoc. It was the biggest blast to hit the area since a local favorite son startled a Fourth of July crowd by dynamiting the Oconomowoc Lake club pier! Decades of dispassion had passed since these two timely events.

Every seat at the Junior High auditorium was sold out for weeks. The night of the performance scalpers pounded the pavement selling tickets for three times their face value. They turned out to be Lonesome Stone stage crew testing promotion tactics! Nobody complained—six dollars a seat was still a steal to see this show!

It was a super production. Excitement extended beyond the stage as the cast ran down the aisles and involved the audience. After the show, Jim Polosaari invited people to accept Jesus.

Superlatives gave way to sadness with the realization that there wouldn't be a second show—many people wanted their friends to see it. Matt Spransy proudly wore his "Lonesome Stone—London to Oconomowoc" T-shirt at the cast party afterwards.

Lancaster, Pennsylvania, proved to be the swan song for Lonesome Stone. The logistics of lugging a sizable safari on cross country megathons wore thin on the skin and the wallet. Lonesome Stone's financial skid rivaled the stock market slide of the Great Depression!

When their Sugar Daddy went into seclusion, the shepherds slipped into confusion trying to combat this cash crunch. Jim Polosaari's pacing put a permanent furrow in our living room rug.

A new Board was formed to prop up the production. However, top-heavy with artistic talent while devoid of business acumen, the new contingent collapsed the shaky structure faster than a hurricane buckles a boardwalk. In the fall of 1974 "Lonesome Stone" lost $20,000!

Adding devastation to destruction, their charter carrier, "Mid East Mozambawae Airlines" went belly up financially. Facing permanent grounding, the Board attempted to persuade another airline to honor the return tickets of the thirty European kids. It was like trying to talk Wisconsin Lutherans into tithing to the Papal Fund—there were no takers!

Consequently the Oconomowoc area was turned into a gospel rock refugee camp. Living Waters became the official "Lonesome Stone Adoption Agency." Many families took one, the Steinkes squeezed in five stranded sheep and we were blessed with six.

Matt Spransy devised an ingenious master plan to solve the immigration mess—marry them! Matt married Siv Algottson from Sweden on December 10,1974. The other bachelors panicked and went into hibernation for the winter!

Our international clan included Robin and Vanessa from England, Anita from Sweden, Rachel from Holland and Klaus from Germany. Henry, the neo-international, spent his childhood living on U.S.A. military bases throughout the world.

At times we had fourteen around the dining room table. Minnie Main's kitchen contortions were so time consuming she couldn't indulge in her favorite hobby—heated debates!

Karen made the Christmas season joyous for everyone. Her special gift of affirmation brings forth the best in young people. In addition to giving practical presents she showered spiritual gifts by hours of listening, sharing and praying with each one.

The scattered flock hoped Santa Claus would nix the North Pole and stay to lead Lonesome Stone out of its financial wilderness. The spirit was willing but the restless reindeers were homesick—Europe was too far from their beaten trail!

Meanwhile, the shepherds were losing ground in their struggle for survival. Racing from crisis to crisis left them no time to corral their own compulsions. In rare moments when no certified crisis existed, they created one. Suffering from battle fatigue, it was time for the burned-out shepherds to turn themselves in for a 100,000 mile checkup!

The Jesus People Army dug in for the long hard winter by pitching tents in pockets along the landscape. One snowy day, Mike Dreyful, the business manager, drove out to a commune near Rubicon bearing more bad news—all the band equipment had been sold to pay bills. The last nail was hammered into their hopes. The effect was the same as seizing the barber's scissors and expecting him to tear everyone's hair out! Lonesome Stones labors were officially over and long locks were all they had left.

The sheep slowly filtered back to Europe as standbys and stowaways during the ensuing months. Robin Newton, relating better to Dick Nixon than Queen Elizabeth, got permanent resident alien status after bureaucracy battles with the U.S. Immigration Service. He kept our property in prim and proper shape for the next three years.

## Highway Missionary Society

Jim Polosaari had been pounded to the canvas but not counted out. Heeding Horace Greeley's advice, he headed west and crossed the border into British Columbia. In the virgin territory of Victoria he started another Jesus People ministry called the Highway

220

Missionary Society. They traded street corner witnessing for res-cuing stranded motorists on the open road. After fixing their flats and charging their batteries, the Society jump-started the weary travelers' spiritual juices.

Jesus Freak mission fields didn't function without music, so Jim organized a new band named Servant. By 1979 Servant signed a recording contract and the entire commune moved to Grant's Pass, Oregon. Matt and Siv Spransy joined the Highway Mission-ary Society and Matt became Servant's keyboard player. The band traveled coast to coast with the Holy Ghost, playing 250 gigs a year.

During Servant's six year run they cut an album every year including their best seller "Shallow Water." Jim split halfway through for bluer pastures on the Big Island of Hawaii. After a brief bask in the Kona sun with Youth With A Mission, he returned to his first love—managing a Christian heavy metal band.

By 1987 the ministry cycle had driven full circle and the High-way Missionary Society was encountering deep ruts. The com-mune became the focal point instead of Jesus! Family members, left to fend for themselves on the farm, were frustrated and feisty. Their elation over Servants' road show was waning faster than wounded wallabies wallowing in wet wax. The "submission sages" had ruled the day and now it was time to pay. With finances fad-ing, faith was replaced by fears of foreclosure. The IRS chased the Highway Society all the way to Cincinnati, which became the commune's last stand.

The community officially disbanded in 1988 and Servant faced the same music the following year. Many of the former flower children filtered into mainstream society. Matt and Siv Spransy chose Oconomowoc for their fresh start. Matt is a low-key high-tech engineer and Siv a successful seamstress in addition to teach-ing home school. Tim Spransy and Michael Steinke are well-known commercial artists.

Jesus People alumni in the area formed a band named Be-lieve It, which performs periodically. Believe It has a super sound, but the era of ear plugs is long gone! So have the Jesus Freaks, but they will never be forgotten.

# 17

# The Kingpin of the Cut-Outs

In the late 1960s, teenagers by the tons turned up at our place on Sunday afternoons. Christian brain trusts believed that physically fatigued kids were fodder for spiritual faith, so my task was to tire them before the evening meeting.

In summer, softball, volleyball and water-skiing were the winners, but in winter, we retreated to a rustic basketball court on the second floor of our coach house. In its heyday the bottom floor stored carriages, cutters, sleighs and wagons. The blacksmith shop, accented by leather-belted power equipment, still exists, but the horses have hit the road.

After I wore out the restless, the rodents and raccoons took over the court. Evidence suggested that they were better dribblers than dunkers.

As "Campus Cop," the cutting cold of winter was a valuable aid in corralling the kids for the 7:00 p.m. meeting. Spring stretched my patience in this perennial pursuit, as warmer weather brings out wanderlust in wide-eyed youth. Most of the teens weren't troublesome, but there were always some Dennis the Menace mentalities running rampant around the grounds.

Jeff Newell was crowned the "Kingpin of the Cut-outs." His contagious smile and easy-going style put you to sleep at the same time his imaginative mind was scripting mischief on the sly.

Jeff's favorite hiding place was the backside of the boathouse. Whenever his sentry saw me coming it was time for their tag team to swiftly squeeze through the crawl space below the boathouse floor. Jeff knew I wouldn't duck into this dark, dismal abyss of silted sand and sea urchins in my meeting clothes. I wouldn't cavort in this creepy crud in Adam's attire either—even our dogs wouldn't plunge into this pit!

Outsmarted by this "Swamp Fox," it was time to burst the bubble that made his head swell. Alternating my route, I attacked from an easterly direction, camouflaged by the woods. With Jeff's comrade in crime setting his sights on the vast Victorian, I crossed the bridge and crept along the shoreline.

Jeff was strutting on the cement retaining wall as proud as a potentate. Closing quickly on their rear flank, a few feet away from my prey, I jumped up and screamed, "Jeff!" Startled, he whirled around to block my body with his forearm, but the impact forced him to fall backwards into the lake. After hitting the water like a downed drowned dirigible, he finally surfaced sporting a sheepish smile. We laughed for weeks over his aquatic acrobatics.

I fired Jeff's sentry on the spot for leaving a gaping hole in their rear guard and paraded my prize catches up to the house. After a quick change of clothes, the three of us occupied reserved front row seats five nose lengths from the speaker. The "Kingpin of the Cut-outs" appeared self-conscious as kids eye-balled him from all sides of the room. The last time Jeff was this far forward was at his infant baptism!

True to form, Jeff could hardly wait to bargain. He agreed to attend the meetings on time as long as he could sit in the back. Only after the deal was sealed did I reveal who would be sitting beside him. The "Kingpin of the Cut-outs" cashed in his crown for a chance at the "keys to the kingdom!"

## Saved by the Stronger Sex

With as much warning as a touchdowned tornado, kids came at all hours during the week. It was rare for any teen to ring the bell. This is why Jesus tells us in scripture not to be concerned about the day or the hour—just be ready! These trying times were a foretaste of glory divine.

One afternoon, Father Bill Wetzel brought two restless wrestlers, Dan Edwards and Doug Dillon, from the high school team. After ushering them into the music room, I retreated to the kitchen to retrieve some Cokes. By the time I returned, the two terrors were rolling on the oriental rug and there was nothing holy about it! Dan, escaping a hammerlock, knocked Doug into the legs of the gold-leafed love seat as he pounced on him. The love seat levitated as the bucking bronco tried to throw his rider.

Our music room, which was designed for stringed instruments, not the pounding of percussion, was being turned into a shambles. Oconomowoc High School was hard up for money, but not even in the Ming Dynasty were wrestling mats replaced by Oriental rugs!

Father Bill, dressed in age-old Anglican garb, tried to break up the battle. I canned the Coke and attempted to assist him. Pinned together like pasted pancakes, these grunting gladiators presented a challenge. If the tumbling twosome rolled under the baby grand piano I could chain saw its legs and body slam both of them with it!

When Karen came downstairs she shrieked in shock at the sight of four on the floor with the entire room shifting! The distinct sounds of a woman in distress caused Dan and Doug to cease and desist. As they sheepishly crawled back to their respective corners I realized that females are definitely the stronger sex. One shrill scream can put two pugnacious pugilists in their place pronto.

The Coke and cookies helped everyone regain their composure. At the risk of turning the teenage meetings into a free-for-all, we invited the boys to return on Sunday nights. Neither one accepted, but Dan came on other occasions with Father Bill—alone!


## Nick's Nudist Camp

By the summer of 1970, the surge of saints and sinners descending on our domicile was in full force. Verna Dunrud, discerning the effect of the force, was led back to the mission field. Panicked, we cut a deal with Daystar Ministries that even St. Vincent of Lombard couldn't duplicate. We traded Verna for Merlin and Ann Severson and Margaret Buhler. Jack Winter even threw in some undisclosed future draft choices!

Merlin and Ann Severson and their four daughters moved into the caretaker's quarters, next to the coach house. Merlin maintained the grounds and repaired equipment. His ministries included praying for the sick, counseling and exorcisms. Ann, gifted with a gentle manner, helped Merlin with spiritual support.

Margaret Buhler, a tall tough-minded woman with a multitude of ministry gifts, hunkered down as our housekeeper. Anyone trying to bluff Margaret had better be prepared for battle. Behind her big smile and darting eyes were decades of waging spiritual warfare with the devil and any other dude dumb enough to take her on. She could discern a devious "druggie" and deliver him of demons faster than he could find his next fix. If a sly saint socked it to her she "slayed him in the Spirit!"

Meanwhile, Mary "Minnie" Main had been moved up to the major leagues of the kitchen domain. Minnie, fueled by gallons of Prussian blood, could muster up a molten metal demeanor when tested. Her mood matched her vivid vocabulary which pierced many a tough teen's ears. She guarded the refrigerator like it was the last life raft and our house was the Titanic. With Minnie and Margaret bolstering our defensive line, all alien activity would be grounded.

A few months after the Daystar deal, we found a situation that sent even these warriors scrambling.

Gladys Gleason from Okauchee was experiencing great pain over her son Nick, who was in the clutches of cocaine. After witnessing many wasted kids set free from drugs at our place, she desired the same for Nick. However, Gladys couldn't convince us that Nick desired to cut the cocaine chains.

Jesus' unrecorded rule for restoration ministry states, "He who pushes a prisoner past the point of his own free will will be rewarded with a rampant recidivism rate!" The Great Physician never waved a wand that violated volition. They who break the rule become burdened with burnout. In Nick's case we didn't break the rule, but we bent it beyond recognition!

Nick arrived on a Friday night with all his worldly possessions packed into a knapsack. I instructed Bill and Jeff to bunk him down in the bachelor quarters on third floor, but spared them the details of Nick's nasty habits.

Wandering into the meeting ten minutes late, he parked his stocky frame on the edge of a chair and sat silently in a semistupor. Three choruses later Nick suddenly leaped on top of the love seat and shouted an expletive that stunned every worshipper, including his mother. Before he could expound on his oratory, I ushered him out of the room in a stranglehold.

After informing Nick that his exhortation wasn't edifying to the body of Christ, I turned our P.O.W. over to Bill and Jeff. I admonished the boys, "Stick to Nick like super-glue or you, too, could become his target!"

They escorted him to the porch where he whipped out a weed and leaped in the air chasing bright-colored bubbles. Nick tried to get the boys to join him in the hunt but they stood their ground.

After the meeting, my attention turned to diverting Nick's. Remembering he played a mean trumpet, I resurrected an old English horn from our catacombs. Lighting up like a firefly on the Fourth of July, Nick snatched the horn from my hands, puckishly pursing it to his lips.

Either the horn was horribly out of tune or he had lost his touch. The piercing product sounded like the last blast before the onset of Armageddon! People held their ears to prevent their lobes from loosening.

Nick refused to surrender his latest weapon. Realizing that reasoning with him was as useless as sawed-off shotguns on a shoplifting spree, I resorted to prayer. Meanwhile he marched down the upstairs hallway blowing a butchered version of "Bugler's Holiday." He had to be mixing acid with the hard stuff!"

Finally when Nick descended the staircase the boys grabbed him at the bottom and bulldozed him into the glassed-in porch. I tossed in three sleeping bags and slammed the door.

Apparently food wasn't Nick's fantasy—he slept through breakfast. Before Karen and I left for Milwaukee, I instructed Merlin to stick Nick in his side pocket for the day. He assured me he would keep him working on the property. Blowing up the flat tire on the tractor with his own lung power would be a good start!

Upon our return, our dream of Merlin driving out all Nick's demons was smashed to smithereens. I had to slam on my brakes to avoid our pickup truck, which was blocking the driveway. The passengers had bailed out to pursue hand-to-hand combat in the creeping bent grass near the lagoon. At least this match wasn't in the music room!

Judging by the chlorophyll stains on Merlin's pants, the grapplers had been wrestling for a while. Nick's arms were frantically flailing to free himself from Merlin's bear hug. Due to Merlin's chrome dome's disease, Nick couldn't find anything to grab on to. We abandoned our car to lend Merlin four hands, but by that time he subdued the spirited sapling. If this was a deliverance, the demons sure took huge divots out of the lawn!

Merlin, with his adrenaline in overdrive, emoted with effervescence as he related the story. "Driving back from the dump Nick suddenly lunged at me, trying to shove me out of the truck on the driver's side! Thwarted, he shifted gears and pulled me towards the passenger door, which he had opened. When I grabbed his arms we tumbled onto the gravel. I had to drag Nick on the grass to prevent him from taking the truck!"

Merlin returned Nick's latest "love object" to the garage as I led this colossal kleptomaniac around the lagoon on foot. When we reached the bridge, Nick stared strangely into the water. If he jumped he was on his own—it would take a derrick to pull him out. He broke his silence with incoherent comments about the freedom of the fish.

When I asked Nick about his fascination for 1962 Ford pickups, he claimed he needed wheels to drive down to the Windy City. The whats and whys were not forthcoming. Biding time on the bridge became nerve-wracking, so I persuaded him to return to the house.

Later that afternoon, Dana Dokken, the young daughter of the Oconomowoc hospital administrator, cut her walk around the lagoon short when she heard thrashing in the water. Too cold for carp in April, she moved closer to the edge to witness an eager beaver swimming towards the bridge in his birthday suit!

A few seconds after she relayed this revealing news, there were six people peering from the porch. Nick was not among them—he was too busy doing the breast stroke! Karen herded the girls into the house while Bill and I headed for the bridge. Nick was churning through the water as if a polar bear was in cold pursuit. I shouted, "Stop!," but he left us in his wake.

Maybe if we nabbed Nick's clothes, he would return to shore—there were none to be found. His Garden of Eden exhibition had begun at the big house! I sent Bill back to dig up some duds while I watched Nick do his thing. Maybe we should open up a Sea World called "Saints and Sinners!"

By the time Bill returned, Nick was lapping the lagoon for the fourth time. Our last gasp before going for the gaff hook was to work on Nick's fears—if he had any. I yelled, "Shag your buns out of the water before a snapping turtle mistakes them for raw meat!" The message sunk into his psyche as the psycho swam for shore. Nick landed twenty feet from where he tussled with Merlin a few hours before. Unfortunately, Merlin had neglected to cast out his beaver spirit!

As Nick climbed into his cut-offs, I reminded him that Living Waters wasn't a nudist camp and cover ups were expected at all times! Charismatic Christians were suspect enough without rumors running rampant about romping in the raw!

Karen cornered me to ask how I planned to harness our headstrong house guest. Many Old Testament practices immediately came to mind! She suggested I sign on as his Siamese twin while she rounded up spiritual warriors.

Camping in the woods was his next adventure. Still bearing beaver fever, he headed straight for the swamp. Nick pitched his tent fifteen feet from the water as I stood guard in the driveway.

Dana Dokken's dad was due to pick her up shortly. Hopefully she wouldn't bother him with the bare facts of her sightseeing. His initials weren't K.O. for nothing! By the time K.O. came for his kid, Nick was sleeping soundly. K.O. greeted me and asked how things were going. Tiptoeing around the truth I replied, "Great!"

Dana must have clammed up about the nudist colony because I never heard a discouraging word from her dad. Nobody from town ever trudged out here with field glasses, either.

Nick, still camping in a corner of his own world, appeared as peaceful as a pine cone nestled in the needles of its maker. After feeling his pulse to make sure everything was still pumping, I appealed to his appetite to halt the hibernation.

Upon arriving in the kitchen, Nick grabbed some grub and fled up to the third floor. I exhorted Bill to keep two beady eyes on him.

Meanwhile, Merlin, Margaret and Ann were in the music room mulling over this mayhem. Moments after Karen and I joined them, we all agreed on two major points. One, we had made a mega-myopic mistake in our desire to set this captive free! Two, Nick could no longer stay here!

However, we differed on proper Christian eviction proceedings. Merlin and Margaret favored more ministry; Karen suggested contacting a treatment center; I claimed we should call Nick's mother and if she wasn't available, the men in the white coats! Ann abstained.

All this discussion proved academic—the die was cast, the disease endemic. Chilling screams cut our confab short! It sounded as if a team of draft horses were racing down the second floor hallway, as grunts and groans gave way to brash crashes against the banister.

Our frazzled five sat frozen until Merlin leaped up the living room stairs. I ran to the other end of the house to make sure our kids were okay. Assured that David and Krista were playing peacefully, I reentered the hallway in time to see the action invade the end guest room.

Bill and Merlin struggled to keep Nick pinned to the floor, but for some ungodly reason they released him when I arrived. Back to his basic birthday suit ensemble, he charged me like a raging bull!

Lacking William Branham's spiritual authority, I resorted to the flesh. Confronting the immediate danger of being merged with the full-length mirror, I hit the bull with a cross-body block which sent both of us sprawling across the soft pine floor! My college coach would have been astounded. Bill and Merlin, seizing the moment, pounced on Nick. I piled on. His adrenaline released surges of super strength as he flailed his formidable frame. Merlin, who was in the midst of his second match of the day, yelled, "You can be free, Nick, Jesus can set you free!" Nick retorted nastily, "I don't want to be free, I don't want Jesus!"

Meanwhile, Karen was on the phone starting the prayer chain—iron chains were more in order. I shouted, "Call the cops, the kid won't give up!" Karen reluctantly complied. To get a psychiatric social worker to fetch the fuzz is like forcing St. Vincent of Lombard to forfeit a football game. Mary Soergel was on her way over, also.

Karen, horrified to see Nick hallucinating in the nude, threw a white sheet over him, which he promptly kicked off.

Vern Kissner, a young visitor from Phoenix, spelled Bill so he could inform me of the details before the police arrived. I also summoned Gretchen Soergel, who was an integral part of this story.

When Bill was distracted by a phone call, Nick disappeared into the nearest phone booth to change his attire. Running naked down the stairs, he greeted Gretchen on the landing, who turned in terror and tore down the hallway! Grabbing Gretchen at the railing, Nick let go when he saw Bill barreling towards him. During the ensuing battle, Nick bashed his head against the banister, which drew blood from his right ear. Then Merlin arrived. Meanwhile the bull was still seeing red as he continued to struggle—he was Superman minus the suit!

The cops came and sized up the situation in seconds. They subdued Nick enough to stuff him in a straightjacket secured to a stretcher. He thrashed all the way into the ambulance.

Mary Soergel arrived in time to join Karen's caravan to Oconomowoc Hospital.

Volumes of vitriolic venom spewed forth in the emergency room as Nick screamed, "I hate God, I hate my father!" He was so violent that blood vessels burst in his eyes as the doctor attempted to attend to his bleeding ear.

The Lord miraculously administered a sedative to Nick through His angels of mercy—Mary and Karen. A few minutes after they laid hands on him, praying in tongues, he relaxed and let go of his struggle. The nurses were amazed and greatly relieved!

In the ensuing days Nick was passed around like a polka partner possessed with pyorrhea. After being transferred to a padded cell in the mental ward of Waukesha Hospital, he was shifted to Mendota State Mental Hospital in Madison.

Two weeks later, Nick's therapist asked us if we would take him back into our home. We made it plain that this was insane unless he wanted Jesus! Nick still wasn't ready to meet our requirements. The love object of his life remained drugs. Swimming in the nude was a close second. Even Lucifer was higher on his list than Jesus!

Choosing to run rather than repent, he escaped to Boulder, Colorado, and wound up on the rocks. Nick was murdered during a deadly drug exchange!

Gladys' life was surrounded by sorrow—another son met a similar fate in California. Using time as a friend, she turned her tears into helping other troubled teens during the turbulent '70s. Learning from Nick's life and death, we were determined to be a brighter beacon of light for those left behind. However, we knew we could never ever attempt to out-love the Lord again!

# 18

# Encounter at Encanto Park

In addition to hosting three weekly worship meetings and housing teenagers, there was a constant flow of folks who visited for various durations. Our phone rang so often that even resident rodents had bags under their eyes. It was hard for our house to remain a home with all these happenings. Running a restaurant has to be more relaxing than managing a ministry in your residence. At least when people get filled with food they flee the place! When they become filled with the Holy Spirit, they never get fed up!

Our favorite way of fostering family life was taking vacations. "Getting away from it all" had real meaning—we never left a forwarding address for fear the flock would follow! One discerning disciple was designated to decipher all incoming calls while we were gone. They were instructed to relay the message only under dire circumstances—such as, 'Your house is in flames, do you desire the fire department to put it out?"

Some of our down-home operators proved to be patsies and fell for phony forwarding requests. Currently God has graced our hot line with a no nonsense honcho named Arlene Czaskos. She has the same nose for stuffing power plays that Ray Nitschke had in his prime. Many winters ago Arlene called us in Phoenix to inform us the furnace blew up in our basement. "It's twenty below zero outside and inside it's so cold the canary is curled up with the chinchilla," was her cry! "The boiler boys claim it's beyond repair; do you want it replaced?" she asked. Not one to panic I replied, "I will call you in two days to let you know!"

December of 1969 also found us in Phoenix for the holidays. On Sunday afternoon we took David and Krista to Encanto Park to test the playground paraphernalia. After punishing every piece of equipment, hunger pangs became the predominant force behind their persuasions. Ice cream was of the essence! Still in good humor, I agreed to hunt down the man in the white coat.

In a clearing nearby I noticed a circle of hippies holding hands. When I relayed the news to Karen she flew in a flash to find these flower children. David and Krista related better to the ice cream. When we finally caught up with Karen the circle was still unbroken—she hadn't crashed it yet, but it was only a matter of time!

The participants were holding a new-fashioned prayer meeting—Jesus Freak style. The long-haired leather-thonged leader stood in the center with hands raised and glory gleaming from each facial pore. Sunbelt sheen shone from his blond strands swaying in the gentle breeze. Decked out in a red-and-white bandaged bandanna, tie-dyes down to the waist and battered blues below, he bellowed, "Jesus," as his followers responded in rapid reply, "Jesus is real!"

After joining forces for five minutes of festal shouts of joy, another elder eased the flock through a brief Bible study. Then the fair-haired one picked up his guitar to sing a rousing rendition of "Knights in White Satin," popularized by the Moody Blues. Sifting the secular lyrics, he slipped in saintly substitutions. His vibrant voice followed with fiery fervor in "Come to the Water." People pressed in closer to hear the guru give the closing challenge to his commune—"Witness while there is time, Jesus is coming!"

Karen, not waiting for the sheep to shag her down, quickly cornered the shepherd. Beaming as if the Lord had just let him in on His best joke, he bellowed, "I am Jimmy, a fool for Jesus; whose fool are you?" Karen assured him we were on the same team but had come to the "cross" from different directions.

Jimmy introduced us to his spiritual siblings who had similar stories. Wasting their youth and bodies in the ways of the world, they were dragged through the dregs of drugs and booze before Jesus bailed them out. Flashing his big, broad smile, Jimmy invited us to their commune for fellowship.

Jimmy Sutherland, a real rag-tag, rip-roaring, holy-bold, genuine Jesus Freak, was instant eternal energy. He was so fired up for the Lord, park security forced the flock to gather on gravel instead of grass! That night, the news reported the account of Jimmy and the Jesus People invading Encanto Park.

234

Jimmy had over twenty sheep living in his fold, plus transients tripping in and out twenty-four hours a day. One new convert named Lester studied scripture without ceasing. He spouted answers on all subjects—even when nobody asked! Ten minutes after we arrived at the commune, Karen and Lester locked larynxes over the role of elders in the early church. His wire-rimmed glasses were still glued to his Scofield Bible when we split.

Once spring sprang, we asked Jimmy to join us up north to help with the pandemic of ex-potheads pouring in. Jimmy replied, "If I'm not raptured by then, I'll be there! I'll bring a few brothers with me.! "Right on," I said, "but leave Lester to his scholarly pursuits—we don't need a born again "Wonder of the Word" who is barely out of the womb!"

One day in mid-May a ten-tone rusted van pulled up in front of our house. Jimmy Sutherland, Paul Coors, Vern Kissner and Pat McQuire came prepared to sow seeds of salvation in Oconomowoc's fertile fields where LSD had passed up corn as the "king of consumption." Meanwhile, most parents denied there was a drug problem.

Paul Coors, part Indonesian, had been passed off as Native American as he plied his silver and turquoise trade in jewelry shops in Scottsdale. Paul paraded throughout our house serenading everyone with high-pitched Indonesian songs that sounded like the wail of a wounded wolf. The first night I heard him, I thought he had been poisoned!

Singing aside, Paul was pleasant to live with. One day during winter he helped Willa Dorsey, who was in town for a Gospel concert. Paul let her lean on his ever-steady arm while she attempted to negotiate the icy walk in front of our house. As they inched forward, Willa's high heels slid out from under her, causing the tumbling twosome to hit the cement like they had been leveled by a low-flying plane. Willa's full weight landed on Paul's loins as he let out a primal scream wilder than his wolf wails!

In a pitched battle against gravity, it took four of us ten minutes to get these acrobats airborne again! During the ordeal we contracted Willa's contagious laughter and came close to going down for the count ourselves. It was reminiscent of a Kathryn Kuhlman meeting. When we finally waltzed Willa to the station wagon, she had only forty-five minutes to recover before giving her concert in Milwaukee.

Paul and Vern both worked in my antique store in Chenequa called the Coach House. Part of the reason for establishing the store was to involve artistic kids who couldn't hack beating brush to death. Members of the "lost generation" weren't motivated to mow lawns, weed gardens or whack wood. Numbed by the new age of exotic drugs, heavy metal and hanging out, the Protestant work ethic was passé.

One kid I asked to cut brush told me he would pray about it. I strongly suggested he spare himself this spiritual sacrifice—I was well-acquainted with the "Christian Cop Out School of Prayer!" I escorted the kid into the kitchen and asked Minnie to pray about whether she should prepare dinner. Minnie, not exactly a monastic monk, appeared puzzled but the message went straight to the boy's stomach!

## Supermarket Salvation

Jimmy Sutherland was his happy-slapping, kingdom-conquering, charismatic self in our community. The kids idolized Jimmy, but the parents put him on hold, at best.

Jimmy presented his testimony at Our Savior's Lutheran Church one night. Despite his heavy Jesus People patina, he was tolerated while he stuck with his own story. The moment he ground the gears by suggesting Oconomowoc had a drug problem, many parents tossed him out of the driver's seat by shifting into denial.

However, Jimmy wasn't put off by persecution—it served as his barometer for living the Jesus life. His witnessing welcomed a wide variety of reactions. He would often shout out a car window at a hiker, "Jesus is real!" If his first volley evoked any response, he followed with, "He is coming soon!" Fortunately there was time for the firing of only two rounds before we were out of earshot.

Jimmy's "high-spirited highway ministry" was just a warm-up to his "get saved in the supermarket outreach!" Invading supermarkets during rush hour, he screamed in an ungodly voice, "Repent, Jesus is coming!" Startled shoppers dropped their bags and looked daggers in Jimmy's direction. Few penitents were produced by this atomic bomb approach, but he gave them food for thought by arresting their attention. He always had the discernment to split before they threw things.

Some people compared Jimmy to John the Baptist, but John has to be given the edge at the end. Both were as wild as the "Wayward Wind" and resorted to radical methods to proclaim their message. Jimmy enjoyed Big Macs, John hit on honey and locusts. Jimmy cashed in on captive audiences, John boycotted supermarkets. Both were blessed with bravado that ballooned into full-blown holy boldness. However, Jimmy never let it go to his head!

Jimmy may have inherited some "Johnisms," but he was in no danger of being confused with Perry Como. His vocal chords came closer to a croaker than a crooner! Playing his guitar like it was part percussion, his eyes gazed heavenward as he vaulted his voice over every obstacle. "Jesus Christ in white satin and He's coming again. Get ready to meet him, He's coming my friend. For He loves you - He loves you -ou-ou. He'll get you in the end." By the second "He loves you -ou-ou," we saw Jesus garbed in a long white robe riding a billowy cloud, coming to receive us. We went out to meet him on the wings of a snow white dove. When reality returned, we realized that Jimmy was already there, but the rest of us had to wait a little longer!

After two months of Midwest ministry, Jimmy became nervous about the brethren and sistren back home. What if Lester's scriptural expoundings had led the sheep into a desert experience near Death Valley's door? It took Jimmy and his rusted van ten days for their triumphant reentry into the Valley of the Sun. Stopping at every supermarket is enough to slow anyone down!

Paul, Pat and Vern stayed with us for the winter, which proved they were serious about serving the Lord—most traveling evangelists headed South with the Canadian geese.

Vern Kissner was the solid silent type, thank God! He restored my faith in a Lord that still valued balance. While the other three were on a perpetual salvation spree, Vern witnessed by example. Utilizing his carpentry talents, he restored furniture for my antique shop and assisted Merlin on the property.

Pat McQuire was a protégé of Jimmy. He steered clear of supermarkets but he knew how to use Jesus People jargon to jolt kids into the kingdom. Pat sang, played the guitar, and gave a powerful testimony. One night at a St. Jerome's CCD meeting he shared how Jesus saved him from serious substance abuse and led him to Jimmy's commune in Phoenix. As a result, thirteen of the sixteen young people present accepted Jesus. Even a Columbian Seminary student committed to climb aboard.

One of the kids who joined Jesus that night was sixteen-year old Matt Spransy. Matt, who had messed with marijuana and hash, walked in a skeptic and walked out a "King's Kid." His parents, choosing to fight rather than see their son switch, forbade him to attend our meetings. Later on they allowed Matt to go to Brian and Mary Steinke's fellowship because they were "good Catholics." In the '60s many Romans perceived the Charismatic Renewal as a Protestant plot to render the Pope impotent!

However, George and Nancy Spransy discovered that the same Jesus who Matt met at CCD was at Steinke's and Living Waters. From then on they were supporters of their son's spiritual pursuits. Matt, hearing about the Baptism of the Spirit at Steinke's, experienced the outpouring in the privacy of his own room, with tongues following. Pleased by the positive changes in Matt's life, his parents let him attend Living Waters in the spring of 1971. He brought out many kids including his brothers Tim and Jim.

Matt organized a band called Salt of the Earth that played at our Sunday night meetings. The original members were Matt and Jim Spransy, Terri and Steve Norman, Sam and Carl Edwards, David Vaughn, Tom Holmes, Perry English, Bo Lohman and Denise Goetzke. They decorated a band room in our basement with memorabilia, flags and Jesus People signs. The sounds of Salt of the Earth penetrated every part of the house!

The band also played at a Christian coffeehouse in downtown Waukesha. Started by Danny Beck and the Jones brothers, this store front was a hangout for long-hairs with heavenly aspirations. One soul. saved there was Kenny Thompson. Kenny's peaceful positive witness won many kids to the Lord in the years to come.

When things slowed down at the store front, the "Christian Coffee Klatch" resorted to the Biblical proverb, "If you don't draw them, chase them!" Reminiscent of Robin Hood's gang they raced through the depths of the Kettle Moraine Forest to give the "Good News" to lost souls. In the Scuppernong section, they encountered head-to-head combat with a band of hippies called the Bummer Mummers. After some jousting for Jesus, heads gave way to hearts, resulting in many Bummer Mummers meeting their Master.

Matt Spransy, David Vaughn and Allen Anderson birthed a Bible study at Oconomowoc High. Considered "cool" in the school, teems of teens gathered every noon for two years.

When Matt graduated in 1972, he joined the Lonesome Stone gospel rock musical production in London. However, the boys in the band played on. In spite of flack from his parents, David Vaughn picked up the slack to save Salt of the Earth. Dave and his sister Diane had to sneak out to the Sunday night meetings at first. Soon after, Wilson and Jane Vaughn "saw the Light" of the life their kids were living. Wilson even asked me to lead an early Sunday morning meditation in Lac La Belle park. It was a summer special for sailors and their sweethearts whose sanctuary was the seven seas during the season.

David went on to study at Oral Roberts University and pursue a career in California's entertainment arena. He is a technical assistant on TV shows, such as Wheel of Fortune. In 1994 David blessed us by his surprise visit, which included sharing his testimony at our Sunday night meeting.

## Royalty Rebels Against
## Rubbing Elbows with Rodents

The Salt of the Earth was heavily seasoned with ecclesiastical flavor from the Nashotah House contingent. Perry English, Tom Holmes and Sam and Carl Edwards were sons of a student, a professor and the dean of this high church Episcopal Seminary.

We were in no danger of the Nashotah House hierarchy beating down our doors pleading for a "prayer language!" Some of their students worshipped with us but the bigwigs remained on traditional turf rather than risk a tie-in to tongues.

It took the pioneering spirit of the Jesus People generation to scale the walls in their search for greener grass. Many who went beyond grass got burned on acid! Perry English became one of these singed souls. He earned the nickname "Nuggets" by toting his treasured drugs in a little leather pouch. "Nuggets'" cache turned out to be fools' gold—it fried his mind! When Perry surrendered to Jesus he dumped the drugs, but he never shook "Nuggets" from his name.

Perry's mind darted in every direction as his thoughts ran through a shredding machine. His voice sounded victimized by a "scrambler." Whenever I asked him a question I quickly braced myself for a barrage of disjointed answers which equaled "None of the Above." Karen pleaded with Perry to slow his pace but it proved impossible. He was a kamikaze casualty of the drug culture!

Perry was a pleasant, popular kid with long sandy hair lapping around his shoulders like a wave rolling in on a beachhead. His limited wardrobe featured faded denim shirts with Levis looking like "rag picker rejects." The patches holding his pants together could have passed for dried potato skins. He wore these wormy wonders at half mast which brought his bulging belly button into full view. Bending over "cracked a smile" as underwear was not part of Perry's apparel!

Perry played a mean bass guitar. When he wasn't performing with Salt of the Earth, he was mixing sound in every town within ten counties. In constant demand by burgeoning bands, he raced across the landscape like a charged-up circuit rider. No one ever knew where Perry was, including himself!

His bandoholic bandying was derailed for one brief shining moment by a Miss Maggie who desired to marry Perry. A slight ecclesiastical crisis was created when they chose our family room for the ceremony. The Nashotah House high church rollers and the Living Waters holy rollers would have to join forces to launch these lovers on the stormy sea of matrimony.

Dean O. C. Edwards was chosen to officiate. Perry and Maggie's Jesus Freak friends outnumbered the Nashotah House contingent three to one, which resulted in a "rainbow coalition" of couture.

One hundred warm bodies heated the room on this cold winter night, as a wicked wind whipped up from the ice-laden lake. It could have been perilous to fire up the fireplace as Dean Edwards would be instantly defrocked if he stepped backwards. The warm glow of candlelight sufficed along with the incense that soothed the senses.

The room was so packed, the wedding party swooped down the aisle sideways. Thank God Perry wasn't wearing his jungle jeans when he kneeled with Maggie on the kneeler! His monkey suit projected an entire new image. The only faux pas wasn't Perry's fault—the boys in the band had painted "The End" on the soles of his shoes.

The reception took place in the adjoining rooms, as everybody survived this epic ecumenical entry into married life.

The newlyweds never left the festivities—they moved in with us for a few months! They occupied a room on third floor while having the run of the house like all our other "angels unaware."

Perry procured a part-time job with a retail electronics outfit and spent every spare moment on the band circuit. It took a tug-of-war team to pull Perry out of the pad in the morning so he could make it to Milwaukee by noon.

His only house duty was transporting garbage in big black bags from the back of our kitchen to a chicken coop. Perry's pussyfooting persisted with excuses extraordinaire. To make matters worse, Maggie protected him as if he was the King of Prussia! I crowned Perry the King of Procrastination!

The third floor became an aristocratic fortress impregnable by the pragmatic proletariat living below. On special occasions when Perry faced up to the fundamental rules of communal living, he chose his car to cart the garbage to the coop, a quarter of a mile away. After stuffing his rusted wreck with bulging black bags, he left barely enough room to wedge behind the wheel.

When I asked him why he didn't use our trailer for transporting these treasures, he replied, "Using my car gives me the same high as hauling the band to a gig!"

The class struggle came to a head when spring sprang and the garbage started germinating in the back room. The peons inhabiting the second floor were writhing in their rooms from the pungent perfume filtering through the floor.

Meanwhile the aristocrats on third remained above it all. Their rationale—why ruin rodents' playgrounds by removing rotten garbage? The real reason was Royalty rebels against rubbing elbows with rodents!

After binging in the back room, the mice discovered other areas of destruction. Chewing their way through my office closet they attacked my memorabilia as if it were Swiss cheese. Busy as bag ladies turned loose on a bazaar, they gorged on baseball cards, photographs, canceled checks and tax returns! Even my old King James Bible was bitten to bits! Hopefully the rodents got religion while feeding on the Word.

I boxed twelve drawers full of shredded evidence and marched it up to the royal couple's penthouse. After viewing the vermins' voracious villainy, they got the message. If the garbage doesn't go pronto, they would be dethroned by a bloodless coup d'état! I stored the relics down the hall as a reminder of their royal responsibilities. Twenty years later the remains remain untouched by human hands. My allergies to mice manure prevent me from sorting it all out!

The boxes are still there but Perry and Maggie are long gone. There was no need to summon the elders as the newlyweds' nirvana was to find a place with more privacy—The rodents found the way to the penthouse and cramped the royal couple's style!

Sky-high they settled in Denver until Perry came down with an acute case of band fever. This time the eternal sound man mixed it up with the big boys—Lynyrd Skynyrd is their name and Southern rebel rock is their game.

The band's three-guitar attack was grounded in 1977 when their getaway plane ran out of gas and crashed into a Gillsburg, Mississippi, swamp! Lynyrd Skynryrd"s lead singer, Ronnie Van

Zant, was killed along with two other musicians. "Nugget's" body was miraculously spared, but his threadbare jeans were totally torn asunder!

Shortly after, disaster hit the home front, marital bliss bled and led the royal couple to the same court as Bill and Denise—divorce. You can throw the boy out of the band, but you can't bind up the battle wounds of a bandoholic with Band-Aids!

Perry returned recently with his adult daughter to check on the rodents. He was greatly relieved when we informed him he had been rescued by Wil-Kill. Perry is presently active in 12-step programs and provides input for an Anglican devotional.

Indoor weddings weren't working well—outdoor ceremonies have proved more lasting. God's fresh air sanctuary cements the relationship so that even the blustery blasts off the lake can't blow the couple apart.

We've had success with live-in singles but married couples are another matter. The nightmare of newlyweds is enough to transform thick-skinned spuds into mashed potatoes! When their first kid comes, bolt down the battens. The adorable munchkin massacres our house while the passive parents appear oblivious to the performance. Faced up with the facts, they feign the denial disease as their little darling carries on the carnage.

## Sucker-Punched by the Spider Man

After Perry split, we switched to the tall, slim, silent type to restore peace to our pacemakers. Bo Lohman, the long dark haired drummer moved in. Bo was so thin that a teenage tough tried to run him through a pencil sharpener. After getting the point, Bo erased the kid from his short list of friends.

Bo, moving around our house like a spider man, would suddenly step out of shadows without warning. Having spun webs in every corner, our challenge was to free him from his entanglements. Through prayer and affirmation his deep hurts and repressed feelings slowly surfaced.

Bo's talents extended beyond pounding percussion—he restored defaced furniture faster than I could haul it home. Some of his antique artistry never left the house. He refinished a fourteen foot multi-leaved maple table which became a permanent fixture in our dining room.

When we were away, Bo often pursued projects without permission. One time the white plaster protruding from the center of our dining room ceiling caught his roving eye. This Michelangelo of Milwaukee gilded it in gold to match the brass chandelier. Bo's unsolicited skills almost cut his career short! I told him, "I admire your masterpiece but it's better to ask the dog if he wants his tail shortened than being stuck with the task of tying one on!"

A month later Bo left his mark on our glassed-in porch playroom. While saying good-bye to his girl an altercation ensued. A statement he made caused her to slam the door in his face. Not to be upstaged, Bo pivoted and pounded his fist through our cabinet door. It was a sucker punch—the door never had a chance! Bo's right hand paid for decades of repressed anger as it doubled in size.

As his hand slowly healed he nursed the cabinet back to health. Despite Bo's skill at covering up his trail, a trained eye can still detect a trace of trauma ingrained in the wood.

Believing that a body shop is a bona fide bonanza for releasing aggressions, Bill Toll put him to work at Holiday Motors in Milwaukee. Bo boycotted the rubber mallets by pounding out the fenders with his fists!

# 19

# Foiled by the Flaky Fawn

Boys weren't the only bane of our bedraggled state. Girls such as Jackie Borden from Beaver Darn, Wisconsin, made sure we would never experience boredom!

Jackie was a lean bean of fourteen whose fawn-like face was a front for living in the fast lane. With her big blue eyes rivaling her long blonde hair for attention, she hit the teens like a turbojet, turning her parents' home into a hangar for high-flying hippies.

Fueled by LSD, Jackie landed at our place with an acute case of lice claiming a lien on her flaxen mane. One of her acid trips terminated with her writhing on our front lawn like a poisoned fawn. It took three grown guys to restrain her so Karen could pray her down.

Once during a special dinner party for Willa Dorsey, Jackie came home late and refused to appear. When I reminded her of the house rules she ran to her bedroom window and threatened to jump. As she opened the window wider I withdrew my request. I had seen what high-flying feats had done for others. It was better to eat crow for dinner than cater to these ravenous birds.

Jackie wasn't dubbed the "Flaky Fawn" due to dandruff. Her propensity for pranks, pratfalls and prattle while exuding an air of innocence earned her this endearment.

One night beyond the bewitching hour, while responding to noises near her bedroom, I tripped over Smoky the Keeshound camped in the hallway. Deciding the dog made the disturbance, I went back to bed.

Two days later I discovered my myopic eyes had failed me. Grabbing the grapevine, I learned that Jackie had snuck downstairs for snacks. To her despair she knocked over a chair upon reentry. Hearing footsteps, she hit the floor on all fours and feigned like a canine. Jackie could hardly control herself when she crawled past me and I called out, "Smoky!"

Karen, pleading her case, argued that the statute of limitations had passed. Agreeing that this sloppy sleuth had been outfoxed by the impersonating pooch, I pardoned her. Indolence has no claim on retribution!

Weeks later, Jackie got back on her feet permanently. Accepting inner healing prayer as part of her solution enabled her to cope better with her problems.

Nine years later, Karen and I were invited to speak at a Lutheran church in Lebanon, Wisconsin, on "Raising Children in the Rock and Roll Era of Sex and Drugs." By divine coincidence, Father Roger Cuzon, a French Jesuit priest headquartered in Beirut, Lebanon, was our dinner guest that evening. Father Roger appeared perplexed when we informed him we were on our way to Lebanon for a speaking engagement!

Much to our surprise, Jackie Borden was sitting in the front row of the church. Karen, who planned on telling part of Jackie's story, quickly altered her talk so Jackie wouldn't be embarrassed. The "Flaky Fawn" had definitely reformed—she sat still for the entire message!

After the service, she honored us with a holy hug and told us about her latest escapades. Jackie, her husband and two children lived in a house on the church grounds. She still possessed that impish look, but had gone cold turkey on canine capers!

Today Jackie has come full circle. She is a licensed counselor, specializing in helping people heal their addictive problems.

## A Hot Time in the Old House

For the sake of our sanity we also accepted kids who qualified for the cool, calm category. One of these endangered species would appear every few years.

Brenda Lewis, who hailed from the "hollers" of Kentucky, fit this description. When her parents died, she and her siblings were raised by their grandparents.

Brenda's older brother Cowley came to Oconomowoc to work at the Carnation Company. Cowley didn't have a wife but he was blessed with an infant daughter named Sandy. When they came to Living Waters, the pre-teens squabbled over taking care of Sandy so Cowley could attend the service.

Cowley told us about his sixteen-year-old sister Brenda who lived in Madrid, Spain, with their eighteen-year-old sister Joy. Brenda needed a breather from the abuse she was suffering at the hands of Joy's middle-aged bad news boyfriend. Cowley, hearing directly from heaven, relayed the message that the Lord had hand-picked our place for Brenda to live! It's futile to fight Abba Father—He can always call in more troops! At least the abusive boyfriend wasn't part of the package.

We expected a tigress, but by God's grace got a tame tender-hearted freckle-faced kid with flaming red hair. Her Spanish was Castilian, but her English had a hillbilly hangover.

A year later, Brenda, homesick for her kinfolk in the "hollers" of Kentucky, left to live with her grandparents. Upon her return to Wisconsin, some of the kinfolk followed. The kinfolk moved in with Cowley, but we reclaimed Brenda.

Brenda Lewis and Beth Wing bunked together in a second floor bedroom facing our driveway. Beth, who attended our meetings in her high school days, chose Living Waters as her field placement while a student at Bethany Bible Institute in Minneapolis. In addition to heading our Youth Ministry, she assisted with music and served in more mundane ministries such as cleaning the house.

By the middle '70s we discontinued the Friday night services and replaced them with Thursday night "core group" sessions. The "core group" consisted of twenty-plus members committed to serving Living Waters Fellowship.

Ruth and Ron Novak from Eagle, Wisconsin, attended the "core group" regularly. Ruth, who had recently given birth to their third daughter, Renee, drove up on a cold winter night despite an infection she was fighting. When the fever escalated, she decided to stay overnight instead of forging over the frozen tundra.

Karen, concerned about Ruth's condition, remained with her and Renee for the night. After pushing the thermostat up a few notches, I retreated to my bedroom at the far end of the house.

Three hours later I was rudely awakened by a rumble in the hallway. I thought Karen must be up to her Wheaton College capers of chasing roommates with cold ice. Nocturnal noises were so commonplace I took no further notice and went back to sleep.

Karen's curdling scream "Jack" bolted me out of bed in the direction of the hallway. Smoke smacked me in the face as Brenda yelled, "Our mattress is on fire!" Karen, with terror in her eyes pleaded with me, "Do something!" Billows of black smoke swirled around the burning bed as I entered the girls' room. Their mattress must be made from rubber tires!

Brenda, a one-woman bucket brigade, hurled gallons of water at the flames, while Karen tried to beat the blaze into oblivion with wet towels. Ruth, wrapping Renee in a blanket, raced downstairs to find a safer sanctuary. Meanwhile, Beth freaked and faded into fresher air.

I startled David and Krista out of sound sleep by carrying them downstairs to the glassed-in porch. After alerting the volunteer fire department, I called Dad Ziemann, who lived in our caretakers' home. Mom and Dad, on sabbatical from the Ghana missions, moved on the property months before to minister in the fellowship and assist in tasks such as mowing lawns.

Dad raced over as if Smoky Bear was bearing down on him. Battling the burning bed like he was challenging a legion of demons from the dark continent of Africa, he yanked it away from the wall barehanded. Despite sputtering from the heavy smoke, Dad joined Brenda's water brigade.

The firemen, who had recently returned from another blaze, were still red hot when they arrived. They doused the mattress and crammed it through an open window in a matter of moments. David and Krista were shocked to see strange men in rubber suits race through their playroom in the wee hours of the morning.

The firemen praised Brenda, Karen and Dad Ziemann for their heroic action in preserving our historic landmark. Everybody went on a frantic search for Beth and finally found her taking refuge in the family room. In times of trouble she tended to stay close to her music!

The next day an article appeared in the Waukesha Freeman lauding the Lord's miraculous assistance. The headlines read, "God Spares House."

Brenda and Beth provided a vivid account of the event. They were sleeping soundly when suddenly they felt their feet warming up. Their first thought was I had a change of heart and turned the heat up in the house! Seriousness sunk in when they saw the bottom of their bed ablaze. Their electric blanket caught fire where the cord connects! Jumping free from the covers, Brenda yanked the wire from the wall while Beth's panic-packed screams startled Karen and Ruth across the hallway.

The celebration over the "big blaze burn out" was tempered by the realization that smoke would saturate the house for days. We coughed up soot like survivors of a coal mine blast! Our draperies, furniture and walls needed a Saturday night bath before the EPA would issue a clean bill of health. Of course, the friendly agent from Employers of Wausau raced in with the boys in the rubber coats ready to foot the bill.

Brenda and Beth wouldn't return to their room for weeks. Fleeing the frying pan, they chose the cool catacombs of the basement to catch up on their sleep. A few nights later Beth barreled out of her basement bedroom for good when a rabid rodent wrestled her for her pillow and won!

Karen's fire flashbacks finally disappeared after days of fervent prayer. Ruth's recovery was on hold—she wandered around humming, "There is going to be a hot time in the old house tonight." She decided that Living Waters was too stressful for the sick and would take her chances at home next time she was suffering. Dad Ziemann brushed off the fire as just another day in the African bush. Compared to hand-to-hand combat with wild beasts of the jungle, a burning bed doesn't have much bite!

By the time Brenda moved out of our house she was so in touch with trauma she entered the Police Academy. She is the prettiest policewoman on the Milwaukee force and her beauty beats out most of the men, also. Brenda is married and the mother of five freckle-faced kids with bluegrass accents.

Beth beat it back to Bethany Bible Institute shortly after the burning bed incident. She slept like a baby there—Bethany, on a strict budget, wasn't burdened by electric blankets. After graduation she gravitated to Florida, before moving back to the Milwaukee area. Beth is still on fire for the Lord but fearful about our place. A few years ago when she came out to help on Sunday nights with the music and the youth, I noticed she never ventured beyond the family room.

Electric blankets were permanently banned from the house and cast into the "Lake of Fire." After many heated discussions, I finally agreed to turn the thermostat up two degrees to compensate!

## The King's Kid Crashes The Kingdom

There is one person that stands out in every crowd. The reasons are as far-reaching as a ripple of gold in a rainbow. For some, height is the highlight; for others, width is where it's at. Some cause a ruckus for recognition; others head up heavy hunger strikes. Some are blessed from birth with charisma; others are just loud in the crowd.

Kenny Thompson stood out in a special way—his spiritual depth made the difference. Not the kind that comes from sitting in seminars, exorcising evil spirits, sharing on street corners or bubbling with Bible verses. In Kenny's case it was written on his face. His relationship with Jesus revolutionized people's lives. Kenny, while never pursuing popularity, was probably oblivious to his captivating charisma. He was simply a King's Kid whose only desire was to walk with his Master.

We didn't know Kenny during his druggie days. We couldn't conceive of him sold out to anything or anyone other than Jesus. Kenny composed music and played guitar. When he sang, the entire room radiated the presence of Jesus. With his blue eyes sparkling and his saintly smile spreading peace, Kenny wasn't worried about the Rapture—he was experiencing it! It was written on his face.

Kenny created situation skits in which kids acted and reacted to real life scenes. Some centered on sharing Jesus in various circumstances. They were so popular, they became part of the Sunday night meetings.

Kenny's only agenda was Jesus' will as he witnessed throughout the area. He assisted at the Waukesha coffeehouse and spent more time in the local forests than Smoky. His favorite sanctuary for spiritual solitude was in the Scuppernong section of the Southern Kettle Moraine State Park.

Once we talked Kenny into leaving the woods long enough to join us for dinner at the Marc Plaza Hotel in Milwaukee. We were hoping he would talk more about himself, away from his natural habitat. However, our waiter had personal problems which Kenny and Karen spent the evening sorting out. Even in sophisticated restaurants, Kenny never lost his angelic smile. If someone hit him with hot coffee, his spiritual endorphins would protect him from pain.

One summer night after the service, Karen and I took a moonlight walk. As we approached the parking area, we heard a familiar voice singing and praising God. Kenny was conducting a one-person praise fest from the hood of his car. We hid behind a large oak to soak in the spirit of the worship. It was love at first, second and third sight—it was written on his face. All the forest creatures should be safely in the kingdom by now.

When we appeared, Kenny acted as if a wise old owl had warned him. He spoke softly about Jesus, the stars and the magnificent moonlight. We asked him to offer a special prayer for peace to reign on every part of our property.

When we suggested a raid on the refrigerator, his smile broadened as he gave both of us a big hug. As Karen and I walked to our house, we looked back at Kenny who was still perched on the hood. The spiritual food he was feasting on was more than sufficient to sustain him. The two of them had a glorious night ahead.

Girls went crazy over Kenny, but he was sane enough to stay single. Heeding the Lord's admonition about the flowers in the field, he was waiting for the Rose of Sharon to select the fairest one. Holding out for a divinely picked Daisy, he bypassed all black-eyed Susans.

Kenny tarried for a time until a girl named Terry tiptoed into his life. Months later they were talking about tying the knot. Treating us like spiritual parents, they desired our blessing before making final plans. Whom the Lord had brought together we weren't about to put asunder. After we prayed together, they left hand-in-hand, beaming beyond recognition.

The celestial couple was married for eight months when their Garden of Eden was rudely uprooted. Kenny had headaches for weeks but his spiritual endorphins deadened the pain. Devastating news ensued—his doctor diagnosed him as having an inoperable malignant brain tumor!

Kenny received more prayer power than the Pope gets from the South side of Milwaukee. Deeply saddened, we went to the intensive care unit of Waukesha Hospital. Kenny recognized us but couldn't talk as we prayed for him with the laying on of hands. A nurse stopped to join in silently. Kenny pressed the picture of Jesus we had brought to his heart. I had a strange feeling he was interceding for us at the moment—it was written on his face!!

We fought back towels full of tears as we left Kenny's side. It cut us to the quick to see the King's Kid as a prisoner of this ward. It was mid-afternoon. Kenny should be in the Kettle Moraine Forest singing praises to Jesus!

We suffered in silence on the way home. As positive praise the Lord Christians, we felt like failures. Our friend was fading fast and we lacked the faith to restore him to the forest. We surrendered all earthly claims to Kenny and placed him in the Father's hands.

Two days later, the King's Kid crashed the Heavenly Kingdom! His change of residence wasn't revolutionary for him—he was always halfway there anyway. It was written on his face. For those of us who loved this lad the loss was larger than life.

As a kid I could never warm up to wakes and funerals. Things hadn't changed much. The Jesus People approach to the passing of a loved one was a prayer and praise meeting. It was borrowed from the Bible— "Death, where is thy sting?" I don't know, but the answer sure hit me! I couldn't work up a false facade to deny the grief. The only smile I wanted to see at the King's Kid's funeral was Kenny's!

The mortuary in Waukesha was packed with a wide variety of people. Kenny affected businessmen as well as Jesus Freaks. The mood was upbeat but I couldn't enter in. When a longhair claimed that Kenny's death was God's will, I cringed. Maybe he was right, but I wasn't relating to his revelation at the moment. I refused to associate a loving Lord with the premature falling of my friend. I'd rather give the devil his due reward!

Kenny's mother and Terry were standing to the right of the casket. Words failed to relay the depth of our feelings as we hugged them. When we moved to the left we encountered the King's Kid. Our friend had never failed us and he wasn't about to now. The sting of death had long departed—it was written on his face! His smile was so peaceful I suspected the Lord might be bringing him back to sing at his own funeral. If only I had the faith to get his guitar.

During the service I kept one eye on the casket in case Kenny needed help climbing out. This contraption could never contain the King's Kid for long.

The eulogies, reflecting Kenny's victory, were a living memorial to the magnitude of his impact among us. Kenny's Kettle Moraine days were over as he passed through the portal of Paradise. There would be no more solos—he was already harmonizing with the Heavenly choir.

Terry gave birth to their son a few months later. There wasn't the slightest question that this was Kenny's kid—it was written on his face!

# 20

# Foul-Up on Fowler Street

As drugs continued to drain the youth, denial disengaged its stranglehold on some parents of the "Newport of the West."

A city committee was formed to arrest the aimlessness of nomadic teen tribes roving the region. In addition to concerned clergy, the committee included Charles Groombridge, the controller of Brownberry Ovens, Fred Spade, the new hospital administrator, Harold Horton, a crack chemical company salesman, myself, and a few others.

Motivated by the constant cry to establish a center where kids could come clean and still have fun, we went to work. In our search for a building that would bend but not break we were led to a recently abandoned house on Fowler Street. The landlord lived in Oshkosh, but by gosh she was willing to send her son Chad from Milwaukee to show the place.

As the committee congregated on the icy steps of this two-story frame Victorian, eagerly awaiting Chad's arrival, two of our men cased the outside as if it was already ours. Seven o'clock passed and her son didn't show. Forty minutes later the mood of mirth turned mad. Chad, the prodigal, must be on a bender in big, bad, Beer City!

Lacking faith for miracles, the committee was overcome by a vigilante mentality. Harold Horton, a no-holds-barred kind of guy, swore he could go in a back window. Frozen toes turned the tide that decided to let Harold have his way. He was in the house so fast, I started to question his real profession—sales could be a front for getting in the rear!

Our fears about forced entry faded as we focused on our mission. The house would make a great hangout—a full basement for recreation with no furniture in the way. Any necessary equipment could be contributed by the community. We decided to bypass the son and deal directly with the mother.

As we were about to leave, there was a rude rap on the door. Convinced it was the prodigal, Harold hustled down the hall to greet him. His hue turned to gray haze as he encountered a cop instead. Three strides later the officer stormed the living room like he had cracked a crack house. The "cold crunchies" crept up my spine as I envisioned the Oconomowoc Enterprise's headlines—"Youth Center Committee Tossed in Clink for Crashing Fowler Street House."

He cut short Harold's hasty explanation with a terse warning, "There has been a forced entry complaint. Vacate the premises immediately before the owner presses charges!"

No one needed a second nudge as we vanished in the night faster than nuns at a nudist camp. Two days later the paper hit the streets with no mention of Harold's house party. It was safe to resurface.

Feeling like a millstone had been removed, we met to mull over our next move. Heeding the old precinct proverb, "Neighbors get nosy when kids get noisy," we abandoned restless residential areas and zeroed in on the vacant fieldstone railroad depot.

Obviously we were on the right track—the only neighbors were St. Jerome's Church and a corner tavern. The pub presented no problems—once the patrons imbibed enough booze, the teens could demolish the depot and nobody would know the difference. The church created a different challenge. We were prepared to propose a deal with the priest, whereby he reserved the right to put any problem punk on the next plane to Purgatory!

## The Brady Street Brawler

Months later we received an S.O.S. Sunday night phone call from the depot. The pastor serving at the center needed assistance in solving a crisis. A bleached blonde bombshell named Bonnie had blown in from Milwaukee's Brady Street that afternoon. She was seeking asylum for the night. In the past, pastors padded out passive freaks in their church basements, but Bonnie acted more like a brazen babe out of the bootleg era.

Our name had flashed across the parson's brain like a bolt of lightning and he wanted to know if there was any more room at our inn! Facing an offer my flesh wanted to refuse, I told him our quiver was full and we weren't conscripting renegade recruits. However, we agreed to pray about it, and call him back in ten minutes.

Reluctantly I rounded up our discernment team for spiritual direction, while my mind manufactured a myriad of reasons why taking in Bonnie would be a mistake! A miracle happened. When Margaret, Merlin, Ann and Karen arrived at a positive answer, I totally disarmed them by agreeing! The Lord had shown me there was something special about this situation.

The pastor was as pleased as a porpoise with a new pool. When Karen and I drove to the depot to collect our door prize, we drafted Merlin as our bodyguard. He had fully recovered from his wrestling matches with Nick.

Bonnie was more bizarre than her advanced billing. Her long blonde hair looked as if it had been snatched off a clothes line after a nap in the noon-day sun. Purple toenails matched her torn blouse, which was slashed in a knife fight on Brady Street the night before. In contrast, her lizard-length fingernails were a calamity of clashing colors. Pounds of rouge ran rampant all over her face. Faded jeans doubled as drug emporiums with extra pockets sewn in to conceal the cache.

Gruff and guarded, Bonnie performed her best "Clyde routine" until she realized we weren't about to lay a heavy rap on her. We promised her one night's lodging if she would check in her backpack at our front door. The "Brady Street Brawler" never disappointed—she was a one-woman show!

The first night we went light on the Lord and heavy on love. As Bonnie's facade slowly faded, she admitted damaging her mind on LSD and doing time at Mendota State Mental Hospital. At the bewitching hour we dismissed our bodyguard, who had been bug-eyed all evening.

The next morning we told Bonnie she could stay if she would dump the drugs and give Jesus a shot. Full of fear, she was ready to try anything. She even turned in her tattered top for a more feminine number.

Through Karen's affirmations and prayers, Bonnie found a friend in Jesus. Symbolic of her spiritual security was a brown shawl she kept wrapped around her twenty-four hours a day. The real Bonnie Newman emerged pleasant, polite and gregarious, with bottomless pools of untapped energy. The "Brady Street Brawler" ceased flashing knives and started sharing the "Sword of the Lord." Back at the depot they couldn't believe Bonnie was the same girl who freaked them weeks before!

Bonnie's rapport with customers in my Golden Eagle antique store was amazing. Not only did sales surge, but she kept accurate records of all transactions!

## Andrae's Army

During Bonnie's stay with us, "Andrae Crouch and the Disciples" moved in while performing Gospel concerts in the area. Andrae's L.A. gang had cut many albums and were one of the top black gospel groups in the country.

On the day of their arrival, Bonnie bounced around the house like a cheerleader going to the homecoming dance with the football captain. Every few minutes she raced outside to listen for the sound of Andrae's bus that was about to round the bend. Finally, the town crier tore into the kitchen with the good news.

By the time we reacted, the silver-streaked Greyhound was already parked in front. Andrae, disembarking bearing a big smile, greeted everyone with a holy hug. His electrically charged meet-the-people personality could jolt deadbeats back to life!

Andrae's bus was packed like the last evacuation vehicle fleeing a war zone—twenty-two characters crawled out in three minutes! Included in the number were Andrae's sister, Sondra; four more Disciples; five from Sonlight, the backup band; and Dannibelle, a recording artist in her own right. Then Reba Rambo stepped out. Reba was the latest Rambo from a long line of Southern gospel singers. Next came Mylan Le Fevre, who became a popular contemporary Christian performer. The rest were sound people, stagehands and Andrae's army of Christian converts, including a former drug-crazed hippie who had been off dope for only four days!

Andrae's concept of "follow-up" included inviting concert converts onto the bus for Bible basics and prayer sessions. Andrae's Army packed such spiritual persuasion even the Greyhound had been converted into sleeping quarters!

Minnie, the head honcho of the "Minnie Main Culinary School for Christian Converts," had to feed this famished flock who had grazed for days on bus fare. Previously, we told her to plan on eight extra. Austere Austrian angst poured forth as she faced the magnitude of our miscalculation. Minnie was a few degrees short of being able to boil an egg on her forehead until I promised her all permanent boarders would do double K-P duty!

Hunger was one hang up, weariness was another. Some got beds and the rest settled for floor space. The family room resembled a refugee camp! Andrae bunked in David's room and the two became instant friends.

Bonnie poured her energy into creating posters for the concerts. She conscripted chain gangs of Jesus Freaks to contribute their artistic talents. "Bonnie's Brigade" produced enough posters to pave our mile-long driveway. Fortified by poster power, she twisted more arms than Gorgeous George for permission to plaster the propaganda on every church, school, store and public building in a ten-county region.

The concerts from Kenosha to Marshfield were colossal successes. Sonlight warmed up the crowd before Reba Rambo changed the pace with down home country renditions. Despite Dannibelle and all the other tantalizing talent on display, there was no doubt about the leader of the pack. Andrae Crouch's performances moved people into the presence of the King of Kings.

Bonnie's poster parties paid off, as the jammed concerts lifted Jesus higher each succeeding night. The highlight for Oconomowoc was at St. Jerome's School gymnasium, where Salt of the Earth, led by Matt Spransy, opened for Andrae Crouch and the Disciples.

The jam sessions continued after midnight when Andrae's entourage returned to our home. Entertaining notable night people who sleep until noon had us grabbing for the Geritol! After devouring Minnie's munchies, the boys in the band worked it off on the basketball court.

Lacking the Lakers Los Angeles Forum, I carted them over to the second floor of our coach house. Upon seeing the facilities, they laughed so hard I feared their food would resurface.

Billy Tedford played as if he was born with a basketball. In addition to dunking with his eyes closed, he dribbled between his legs. At six-foot-five he was forced to relax his rebounding antics after a run-in with the rim! The only thing that slowed Billy down was when his right foot went through the floorboards.

After two hours of barn beam basketball in high humidity, we appeared as if we were products of a pestilence. Sweaty clothes clung to our fatigued frames like loose skin after a forty-day fast.

Hauling everyone to the house in our rusty Buick wagon, we partied on Pepsi and potato chips. I dropped out at 3:30 a.m. to bathe and hit the pad. Four hours later I was headed east on I-94 in my perpetual pursuit of antiques for the Golden Eagle.

The excitement of hosting this traveling troupe carried us this far, but now we were fading fast. Minnie, appearing more like a victim of Valley Forge than a culinary queen, threatened to return to Austria if things didn't slow down!

Three early morning marathons of "big barn buckets" rendered me too tired to trek to Marshfield for Andrae's final concert. Karen was prepared to pass on the trip, also, but her penchant for adventure and Bonnie's power of persuasion prevailed. Playing pseudo-psychologist, Bonnie hinted she might hitchhike in a pinch.

The girls pulled into Marshfield in time to put up more posters before heading for the auditorium. After the concert, Karen's contingent crashed at the nearest motel, while Andrae's Army headed for the Twin Cities.

Bonnie was revved up for weeks. The best way to keep her on an even keel was working her hard at the Golden Eagle. I steered her clear of the glass to prevent a career-ending crash.


## Hitchhiking on the Highway to Heaven

For months Bonnie expressed her desire to hitchhike back to Boulder to share Jesus with her Colorado cronies. Believing her proposed Pauline missionary journey to be premature, we encouraged her to stay, but her wanderlust won out. Dreading her hitchhiking on hazardous highways, we made an offer she couldn't refuse—promised prayer support in addition to allowing us to buy her a bus ticket to Boulder.

The morning of Bonnie's departure she failed to find room for all her earthly possessions in her backpack. We felt better when she left two sweat shirts behind, promising to reclaim them before Christmas.

As the "Brady Street Brawler" boarded the bus, all of us beat back tears. Even the dogs were depressed—Cedric the basset and Charlie the lab had both played a part in Bonnie's healing.

Ten days later, her first letter arrived. Bonnie lived in a Christian commune near campus, while working at a fast food joint. Spare time was spent working on friends to "junk their joints" for Jesus. The Lord's presence was powerful in her Pauline pursuits.

Bonnie's second letter was cause for concern—she said she was being lead to Northern California to spread the "Good News." Harder to reach than a kite and twice as flighty, we finally caught up with her. Euphoria reigned—"California here I come" was her call! Convinced it was hopeless to keep her in Colorado, we hit her hard on the hitchhiking. Bonnie had enough bread for a bus, but made no promises.

We arranged to meet Bonnie in San Francisco on our return from Hawaii. August 23rd at the Hyatt on Union Square was the appointed time and place. Hawaii was always a winner, but this time the anticipation of seeing Bonnie was a bigger hit than hula dancers.

The morning of the 23rd we rode a cable car to the Wharf to see some sidewalk entertainers. Our favorite was the "Human Jukebox," who camped outside the Cannery. He resided inside a rectangular box while jukebox junkies fed him currency to force him out of hibernation. Addicted more to paper products, he would also binge on coins, to ward off hunger pangs.

Responding to his reward, this bearded hippie, with big bulging eyes, bounded out of the box and broke into a rabid rendition of, When the Saints Go Marching In. Flying high, he waved his trumpet as if he was flagging down a rescue plane on a remote island!

When the "Human Jukebox" crawled back in his box, we headed for the Hyatt hoping Bonnie would be arriving shortly. Six o'clock came along with crummy thoughts. Hopefully it was a case of the wrong hotel and would soon be solved.

Meanwhile our attention was diverted by a bellhop who tipped us off that Benji, the canine king of the silver screen, was perched in the penthouse three floors up. His trainer, Joe Camp, was about to bring him down in the elevator for his nightly stroll through Union Square.

Bonnie took second place to Benji as the four of us rushed downstairs. Benji boosters paced all over the lobby anxiously awaiting his arrival. It was definitely not a Tony Bennett crowd. Blowing the whistle on Benji was big time bellhop business at the Hyatt! The question was, who was tipping whom?

Benji didn't disappoint his fan club. Joe Camp, evacuating the elevator with his charge, headed straight for the door. Kids led their parents in hot pursuit as the canine caravan raced across the street. When Benji hit the bushes, Joe fielded questions to protect his star's privacy. After a brief petting session, Benji sniffed a few permanent park residents who weren't privileged to have penthouses.

Benji wasn't at breakfast and neither was Bonnie. Two days later we left for Milwaukee, but our hearts were still in San Francisco—wondering what happened to Bonnie.

Back home it was business as usual. The mail was piled so high against my office door I couldn't see the keyhole. Crises were crawling out of the carpets. Characters competed to see who could lay the heaviest headache on us. One kid complains about K.P. rotation, while another flash flushes Bible tracts down the toilet causing the lift pump to levitate.

Three weeks later, while I was cutting brush in the woods, Karen called from the top of the hill. No further words were needed—her tone told the story. Dark clouds of reality had replaced denial days ago. Sobbing, she handed me a crumpled letter stuffed back in its envelope. It was from Bonnie's parents. As

I reached the second line, Karen screamed, "Some bastard killed her!" Ten thousand volts jolted my body as I tried to comfort her. She kept crying, "I loved her so much; I loved her so much...." Each line was laced with more pain, as I envisioned Bonnie bounding around our property in perfect peace.

The Ukiah, California, police pieced the puzzle together to produce this probability. Bonnie was hitchhiking south of Ukiah when a serial killer picked her up, strangled her and dumped her body in a deep ravine hundreds of feet from the main highway! Many young girls suffered a similar fate in that part of the state.

Bonnie leaped into the Lord's arms, but the lunatic was still at large. I believe her last breath was an attempt to save her attacker's soul—she's that kind of kid.

Her parents, grateful to us for helping Bonnie, sent a most prized possession—her high school picture, which occupies a prominent place in our hallway gallery.

Bonnie's spiritual beauty engraved a soft spot in our hearts. We kept her sweatshirts for a long time, hoping all of this was a nasty nightmare. A case of mistaken identity might miraculously transport her to a Sunday night meeting to share her story. It's been over twenty years and we are still waiting. If there is a way, Bonnie will find it—she's that kind of kid.

We finally gave away her sweatshirts, but not due to lack of faith. A young girl traveling the same road that brought the "Brady Street Brawler" here needed them. We don't believe in lucky charms, but we know the Holy Spirit can make inroads through the sweatshirts of a martyred saint!

# 21

# Bringing in the Sheaves

As a child, I was confused by the words of the old hymn, "Bringing in the Sheaves." For a while I thought it was sheep they were singing about. Whatever was being brought in, it was a time for rejoicing. After hearing the hymn hundreds of times I finally asked my Dad, who replied, "Sheaves are cut stalks of grain bound with straw and brought in at harvest time."

The mystery remained. Northern New Jersey was a concrete jungle and the congregation could hardly pass for farmers. Dad quickly explained the spiritual application and was pleased that I paid attention in church.

I often think of this hymn when we are bombarded by people seeking help. Other laborers in the Lord's fields bring the harvest to us. Some of the sheaves are so bound up an exorcism is in order!

Occasionally a sheaf was literally carried in. One Sunday night three long-hairs came shouting that they had an accident victim sprawled on the back seat of their car. I rushed to their rusted relic to get a glimpse of this young man bleeding through his blond hair.

When I asked why they hadn't taken him to the hospital, one replied, "Someone told us Jesus healed people here and we came straight away! We found this guy in his car which had sideswiped a tree on Sawyer Road."

I couldn't argue with their orthodoxy even though I doubted these hippies were familiar with James 3 where it says, "Seek the elders of the church if there are any sick among you." I simply replied, "The Lord will honor your faith, but after we pray for him, you get this poor boy to the emergency room pronto! The "Good Samaritans" got the message!

Laying hands on the lad's head, we beseeched the Lord to heal him in the name of Jesus. I sensed He worked wonders in this wounded wayfarer.

We never saw the bloodied boy again, but received positive reports from his friends. The next day he was released with superficial head wounds that healed quickly.

Reminding everyone that Living Waters wasn't a substitute for hospitals, we implored them to seek medical help for serious cases and we would provide prayer support.

## The Lowdown on "High Adventure"

In spite of our intentions, our home continued to be a trauma center. One winter's night with peace reigning inside and a blizzard raging outside, Bill's dad was our dinner guest.

Willard Flint, an executive with American Can Company, came periodically to observe Bill's progress or lack thereof. Willard also invented products he peddled through small companies. He desired for Bill to run a business some day, but at the moment Bill was running his own way.

After dinner, Karen told Willard about George Otis, a Christian businessman from California, who wrote the book "High Adventure." We just happened to have a copy in our family room.

When I turned on the lights in the dark ,cold room, I explained that I kept the thermostat at 45° to conserve fuel. With wall-to-wall windows on three sides, the winter winds take their toll on our heat tab. When I assured Willard that I turn the dial up ten degrees for the meetings he appeared relieved!

As Karen looked for the book, I showed him our new entrance way. Before flipping on another light, I tripped over a pair of snow covered boots peeking around the corner of the cloakroom. Normally that would not be a problem, but these boots were belly down with feet in them! The left boot moved slightly which meant there were at least legs attached.

Karen abandoned her search for "High Adventure" to assist in solving the cloakroom case. Cautioning her to remain calm, I located the switch which shed light on our subject. The large prone body was encased in a frayed coat with a fur collar hiding most of the head. The length of this stranger in the night convinced me we were leaning over a male of undetermined age or origin.

Aware of Willard's weak heart, I waved him back a few paces. When verbal communication failed with our floorman, I chanced he would turn into a leaping lizard by rolling him over. It was Jay Johnson, a teen who attended our meetings!

Karen gently rubbed Jay's face as she prayed over him. His eyes gradually opened but they appeared distant. He mumbled something about the snow but then drew a blank.

Apparently Jay had overdosed on drugs before battling the blizzard on foot. Overcome by exposure to the elements he found his way to the floor of our cloakroom! Jay was checked out at the hospital and released later that evening.

Willard, appearing close to caving in himself, was guided to the living room couch while Karen continued her search for "High Adventure." I hadn't read the book but it was a long shot to beat what Willard had just experienced.

Following this episode, we always locked the west entrance at night. Next time the bloke in the black boots might be "Bad, Bad Leroy Brown!"

## Elephant Dust Downs the Class Clown

Not every "stranger unaware" came stretched out —some walked in willingly under their own power.

One spring night after dinner, four drug cultured teens detoured our doorbell to do their thing. Discerning that they were tripping on more than their feet, I headed them off in the playroom. Jeff Newell had sent them.

Passing preliminary perusal, the party advanced to the music room where Karen joined us. Scott Sibona looked familiar, but Tony Valone, Wylie Hinton and Sue Brown sure didn't.

Striking features, combined with charisma, confirmed that Tony was the ringleader of this rag-tag group. His Roman nose was partially exposed behind long, dark hair which he snapped like a horse's tail attacking flies.

Meanwhile, Scott avoided eye contact at all costs until suddenly my radar remembered who this rebel was. He was the "Son of a Sea Biscuit" who beat on Jane Wagner when she witnessed about Jesus in Lac La Belle Park! Scott knew his cover was blown the moment I mentioned Jane's name.

Wylie, wordless and wasted, bobbed his head back and forth as if tuned into his own antenna.

Sue, who claimed to have blown in from Boulder, was a sorry mess, also. Her arms were branded with cigarette burns! If this ancient ashen art wasn't self-inflicted, the engraver should do time as the eternal torch in Arlington National Cemetery! Sue needed a place to crash for a couple of days but had trouble passing our acid test. Her knowledge of Colorado cracked me up—if Durango is a suburb of Denver, and Central City is the capital, then Boulder must be in Estes Park!

The high which Sue was on wasn't fueled by the Rockies. She was more likely a local runaway running out of options. We offered her a few, but there was no response.

Tony was the only one who listened to the "Good News." We encouraged him to seek the Lord's help, but he made no promises.

Later we learned from Jeff Newell that Tony was an acid head who was well-liked and played class clown in high school. At graduation he wore Pluto-type tennis shoes, topped off by a hat with long doggie ear flaps!

Months later, when Karen encountered Tony downtown, he expressed a desire to study architecture. Before they parted, she again shared the love of Jesus and His power to set Tony free.

Shortly afterwards, the class clown celebrated his birthday with a big blast at his home. One of his guests came bearing elephant tranquilizers called TCP, which Tony promptly tore into. Severe depression drew him to Lapham Peak Park in Delafield where he raced up the lookout and leaped from the top as his friends stared in shock!

The jolt of Tony's death derailed the "druggie train" briefly. However, before long the passengers were back on track continuing their trip. They saw no other way to deal with the demise of their class clown!


## The Jesus Look-Alike

The sheaves showed up straight from the highways and by-ways, also. A Jesus Freak picked up a hitchhiker on Highway 16 and unloaded him at our house. Don Sellers was his name and hitting hippie communes was his game.

Hawaiian beaches had been Don's abode and bananas were his sustenance mode. He was on his way back East to visit his mother.

Karen, home alone, had a hard time turning away this wheel-less wayfarer. She tested his spiritual temperature instead!

After Karen shared some of her story, Don claimed similar experiences smoking marijuana! Dipping into his cache of grass, he gave her the chance to cash in on these encounters. Refusing his offer, Karen countered with the promise of a crash pad for the night if he would ditch his drugs. Don could have refused the offer, but he didn't.

Upon arriving home from work, Karen hit me with this "happy hitchhiker story." Reminding her we were border burnouts who couldn't harbor every Tom, Dick and Hippie tripping through the territory proved fruitless. Soothing me with psychological sweet talk, she claimed our beach bum looked like Warner Sallman's portrait of Jesus. The main difference was Sallman's Swedish version had slightly lighter eyes. It would be sacrilegious to turn away a flower child as fair as the Jesus hanging over our fireplace!

A face-to-face encounter confirmed that Karen was correct if you could get past the faded tie-dye aloha shirt! The long brown hair was there, the sandals in place, but the most striking features were in the bearded face.

Karen ceased her sales pitch when she saw I was sold on Don Sellers, also. Anyone who laughs at my jokes is automatically in anyway—it shows superior intellect combined with a proper upbringing!

Don proved to be polite, soft-spoken and blessed with a contagious smile. He gave up grass and other garbage when he jumped on the Jesus wagon. The Holy Spirit showed him as long as he looked like the Lord he might as well join Him. Before long his diet broadened beyond bananas.

Don worked on the property in the mornings while he still had energy. David sapped his strength later in the day by turning him into a camel.

Girls went dizzy over Don, but he always maintained the Jesus approach to dating—plead claustrophobia and row across the lake for reflection!

Don was a Christian Crusader in the same untiring tradition as Karen and Bonnie. Believing in a cause caused him to support it to its ultimate conclusion. Upon taking Don to a FGBMFI meeting in Milwaukee, he caught the same passion that prompted Bill Toll to promote their upcoming banquet.

Don didn't have a clue who the featured speaker Joe Ninowski was, but he pushed the event as if it was the Super Bowl and there were only a few tickets left! This former flower child, a few weeks removed from the beaches of Hawaii, poured his soul into the "blue suit brigades'" big banquet. Posters, spiels and appeals were all part of the effort. Don was so sincere, people would have attended even if the main event was Walter Winchell reading want ads!

Don's stay at our home was cut short when he decided to enter Bible School out East to study the fundamentals of his newfound faith. After a brief bit with a band he became a successful businessman in the gorgeous Garden State of New Jersey.

About the same time a young lass, by the name of Delores, snuck up on Don while he was sleeping and put a scissors to his hair. With his strength sapped for rowing, the ex-banana binger was wide open for wedded bliss. Don, Delores and their kids keep in contact and have promised to visit us some day soon.

# Busting Up Bubba's Bar

Robert Brewster from Boston fought a bigger battle. The demons dragging him under were doing the deadly duo of illegal and prescription drugs belted down by booze. His creative combinations were more volatile than a Molotov cocktail! Compounding the problem was that Bob suffered from epilepsy but often refused to take his medicine. His many scars told the story of his mind-altering altercations with alien forces!

Father Bill Wetzel brought Bob to our home after he crashed through a plate glass window at Bubba's Bar in Chicago. Too small to do battle with the bar behemoths, Bob's bouts were always with metal, glass and wood.

We took Bob on a trial basis and shortly after we were the ones on trial! We gave him more pep talks about popping pills than Lombardi ever unloaded on his legion. Whenever he ceased it caused a seizure—at least we had carpeting. With all the crashing and thrashing going on, he came close to swallowing his tongue a couple of times. Prayer usually brought him back on his feet, but the whole household was on edge because no one could predict when Bob would hit the floor again.

One day, when a Nashotah House Seminary graduate returned for a visit, he asked me, "What has been happening here lately?" I was answering Father Ted as we walked down the hallway when suddenly we were interrupted by a commotion from the kitchen. Bob, abandoning the sink, was headed in our direction with pots and pans. Desperately fighting off a fit, he staggered across the floor with eyes appearing as wild as a winter storm. Pitching a pot against the metal cabinet, Bob managed to stay airborne until he collapsed on the hallway carpet in front of our feet, with a pan still firmly entrenched in his hand. I pointed to Bob and said to Ted, "This is what has been happening lately!"

He didn't flinch an inch—during his chaplain days at St. John's Military Academy, he had seen it all. Father Ted quickly assisted Bob through his seizure and had him back battling pots and pans within twenty minutes.

The longer Bob lived with us, the deeper two realities sank in—he had affection for us but no positive feelings for Jesus. Bob sought human help but sidestepped spiritual solutions faster than he had seizures. Bordering on burnout from his S.O.S. escapades, we resigned from the "Enablers Union" to concentrate on captives that wanted out!

Bob begged for another chance but it was time for tough love. Father Bill Wetzel agreed it was back to Boston for Bob. He called us many times, but never seemed ready to dial "Abba Father" direct. We guaranteed the most it could cost him was his life!

## Targets of a Teenage Terrorist

Not every kid crashing our house was a hippie—some were just old-fashioned juvenile delinquents! Lenny Bender over-qualified for this category—his specialty was stealing cars. His joy rides ended in juvenile court which passed him on to us.

Lenny's dad, Dr. Carl Bender, was a Child Psychology Professor in the University of Wisconsin system. Conditioned to studying family crises the educator's theory leaped off the pages and landed in his living room in the presence of Lenny. At fourteen years old his son seized the opportunity to publicly demonstrate the extent of his emotional deprivation—doing donuts with pilfered cream puffs was his vehicle.

Dr. Bender, diagnosing the path of Lenny's pathology, wanted him out of his home and placed in ours! The Juvenile Court accommodated. The next day Dr. Bender brought Lenny out to get acquainted—it didn't take long.

The moment Lenny moved in his compulsions changed from cars to canines. He took to our black lab Charlie as if he was a Buick Riviera! His day and night affinity was fine with us as long as Lenny didn't ride him.

Lenny was a likable kid if you looked beyond his idiosyncrasies. He possessed a high I.Q., but the application thereof caused constant consternation. This tall gangly kid with acute acne was a genius in the classic art of negative attention. Traveling the hyper-highway, his glasses nudged down his nose from nervous vibrations. Premature signs of Parkinson's surfaced when he poured milk on his cereal and only half made it into the bowl!

Lenny's love for Charlie didn't extend to all animals—the drop-off rate revolved around the size of the creature! Gophers were flushed out of the ground with a garden hose under the guise of giving them a drink. When the "little guys" surfaced waving white flags, Lenny's sadistic side faded, allowing his St. Francis' spirit to take charge. Grasping the gasping by the tail, he toted them into the house for first aid. Karen, aghast at the sight of these water-logged creatures, miraculously saved their skins. However, Lenny's was in jeopardy at the moment!

After a few tongue lashings, Lenny left land rovers alone and shifted his shadow side towards our fine feathered friends. After knocking down a birds' nest, he presented Karen with two fuzzy balls of feathers to nurse back to health. Karen's record remained intact but Lenny's continued to be tarnished.

Bobby Huffer from Chicago shared Lenny's room on third floor with Charlie sleeping between them. One night we were awakened by seismic-size screams from upstairs that shook the entire house. By the time we arrived, Bobby was thrashing about the mattress in extreme agony. Lenny's attempt to alleviate the pain by making funny faces was failing miserably.

Appendicitis popped into our minds as we rushed Bobby to the emergency room. When the tests returned negative, we searched for other clues. All fingers pointed towards Lenny who was four years older. Apparently Bobby had been traumatized by this bully's tauntings. Teasing, tickling and spitting produced gut-wrenching reactions in Bobby's solar plexus!

We begged Bobby's forgiveness for teaming him up with this wild "brutenik," and moved him to another room where the big boys could be his bodyguard.

Lenny was operating on such thin ice he would need water wings to survive. His barbarous behavior with animals, birds and Bobby had already cost him his companionship with Charlie. A vision of Charlie appearing some morning minus a tail didn't turn us on! Lenny never argued or defended himself—his insatiable desire for negative attention welcomed more chastisement!

On meeting nights our music room looked more like the floor of the New York Stock Exchange. During the summer we used our large porch, but some of the screens were screaming for attention. Mosquitoes always took unfair advantage, followed closely by bats barging in. Spiritual warfare was one thing but fighting flying rodents was enough to undermine a prayer meeting!

We tore down the strongholds and constructed an all-weather room with wall-to-wall windows on three sides. It featured a separate entrance with a cloakroom and bathroom.

Lenny, fascinated by the building activity, paced around the perimeter with his eagle eyes focused on each operation. I warned him never to transgress the threshold of the construction area!

Three days later, Kurt Kretchmer, the general contractor, collared me with a heated complaint. Meting out his message with his strong German accent, he claimed that two of his men were targets of an avid arsonist operating out of a second floor window! The head honcho had been beaned by burning matches! Kurt ranted, "Dis has to stop immediately, there are flammable materials all over!"

After assuring him I wasn't the offender, I shouted, "It won't take the FBI to find him—my suspect list has been narrowed to one!" If Lenny wasn't the fire bomber, I would swallow a flaming sword at the next Living Waters Christmas Banquet!

Second floor produced no sign of the arsonist, only his arsenal. There was enough fire power to keep the boys below blazing all afternoon! Evidence suggested that the suspect was switching to long wooden matches filched from the fireplace mantel. If this guy wasn't stopped soon our addition would become a subtraction and the rest of our historic house would be history!

My inner ear heard the kennel calling. When I arrived, Lenny was leaning against the chain link fence fidgeting with Charlie's face. He acted as if he was expecting me.

I marched him up to the second floor to familiarize him with my findings. Denial was just a large river in Egypt as far as Lenny was concerned. His main claim to infamy was pride in his performance! Lenny was a legend before his time! It would be another ten years before international terrorists started competing to claim responsibility for the next heinous crimes!

After we gathered all his kindling, I confined this teenage terrorist to third floor. Lenny was lucky I didn't sic Kurt Kretchmer on him—they know what to do with kids like this in the old country!

When we paid our resident pyromaniac a visit he was resting comfortably on his mattress minus Charlie. Confronting him about his latest offense was tantamount to placing him on a pedestal—he ate up the attention! Now he had the entire house hopping, including Kretchmer's crew.

Lenny, sensing this was his "last hurrah," put up no resistance when offered spiritual solutions. Mary and Norman Soergel helped us lay hands on the lad, asking the Lord to deal with his destructive forces. After we prayed that he would open up to the Holy Spirit, there were rays of hope written on his face.

One significant sign at breakfast the next morning was that most of the milk made it into his bowl! After three weeks of weaning from menagerie mayhem, Lenny got Charlie back. House-breaking started from scratch but the canine kid was equal to the task. Even the gophers went through their daily routine with less stress. There was spring in their steps as they gathered fall food for the long winter ahead. The spirit of St. Francis returned peace to our property!

After numerous family counseling sessions, Lenny returned to his dad's home. He wasn't monk material yet, but he was miles away from returning to Juvenile Court. Lenny came to Living Waters like a looney and left a living legend!

The former fire bomber stays in constant touch. He was a painting contractor for many years but gave it up for fear some crazy kid would drop live matches on his ladder-laden crew! Lenny ultimately made the transition from teen terrorist to taxi titan. He adds to his Milwaukee fleet the old fashioned way—buying them!

Before Lenny got married, he brought his fiancee out for our approval. We didn't dare reminisce about his rebel days until after the reception. All of their kids have been baptized at our home by the late Father Joe Hunt, our beloved friend from Nashotah House.

# 22

# Deprogramming a Kleptomaniac Cult

Sandi Warren, who had a history of being abused by her brother Hank, moved in with us to escape this harassment. Living in constant fear stunted her self-worth. Sandi's mousy brown hair matched her dowdy appearance.

Her hideaway turned into a hellhole—Hank followed her to our home. After hitting his favorite hangouts, he crept down our driveway in his dilapidated pickup to camp in front of our house. Killing the headlights, he positioned himself so he could draw a direct bead on Sandi's bedroom.

We were reluctant to call the cops as Hank's temper was hot enough to set the woods on fire! He even looked mean in the moonlight! Big brother's nightly stakeout let little sister know he was still in control. As long as Sandi was in his sight, no one else could steal her.

We encouraged Sandi to alert the authorities about her abuse, but she cringed at the thought. She acted as if she would dive into a dungeon of denial if someone else blew the whistle on her brother. She felt safer under his surveillance than facing Hank head-on in court.

Hank changed the pace as time wore on—his visits became sporadic. Even a drive-in movie loses its allurement after you've seen the same flick fifty times!

The stalking ceased the moment Sandi moved in with a girlfriend. Shortly after Sandi split, Karen noticed some of her summer clothes had followed suit! A serious search of our sizable house proved as fruitless as hunting for Jimmy Hoffa in the Meadowlands. All fingers pointed towards Sandi and the dresses driving off under the same influence.

There was only one way to make sure Sandi hadn't joined a "Christian closet cult" that encouraged kleptomania! Karen paid

Sandi a social call which was more like taking inventory than a house warming. Sandi flashed her abashed smile when faced with the fashion filching. There was no need to call the cops. She walked straight to her closet and produced the prodigal raiment as if they had come right off the rack at Saks.

As Karen carted her clothes out the door, she spied two of Krista's stuffed animals cuddled on the couch. Split second intuition told her Sandi needed these "Care Bears" more than Krista. Hopefully they would be part of her healing. Krista's bears were replaced the next day at Uncle Paul's toy store in town.

Two years passed before the next inside job. This time the ante skyrocketed—jewelry was on the agenda! Three of Karen's rings vanished faster than veracity at a volleyball game. We had suspects but no concrete clues as to who the culprit was.

Five months later, Mary Simpson, a girl who had lived on our property, rang our doorbell. As Karen ushered her in she noticed Mary's fingers were flashing two recognizable rings. Shocked to see her grandmother's gold and garnet on someone else's fingers, she sneaked another peak for a second opinion.

Convinced, Karen popped the $64,000 question, "Where did you get those rings!" Sobbing, Mary slowly slipped them off and placed them in Karen's palm. The Lord had convicted her and she came seeking Karen's forgiveness. With this issue settled, the two of them were free to fellowship.

The other ring never returned to its rightful owner. The "new wine grapevine" suggested that a lad we knew lifted it to preserve his drug supply line. Our theme song, paraphrased from scripture, became, "Silver and gold have I none, but such as I have, taketh thee. In the name of Jesus Christ, rise up and offer restitution!" The lad missed the message and we beefed up security which was centered in the Lord.

## Mixing It Up With A Mafia Moll

Sandi wasn't the only stowaway to stay at our house. Reverend Merlin Bradley, a Baptist minister from West Allis, brought out a Chicago girl named Jeanne. Pushing thirty, she looked more like a mid-life crisis. Jeanne was a Mafia moll who turned state's witness against the mob. They were after her hide, but would settle for an arm or a leg! One playful prank they pulled was prying the lugs loose on her car wheels to see which tire would tear loose first. The right front was the first to go, which resulted in slamming into a light post. A few steps away from paraplegic status, we assisted Jeanne's every movement.

She responded well to prayer, but needed more time. Concerned the Mafia might show up any minute, we searched for a remote hideaway for Jeanne. Soergel's Ashippun farm was fifteen minutes further and their horses should spook any city slickers who showed up.

Thirty seconds after Mary and Norman said, "Yes," we stashed our stowaway in the car and headed north. As we drove in their driveway, guilt gripped me, but I didn't dare give in to it. After all, what are friends for if you can't drop a Mafia dolly in distress on their doorstep?

## Karl Cracks the Kingdom of the Cults

Maneuvering through Mafia minefields hastens mortality, but being captured by the kingdom of the cults brings spiritual death!

Karl Voelkner wasn't hit by hippie hairstyles; he was a hairless Hari Krishna. As a loyal subject of the Hindu God, he specialized in standing on San Francisco street corners, chanting Hari Krishna, Hari Krishna. His personality made him a candidate for a cult. As a rigid, serious, sensitive kid, he internalized all his stress. With every known constant coming apart in the '60s, Karl found a haven with the Hari Krishnas, where gurus made his daily decisions. Going with the flow, he disregarded the flaws in their system.

Finally getting fed up with eating out of little brown bowls, he bailed out of this brainwashing bind. Repenting, he rent his orange robe into fragments and sought us out for spiritual asylum.

Pleased with Karl finding Jesus, his parents started attending our prayer meetings. Karl's dad, Mel, contracted cancer and we prayed for him at every service. Mel made many gains, but his greatest victory was spiritual—he moved up to first string on Jesus' eternal team.

Merlin Severson became a father figure for Karl and helped disciple him. Months later, Karl desired structured Bible training, so Merlin introduced him to Daystar Ministries in Minneapolis. He was the third kid from Living Waters to make that big move.

## Hand Walking With the Lord

Gray is so degrading for some people they see everything as either black or white. Barry McBrien from Brookfield, Wisconsin, was such a boy. He was a handsome talented, sensitive kid, born into a brood of bodybuilders. His brother Tom, who attended our meetings, became a champion. Barry possessed the physical potential to build his body; but his internal clockwork cringed at the thought.

Traditional Catholic mothers pray to have at least one priest in their family. If the prayer goes unanswered, she will usually settle for a poet. Barry was the bard of the McBrien family. Every week he brought us his latest lament about his longings to be freed from the dark demons of depression. His well-written works were riddled with emotional wounds.

Not only was Barry down on himself, but he refused to believe anyone else could see his bright side. We spent hours trying to convince him he was a beloved son in the sight of God, who hadn't shortchanged him. Not able to accept love, he believed the lie of the evil one that he was wretched without worth.

Barry slipped in and out of suicidal considerations. It didn't help that his partying peers portrayed this bard as a deadbeat. Any high school kid who gets high on the arts isn't about to win a popularity contest!

A living faith in a risen Lord was Barry's only hope. He talked about faith but ultimately freaked out because he couldn't feel it. He desired a sign from above, but felt too unworthy to see anything. He believed the Lord loved others but wouldn't bother with him. If only God would thrust his strong right arm through the ceiling, grab Barry by the breeches and turn him upside down!

He would probably dismiss this supernatural act as the work of one of his bodybuilding brothers.

After hours of listening to, agonizing with and praying over Barry, he felt nothing. We encouraged him to pursue areas of interest. Divergent activity often deals with introspection and perfectionism. Although he avoided athletics, he was an excellent acrobat. He walked down stairs on his hands faster than most people can on two legs. Barry's blood was about to burst through his pores when he hit bottom but he always recovered nicely. Walking upside down is the therapy of the future—it changes your whole outlook on life!

Barry was the only teen trusted to cut brush in tree planting areas. He loved living things as long as they didn't have legs and a large mouth. Trees were always accepting and rarely talked back. Barry battled brush bullies such as buckthorn, honeysuckles and various kinds of vines which were attacking the pines. It paid to know the territory as poison ivy was plentiful.

The seriousness of this earth-shaking operation was implanted in Barry's brain after I told him my trials with a teenager named Stanley the previous summer. Stanley's talents were more suited for a land leveling expedition. Hours of intricate instruction on the delicate art of maintaining an arboretum didn't make any difference. Stanley massacred everything in sight with machete-type precision! It was jungle warfare at its worst. All sides suffered so many casualties it took a computer to tally the final body count! White pine and Colorado blue spruce were slaughtered side by side, along with the dreaded buckthorn, while wild vines maintained their strangleholds.

When the proud parents of these transplants confronted Stanley, he pleaded confusion—needles and leaves looked alike to him. Thank God he didn't weed our flower garden! It was too late for Stanley the Ripper to repent anyway—he lacked the resurrection ministry required for reparations!

However, the most barbaric bushwacker to ever set foot on our property was the infamous Jeff Charles Hupe. "Hoops", as he is called, mangled more brush cutting equipment in a month than May's Garden Center sold in a year! At six foot three inches and

260 pounds, even the stately cedars shook down to their timbers when they heard "Hoops" huge hulk lumbering around the bend.

Greg Gesch, Dennis Gorecki, Scott Lyle, and Kurt Konicke also contributed to the onslaught. Jeff Hartman, my loyal maintenance man during the "decimation decade" spent half his time in our blacksmith shop welding equipment.

"Hoops" hacking career was cut short by a crushing blow to his knees during an Oconomowoc High School football playoff game. The culprit was Keombani Coleman from Milwaukee Tech, who later played for the Packers. "Hoops" has settled in Chicago selling T-shirts and assorted sports paraphernalia for his colossal promo company—Corvelle.

Barry worked wonders in the woods. His approach to my prized possessions resembled a skilled brain surgeon. Perfectionism turned outward produced a positive practical result. Acing the tree test was a Rite of Passage for this strapping young man.

Barry's new sense of pride propelled him into taking flying lessons—with the aid of a plane, of course. Krista, who had a crush on Barry, helped him prepare for his pilot's license. However, he never found the Lord up there, either, as he continued to have a faith crisis.

The next summer Barry ventured out West with Outward Bound and came back with the victory after thirty days of vigorous survival training. Outward Bound gave birth to Barry's faith! In addition to his witnessing for the Lord, he formed a small Bible study group in the evenings.

The Navy was next on his worldwide tour. The kid wasn't playing favorites—first it was air, then by land and now by sea. We were concerned how Barry would react when some wacko from Uncle Sam's fleet flogged him with his foul mouth.

After basic, Barry boarded a ship set to cruise the Pacific. He endured one bout with the brig for refusing a command that violated his conscience. After sitting in solitary a few days, his principles became more pliable.

Barry entertained the swabbies on deck by walking on his hands from stem to stern. When the seas roared, his friends formed a phalanx around the rim of the ship to preserve this fine art from a fate worse than walking the plank. We found out the real reason Barry rejected the Air Force—planes put a cramp on his time-tested talents!

Barry's bravado blossomed off board, also. Each port presented an opportunity to keep his comrades from serious sailor sins. In Sydney, Australia, he was the first Yankee to walk the width of the opera house on his hands. Bewildered buffs believed Barry was auditioning for a modern Madame Butterfly! Shouts of "bravo" eased his burgeoning blisters.

Defeat finally found Barry in a remote port beyond the blue horizon. While hand walking down a flight of slippery stairs, above a concrete dock, his left hand slid and his bean bounced off the cement like a billiard ball. Good Samaritans rushed to his assistance as he lay motionless. Before long, Barry was back on his feet with only a gash in the forehead. A few days later he was back on his hands vowing to never backslide again!

To complete a clear break with the past, Barry legally changed his name to Hezekiah. The crew called him Hez for short. Hez encountered harassment when he set up Bible studies on board. However, persecution paved the way for respect when the sailors saw the sincerity of his faith.

Walking by faith as well as hands, Hezekiah was no longer a slave to feelings. His head trips were behind him as Jesus turned his life upside down.

Hez visits periodically to make sure the trees are still standing tall. Last time we saw him he was heading for Chicago to be trained as an engineer. He desires to design bridges he can walk across on his hands without interrupting the flow of traffic!

## The Holland Hurricane

When the Lonesome Stone gang moved in we were one up on the ark—there were three of each species. Vanessa from England, Anita from Sweden and Rachel from Holland rounded out the girls. The boys were Robin from England, Klaus from Germany and Henry from everywhere in the world—his dad was a military man.

Rachel was a rangy, big boned babe with blazing brown eyes darting in every direction. Raised rigidly by a no-nonsense father, she reacted to life like a wild bronco released from the stall. Breaking loose, she bounced around unbridled in a life debased by drugs. Rachel ran down Lonesome Stone in Holland and cleaned up her act long enough to earn a spot on their traveling squad.

Rachel's rage was still rooted in rebellion when she landed at Living Waters. Rachel and house rules mixed like a halo in a head shop! I marched her down to my office daily for a meeting of the minds. She tried to hide hers behind a language barrier. Once, when my patience was tested to the tenth degree, I shouted, "You understand more English than the Queen and are twice as cunning!" Both of us being 5 feet 10 inches made us nose to nose. Each session ended with Rachel pleading the fifth.

Rachel was a tomboy turned into an unholy terror—she would try anything for thrills. One day she joined us on a cross-country skiing expedition in the Kettle Morraine Forest. Rain ruined the snow by turning the terrain into a sheet of ice. Wax was hopeless, but klister would keep the skis from sliding sideways. However, it was Hades when you got home—klister clings like Super Glue and needs to be sand blasted off the bottom.

Rachel rejected klister as kids' stuff that would cramp her style. The klisterless miss covered the Kettle Morraine like a runaway toboggan. Oblivious to the conditions, she careened off trails and bulldozed through brush without so much as a bruise.

I had no such hope for my extra pair of skis she borrowed! I envisioned a year's supply of toothpicks laid at my feet. The "Holland Hurricane" finally hung it up when she pulverized my wooden poles into the frozen tundra at the end of a "Flying Wallenda" act. It sounded like a Rice Krispies ad—snap, crackle and pop! The skis showed signs of battle fatigue, but survived another day's onslaught.

Rachel rose early the next morning with her adrenaline still in overdrive. She tested my skis on a monster mogul jump she built above the shore of the frozen lagoon. With her weight shifted too far forward on her third attempt, the right ski dove headfirst into unforgiving ice, resulting in an instant severing of the tip.

Rachel rejected the urge to continue her routine on one ski and turned over her fractured trophy to the rightful owner. The only redeeming feature of this fiasco was to use the skis for kindling.

Rachel's patented approach to apologizing was suggesting that my ski was defective! She was right about the defect, but wrong about the ski. It was a classic case of projection! After reaping the rewards of this renegade racer, I was desperate for a respite.

However, Rachel's reckless abandon wasn't restricted to the slopes. Her major mania was mood swings! We needed a "Major Prophet" to predict which mood she would swing into next! Once when we were gone, she dropped into depression and overdosed on Minnie's sleeping pills. Pilfering the pills from her purse, she downed them like M & M's. Rachel was rushed to the emergency room, but her resiliency resulted in a rapid recovery.

Of all the continental kids, Rachel resisted returning to her homeland the most. Immigration laws were loathsome to this lass. A throwback to the "femme fatales" of the frontier, she fought fiercely for squatter's rights.

Finally feeling empathy, as she didn't have much to go home to, I pleaded her case with immigration officials. These turkeys remained as stubborn as frozen Beef Jerky! Meanwhile Rachel's visa was running out. Desperate, I brought Rachel to the Milwaukee Immigration office to knock heads with the honchos. Las Vegas would have declared this match even odds.

The four corners of the Earth were well-represented in the aptly named "waiting room." Each foreign face exhibited a fantastic story waiting to be told.

Finally we were called to the counter by a harsh voice which herded us to a side room. Fifteen minutes later a stone faced official emerged, appearing as if he had overdosed on Fiber One! When he demanded the nature of our visit, I related Rachel's story until she interrupted to plead her own case. My diplomatic approach aroused her anger.

Her initial volley, in broken English, was returned by the party line. Beaming slivers of steel she retaliated shouting, "I vant to stay, I vant to stay!" He reiterated, "You can't stay," and returned to his canned spiel. Nose to nose, but miles apart, Rachel stomped on the floor, bellowing, "I dun't understand vhat you do to me!"

Fearful that this cat was about to whip out the cuffs and throw Rachel in the slammer, I pulled her away and apologized for her outbursts. Rachel was ready for another round, but I convinced her it was time to split—we had been hit by a "technical knock out!"

Two weeks later, the "Holland Hurricane" reluctantly returned to her native land, vowing she would be back. She possessed the mettle of General Douglas McArthur, but lacked the connections.

The following January Rachel made a valiant attempt to fulfill her promise. We received an S.O.S. phone call while she was at the Toronto airport. She and her boyfriend were stranded and needed help crossing the border! With trepidation I asked, "Where are you headed?" When Rachel replied, "Your place," visions of splintered skis sent spasms through my sacroiliac!

The "Holland Hurricane" had seen too many Hollywood Grade "B" movies—she requested cash to grease the official's palm! I reminded her she wasn't in Chicago seeking a driver's license—Immigration held out for higher stakes!

Her next proposal was for us to call President Carter to persuade him to intervene. "Just because we voted for him, doesn't mean he remembers us," I replied. "Besides, he might have a few other things on his mind at the moment!"

My answers went over like castor oil at a wine tasting contest—Rachel couldn't stomach them. Remembering the call was collect, I attempted to end the conversation, but Rachel kept on ranting! When the "Holland Hurricane" refused the name of a Toronto friend who might have been able to help her, I hung up! The only way to stop a storm is to pull the power.

We haven't heard from Rachel since, but we know she is all right—as a seasoned survivor she is too stubborn to succumb!

## Left in the Lurch Lonesome Stone Gang

Vanessa did dope on the streets of London, before joining "Lonesome Stone." Down to 98 pounds, she was slowly slipping away when the Lord pumped new life in her veins.

Vanessa's style was more reserved than Rachel's, thank God. This perennial couch potato curled up in front of the T.V. transfigured by the tube. The only thing that tore her away was the smell of savory food filtering from the kitchen. As long as Minnie was in charge of culinary concoctions, Vanessa would never have to worry about wasting away.

Anita, a shy blue-eyed blonde from Sweden, had been a heroin addict. Abused as a teenager, she suffered a miscarriage and couldn't have kids as a result. Speaking in low hushed tones, she moved about the house like a delicate piece of china. The only time Anita talked a ton was when she spoke to God—she offered up lengthy prayers at dinner table devotions.

Anita received spiritual and psychological help through inner healing ministry while living at our home. Karen and Sister Arthur Minton, from the School Sisters of Notre Dame, spent hours praying for Anita's wounds.

Klaus, from Germany, was a stagehand for Lonesome Stone who exhibited the characteristics of a Bavarian Boy Scout—trustworthy, loyal, helpful, friendly, courteous, kind, obedient, cheerful, thrifty, brave, clean and reverent.

Klaus's sweet smile melted Anita's frozen feelings. They sat silently on the settee in the music room for hours like an old-fashioned courting couple. A tornado would have had trouble disturbing their total focus on each other.

Six months later they were married in a centuries-old monastery in Germany. Thanks to the Lord's healing power, Anita gave birth to three sons in the ensuing years.

Henry, who was also a stagehand, made so many moves during his dad's military career, that shifting scenery on a small stage was a snap. He helped with chores in our home and related well to David and Krista.

However, addicted to faraway places, Henry married a Wisconsin girl and they settled in Alaska. We see them when they return to the Badger State to visit relatives.

## Saint Francis of Sheffield

God blessed us with stagehands because he knew we had already been blitzed with enough actors to make Abraham Lincoln triple his life insurance!

Robin from Sheffield, England, was the third Lonesome Stone stagehand to set foot on our land. Robin, pleasant but reserved, was harboring hurts from childhood. His stoical face gave way to a gentle grin when we touched his deep-rooted sense of humor.

Robin's elf-like qualities related well to animals. He played with our dogs as if he had been a pup once himself. They were his constant companions when he worked on our grounds. Robin's best friends included birds, fish, hampsters, rabbits, iguanas and chinchillas. However, I never summoned Robin for rodent control—conclusive evidence suggested he would side with Karen and the varmints would take over our vast Victorian!

Robin related to money as if a pyramid of pounds were required to pass through the pearly gates! He saved every cent he ever earned. When his working gloves wore holes in the fingers, he simply reversed them for another round. CARE packages from concerned friends was the only way to add to his wardrobe.

Robin's only known pleasure, outside of nature and animals, was British edibles. If he was a violent man, he would have killed for kidney pie. Minnie only made it occasionally; as kidneys were hard to come by!

Robin was akin to Rachel in only one respect—they both possessed a strong desire to stay in the States. Fortunately, efforts on Robin's behalf resulted in a positive ending. After many rounds of haggling over rules and regulations, we achieved this "Round Robin" victory over Immigration. I slipped Robin in under a "religious clause" whereby he instantly became the Living Waters Youth Pastor. This ministerial maneuver scared the shell off of this ingrained introvert!

In reality, Robin related to trees more than troubled teens. As my right-hand man, he worked on the front forty with the same fatherly feeling I had for the land. Robin's primary approach was preservation, which was worlds apart from other weed-whacking warriors I had battled with. These pompous primates, whose primal scream was procrastination, believed God sent his only Son to set them free from manual labor! Warping the Word, they concluded wiping out weeds was worldly!

Robin always informed me about property-related problems first, not last as in the past. His senses were saturated with a Scotland Yard psyche.

After Robin received "permanent resident alien status" in the States, he worked for the Richard Erdmann's family business, World of Wood. They make exquisite Victorian furniture and have branched off into "Historic Registry" restorations. Robin also put in time at Ellen Strommen's Culligan Soft Water operation before joining the Oconomowoc Fire Department.

Saint Francis of Sheffield found a female fawn he took a fancy to and they settled down. Robin and Celinda come out to the house occasionally to wrestle with the animals.

Lonesome Stone left their mark on Living Waters—sometimes it was left of center, but usually they were right on target. For every soul that lived here, there were six more who entered our door for daytime excursions. We shared the good times, as well as the grief when the group was reduced to an immortal memory.

# 23

# The Mascot of the
# Milwaukee Jesus People

Not all Jesus People were products of the '50s. Many balding believers from the '20s had their roots bale out by the '60s. Lacking long hair and love beads was no sin, even a born-again businessman could get in.

Herbie Goldfine, who became the Milwaukee Jesus People mascot, was such a man. The first time I met Herbie was when he came out to our house with a bus full of Jesus Freaks. This man in the gray flannel suit looked more like a Wheeler Dealer from Maxwell Street than a heaven-bound hippie! He seemed smooth enough to have sold Soldier Field a few times and thrown in Moody Bible Institute to close the deals!

Herbie's chrome dome shone like the Sea of Galilee in the mid-morning sun. Rumor had it he had been recently banned from O'Hare Field for fear a pilot might mistake his head for a runway! Falling the wrong way during a "Slain in the Spirit" session, bent Herbie's beak so bad that when he sneezed he showered his right shoulder!

Herbie became aligned with the Brady Street bunch under the "Grandfather Clause." His childhood stomping grounds in the Windy City were a few blocks from Maxwell Street. In his mid-fifties he met his Messiah at a Billy Graham rally in Soldier' Field. However, Herbie didn't turn into a saint overnight—there was still a smidgen of Maxwell Street in him when he hit Milwaukee. When a friend brought him to the Jesus People Power House on Brady Street, he bonded so quickly, he moved in!

Herbie had a habit of picking up hitchhikers, hitting them with the Gospel and unloading them at our place. When Herbie negotiated the Lord's business, he could talk the talk, but wanted us to firm up the final walk.

One June afternoon Herbie showed up with two curious-looking creatures who could pass for prison escapees. They not only needed the Lord, they needed the lake! Herbie was winded from witnessing and wanted me to take over. Karen wasn't home and I was shoveling sand along the shore to combat erosion problems.

Playing hard nose with Herbie, I informed him, "Witnessing has to wait until all the sand is shoveled. It will be four hours solo, two hours with help!" The three fellow travelers opted for the sandman approach—a siesta on the hillside. Occasionally, one would wake up to watch for a while, like I was Samson at the Milwaukee County Zoo!

Two hours later Karen returned to rescue me from these Rip Van Winkles. Karen, stepping in where Herbie left off, closed one deal quickly. The other guy was more interested in food than in faith! After dinner, Herbie and his hitchhikers departed and I shoveled sand until sunset.

As mascot of the Milwaukee Jesus People, Herbie coveted the kids' freedom to strap all their earthly belongings on their back in a moment's notice. Electing to be a new man in the old suit, rather than the old man in a new suit, he desired to dump all his material possessions accumulated during his dealing days.

A week later Herbie and Jim Palosaari pulled up to our house in a rickety school bus packed with exquisite antique furniture, icons and paintings. Desks, cabinets, chairs and a mammoth 18th century German inlaid wood bookcase replaced the kids on the bus. Herbie asked me to peddle his paraphernalia pronto so he could give the proceeds to the Jesus People's cause.

My problem was where to stash Herbie's haul which had been appraised at $25,000 in the middle '50s! European antiquities wouldn't mix well with the Early Americana at the Golden Eagle. Anything stored in our house was subject to sudden destruction. As long as Andrae's Army didn't return soon, the basketball court in the coach house would suffice. It took us hours to carry the furniture up the creaky stairs. Fortunately, the bookcase could be carried in sections. The total package, which looked great on the bus, was beyond belief on the basketball court. If the rodents and raccoons remained on sabbatical, Herbie's stuff would be safe!

The next day I came down with the dreaded disease, "Antique Dealer's Dysfunction." With no known cure for the affliction, you just give in to it! The most severe symptom is the seller switching roles and becoming the buyer.

I peddled the pictures, icons and a portion of the furniture, but haggled with Herbie over a long term contract for the remainder of the loot. The Maxwell Street shark was much easier to deal with after he met his Messiah!

The 18th Century bookcase was the prize of the purchase. Bailing it out of the basketball court before the bats bombed it, I assembled it in my office. Often when I open its creaky cabinets, I think about the day Herbie hauled it here on that broken-down bus. Unencumbered by earthly possessions, Herbie was finally free to move with the Jesus Freaks at a moment's notice!

## Never Fear, Herbie is Here

Herbie always appeared unannounced. The flip side was, I could call him at the last second with some problem and he would come up with a solution. It wasn't always the answer I envisioned but his heart was right.

One Sunday morning I received an S.O.S. call from our scheduled speaker for that night. His car broke down in Kansas and he would be forced to cancel. Chances are he had latched onto a larger meeting with a more liberal love offering! We had promoted this brother for weeks and expected a big turnout.

When I phoned Herbie about our predicament, his word was, "Never fear, Jesus is here!" I replied, "Jesus is here, but our speaker isn't!" Then he said, "Never fear, Herbie is also here, ready, willing and able to work it out."

Herbie raved in raptures about a musician friend from Chicago who would fill the bill. I was hoping he wasn't referring to one of his hitchhikers!

By 7:00 p.m. there was no Herbie and no musician. Forty-five minutes later, the worship was interrupted by a stir in the rear of the room. It was Herbie and his friend, Seth Worth, who was lugging a cello behind him. Decked out in a full tux with slicked-back black hair parted in the middle, Seth appeared more suited for the Philharmonic than for a prayer meeting!

I introduced Herbie, who interjected a rambling testimony before calling his cellist friend forward. Seth played for all he was worth while periodically preempting the music with short messages. He revealed he is a seminary student at a conservative Bible Institute, which believes the gifts of the Holy Spirit are not to be manifested in this dispensation!

When Seth attacked tongues I looked daggers at Herbie who was hanging his head at half-mast! Victimized by this vitriolic vignette, I cut the concert short before the crowd separated Seth from his cello and tied into his tux! Thanking Seth for his music, I reminded everyone how God isn't finished with us yet.

I rushed Herbie to my office where we had an impassioned powwow next to his beloved bookcase. He apologized while admitting he hadn't known Seth very long. My guess was that he was one of Herbie's most recent hitchhikers. I forgave Herbie but canceled his contract as Living Waters number one booking agent!

## Topping the Ten Most Wanted List

Shortly after moving into this vast Victorian, we received mail addressed to various friends of the former owners, Mr. and Mrs. A. D. Braun. Soon all the correspondence stopped except mail sent to Rabbi Samuel Perlstein. Because the Brauns were Jewish, we assumed the Rabbi was a family house guest.

At the outset it was mainly junk mail, but then things took a more serious turn. Business letters, credit agency requests, correspondence from attorneys, unpaid parking violations and delinquent bills arrived. Next came little love letters from the courts.

The name of the game had dramatically changed. Rabbi Samuel Perlstein was not only alive, but currently using our address for some unknown reason! Because the Rabbi was also unknown, we launched a full-scale search for the real Rabbi to step forward and identify himself.

Meanwhile, we turned all his mail over to the local police who were getting inquiries about Rabbi Sam from other law enforcement agencies. Cops came to our door to interrogate us on the who, what, why and whereabouts. Scotland Yard types tiptoed through our tulips, trying to turn up tidbits. We volunteered everything we knew, which took ten seconds.

One cold December night two of our girls were panicked by blinding search lights leveled at their bedroom from below. Our village police closed in on the culprits, who turned out to be county cops seeking the runaway Rabbi! No arrests were made! Feeling like felons ourselves, we encouraged the sheriffs to search our house. We would offer them a reward to find him! The local police convinced them we were law-abiding citizens, not in the business of harboring criminal clergy.

Our reprieve lasted four months until reinforcements came to check us out. The police asked their standard list of Rabbi questions and were ready to split when suddenly the case took an ugly turn!

Father Bob Bales from St. Jerome's had brought Mike Hentges, a trying teen, to our place six months before for R & R— restitution and religion. As a confirmed fuzz buster, cops made Mike nervous.

Mike, having overheard the questioning while on K.P., pieced together in his mischievous mind a quick solution to the case. He marched Herbie, who was visiting, into the presence of the police and shouted, "This is the Rabbi, this is your man!"

It was paramedic time! We had spent years establishing credibility with the cops, denying we even knew the Rabbi, and this punk produces a live body who looks like he just bombed in from a bar mitzvah! One sneak peak at Herbie's beak caused me to realize how badly our credibility had crumbled.

Herbie was speechless for a change, but it didn't last long. Swiftly shifting into his Maxwell Street smarts, he produced reams of paper to prove his identity, while shouting sweet sentiments at Mike! If Herbie had a hammer he would have wound up in the slammer! The cops eventually got off Herbie's case when we confirmed his story for the tenth time.

However, we suddenly had a new candidate for confinement—Mike! After promoting him from K.P. to the cooler I served him the appropriate papers. Restless as a rattler on his first bungee jump, everyone agreed he needed a setting with stricter structure. Merlin brought Mike to a bible training school up north.

Herbie, having developed a clergy complex, didn't come around as often after the Rabbi run-in. The last time he came he complained of a persistent cough. It's been eighteen years since we have seen Herbie and we have never seen the Rabbi! It's safe to come back now, Herbie—the Rabbi's fan mail has fizzled!

This case still heads up our "Unsolved Mysteries." There are no clues as to where they are hanging out. The Milwaukee Jesus People are long gone and Maxwell Street is a shriveled shadow of its former self. If Herbie and the Rabbi are not in hibernation, or in the hands of the powers to be, I would bet they are booking agents for the Heavenly powers. Then again, they might be stranded in Purgatory, finagling for a ticket to the next station!

## Reformation Roller Rink

Brother Andrew Ulrich was another Jesus kid from the Depression era. Riding high on his Harley, bound in black leather, he looked like the "Fonz" without the fuzz. The reason Brother Andrew lacked long hair was by the time it was in, his roots were out! However, his flair for far-out outfits fully compensated. He mastered mixing black leather with bright plaid shirts and striped pants.

Despite Brother Andrew's classic Pentecostal past, he possessed an ecumenical spirit. Following in his father's pastoral footsteps at Church of the Risen Savior in Milwaukee, he opened the doors to all comers. Jesus Freaks flocked in as if they had found the fountain of forgiveness! In addition to his powerful preaching, Andrew captivated them on the keyboard with his rocking, "Reformation Roller Rink" renditions. When the overworked keys went kaput, a special "Keys for the Kingdom" offering was taken to replace them!

Brother Andrew shared his piano prowess with Living Waters, gave prophetic words and prayed with people. This pedigreed Pentecostal Pastor was never pushy, but peacefully let the Holy Spirit lead mainline Charismatics.

One Friday night a Protestant puritan, with old world worries written all over his wrinkles, plunked a problem in my lap. Paul Barrons was bothered by Brother Andrew's free-wheeling spirit! High on his hit list were Andrew's motorcycle maneuvers, his way-out wardrobe and the souped-up syncopation of his keyboard capers. Paul's ultimate concern was that recent converts would be scandalized and backslide to the other side!

My perception about Paul's prudish prattle was that he had overdosed on prunes! However, he was so persistent, I reluctantly agreed to talk to Andrew about it.

As I led Brother Andrew to my office, I pondered—who was I, a 28-year young Charismatic, questioning a progressive Pentecostal pastor put to the test for decades! I quickly came to the point without mentioning names. As I ran down the loaded list of grievances, Andrew broke into laughter, acting as if I had bombarded him with a barrage of Milton Berle's best jokes! "How can you maintain such a mirthful spirit about these accusations?! I asked. He replied, "As you were speaking, I saw the face of the Father and merely mirrored what He was doing. It's not fair for our Father to have all the fun!"

I reassured Brother Andrew we liked him the way the Lord made him and would continue to welcome him at our "come as you are" Friday night gatherings. With a twinkle in his eyes, Andrew jumped on his Harley and sped off like a man on a mission to spread the "Good News" of love, joy and peace in the Holy Ghost.

I informed Paul that the jury, under Jesus' influence, rendered a not guilty verdict. Paul couldn't catch Brother Andrew's vision of melting the frozen chosen and made himself scarce.

Brother Andrew's ecumenical umbrella included carting vans full of "Separated Brothers" to the Charismatic Conferences at Notre Dame for a triumphant reunion in the football stadium with 50,000 card-carrying Catholics!

Brother Andrew knew no fear in ministering healing prayer. Once while shopping at a furniture store he overheard a lady complain about back pain. Before she could cry "Brother," he eased her into a chair in the display windows. Passers by saw prayer in action as her left leg grew instantaneously. Forgetting about furniture, the lady left the store walking, leaping and praising God!

However, not even leg lengthening could extend Brother Andrew's life—the big Jesus Kid crashed the kingdom shortly after. He became sick one afternoon and three days later he was gone. The Lord must have needed a peppy pianist to enliven the saints marching in.

Trying to replace Brother Andrew was useless—"Reformation Roller Rink" wasn't offered at religious music schools! Andrew paved the way for Jesus People bands to have their day. Talk about syncopation: the blatant blasts of the Jesus bands were enough to make Paul Barrons plead for Purgatory!

## The Wicked Shall be Cut Off Short

It became increasingly evident that Charismatic Christians possessed no guarantee against an early exit from this life. Some eager exhorters, influenced more by exegeses than Jesus, got carried away with the Elisha story by suggesting we were going straight up without paying our dues to the undertaker. Grave situations were created when Charismatic circuit riders roamed the country proclaiming people to be healed!

We opted to follow the New Testament example of laying hands on the sick and letting the Lord complete the work in His own way. When someone has experienced healing, it's redundant to inform them!

Many people recover instantly and others receive their ultimate healing—a resurrected body. Phil Matt met his maker in this manner. By the time his wife Joan brought Phil to Living Waters for prayer, he was suffering from severe stomach cancer. After beseeching the Lord on Phil's behalf, his life was extended long enough for his spirit to embrace Jesus. We ministered to Phil's family for months after he died.

A year later Joan came for the weekend with her new boyfriend John. Shortly after they arrived, John was overcome by his acute carpentry compulsion. Insisting that our Victorian doors needed shaping up where the house had settled, he carted his tools in from his truck. Persuaded by John's professional patina and volunteer price, we permitted him to perform surgery on our doors.

One by one he lugged each large work of art to the basement. Two hours later, when I went to check on John's progress, he already had seven finished doors lined up along the cellar wall.

When I suggested we return some of the doors to their roost before rigor mortis set in, John responded in the negative. Putting his artistic temperament to the test, I insisted we try one for size. It didn't take long to see the light—it was streaming under the bottom of our bedroom door! The measurements must have been made by a myopic madman! No respecting rodent would require a pass key for unlimited entry!

Hoping this was an anomaly, I inspected the next door—it was deja vu! John cut the bottom off the door straight across, ignoring the arched floor. It looked like a bow-legged cowboy straddling a wooden gate. The rest of the doors had also suffered various traumas. It was like they had been dealt the Biblical sentence, "The wicked shall be cut off short.!" John obviously hadn't been trained in Jesus' School of Carpentry—his work resembled a scissors sorcerer's who specialized in short pants!

John was too deep into denial to see the error of his doors. He explained, "I left a little leeway in case the house settles some more.! This was as reassuring as a sales clerk pushing a suit five sizes too big in case you gain fifty pounds! It's been twenty-five years and the house hasn't shifted. If you ever visit our home, make sure you see the doctored doors—they are the eighth wonder of the world!

In this lifetime there are some things we will never fully understand—premature deaths and short doors are two of them. After the grief period passes, acceptance is the healthy way to deal with it.

# 24

# The Clergy Klatch

For the most part the Charismatic Renewal was run by a brave band of fired-up laymen. Clergy were as common as babies born in bib overalls. The cleric clique drew their covered wagons tightly outside the circle fearing that flaming arrows would find their way from Charismatic campsites. Meanwhile, the hierarchy fortified their faithful with fireproof vestments!

Clergy who allowed themselves to be singed by the Holy Ghost became instant infamous celebrities. Some of the saints who dared to march into the camps during the '50s and '60s were Rev. Harald Bredeson, a Lutheran who became a Dutch Reformed pastor; Rev. Larry Christenson, who remained a Lutheran; Rev. James Brown, a Presbyterian; Father Richard Winkler and Father Dennis Bennett, Episcopalians.

Continuing attempts to corral pastors and priests proved counterproductive, as their escape plans rivaled Harry Houdini's in his heyday. Pastors used golf clubs to ward off wired sheep, while Priests closed confessionals to Charismatics to avoid catching tongues! Most clerics who came to Holy Ghost gatherings had been collared by a big-time contributor from the congregation!

## Sorcerers and Search Warrants

The only time local clergy called our number was to challenge us with questions from perturbed parents. One day Father Aiello from Saint Jerome's summoned us to his office to face a furious parishioner whose daughter dared attend our meetings.

Mrs. Wentworth, who was known to engage in occult practices in her home, was eagerly awaiting. Her dark demonic eyes stared daggers at us as she ranted about her daughter Cindy receiving Jesus. When we replied that our ministry was orthodox New Testament Christianity, she became irate. Her disheveled black hair swirled around her head with each jerky gesture as she fired a few more rounds.

Fortunately, Father Aiello remained calm during Mrs. Wentworth's tirade. After she left he asked us if we were starting a church. We assured him our vision was to renew the spiritual life of the church from within, including evangelizing the baptized and confirmed. Christians already had more choices than shoppers at a mega-mall. Father Aiello seemed satisfied with our response.

Cindy's Sunday night surveillance intensified after the encounter with her mother. There were reports of physical abuse. Three weeks later, Cindy disappeared!

After Mrs. Wentworth alerted the entire town, she sent bloodhounds after Cindy's scent. Leading Oconomowoc police to our place, she barged in our door to accuse us of harboring her daughter. While we were protesting this invasion she ordered the cops to search our entire house! Mrs. Wentworth was livid when they lumbered back fifteen minutes later empty-handed.

Within the hour we received a call from Cindy's friends saying she was running away. Momentarily they had her hide out in the basement of Our Savior's Lutheran Church and needed Karen's help. Karen and Sister Regina, a visiting nun, flew out of our house faster than B-29's on a bombing mission.

Upon arriving at Our Savior's, they found Cindy stashed in a basement closet with disarmed guards standing by. While Karen counseled her a bat bombarded them! Cindy agreed to return home if Karen and Sister Regina ran interference.

As they approached her home the search party was still sweeping the neighborhood. Karen convinced them she was taking Cindy home and the vigilantes vanished.

Upon reentry, Mrs. Wentworth berated Cindy for splitting and pinned her against the wall. Karen pleaded Cindy's case and the storm passed as they proceeded to the parlor.

Karen couldn't forget the time Cindy was caught playing with matches at 6 years of age and her mother seized her hands to hold them over a flame from the gas stove. She paraded her poor kid to the police station and insisted Cindy be slapped in the slammer to reflect on her pyromania practices.

As Mrs. Wentworth boasted about contacting spirits of the deceased who appeared at the foot of her bed, Sister Regina looked as if she had just seen one herself. Sister's silent retreat at our home had turned into chaos controlled by a mad woman who conjured up evil spirits!

In the following months Mrs. Wentworth mellowed out some and permitted Cindy to come to our home on occasion.

A few years later Cindy's mother had no more need to contact the dead—she joined them! Her life was shortened in a fiery traffic accident.

## Did Martin Luther Speak in Tongues?

Charistmatic fellowships continued to play "capture the collar" with cold-feet clergy. The more liturgical the booty, the better. Living Waters' main claim to clerics had been Brother Andrew Ulrich. It was time to seek more shepherds.

In March of 1971, a Missouri Synod Lutheran pastor from Milwaukee, Reverend Ferdinand Bahr and his wife Doris miraculously appeared at our Friday night fellowship. We were out of town at the time. Merlin Severson, who led the meeting, made such a favorable impression on them they returned a month later to meet us. It was obvious to me the Father had sent them— Pastor Bahr wore an ecclesiastical collar! I envisioned the first Lutheran pastor led our way would be from the more liberal LCA or ALC synods, but the Lord has the last laugh. If Pastor had been from the Wisconsin Synod I would have started revving up my Rapture wings!

Ferd and Doris Bahr were still feeling their way through unfamiliar territory. They passed over the guest book on the piano, probably suspecting it might be a hit list planted by their hierarchy! As Ferd browsed through a few books on display he was drawn to one entitled, "Did Martin Luther Speak in Tongues?" He approached the publication the same way a curious Curia

Cardinal might converge on Playboy at the Vatican newsstand—one eye on the book and the other roving the surroundings.

Reverend Ferd Bahr is the shepherd of Divine Shepherd Lutheran Church in Milwaukee. Originally from Sheboygan, Wisconsin, he attended Concordia Seminary in Springfield, Illinois, in the mid '50s. A few years later Ferd latched onto an article on the "Baptism of the Holy Spirit" written by Reverend A. Dornfield, a Wisconsin Lutheran Pastor living dangerously. In the '60s, Reverend Don Pfotenauer was added to the fold.

Soon after a faith encounter with the risen Lord Jesus, Ferd was baptized in the Holy Spirit, during morning meditations. By the fall of 1970 tongues came forth without formal instruction or the laying on of hands. Doris had a similar experience the week before. Desiring more knowledge, they read, *They Speak With Other Tongues,* by John Sherrill and *Aglow With the Spirit,* by Robert Frost.

Upon hearing about Living Waters from Milwaukee Lutheran High School students, it took the Bahrs nine months to brave coming—with good reason. A fellow Missouri Lutheran Pastor from Green Bay was put on trial by his synod and removed from his church! "The Trial of Reverend Merton Jannusch" was published in pamphlet form but never made the New York Times best seller list. However, it did hasten the graying of hair of Lutheran pastors in the Heartland!

Reverend Jannusch was baptized in the Holy Spirit in 1969, but "Salvation" became the real issue during his interrogation. Was salvation pure passive grace or did a person have a right to respond to Jesus by faith! Did standing up for Him seal the decision or sink the ship? The hierarchy acted as if "altar calls" were instituted by the Draft Board to replace fallen comrades! Reverend Jannusch's suggestion that shepherds were lost if they didn't find Jesus didn't help his case!

Merton Jannusch was banished but not silenced. His message has gone forth over the airwaves since 1970.

Ferd, undaunted by the demise of his compatriot, invited Reverend Jannusch to conduct renewal meetings. Over seventy parishioners accepted Jesus as Lord and Savior! The next year, Campus Crusade came to hold meetings on how to receive the

Holy Spirit. In 1971, "tongues of fire" fell on the lips of the redeemed as Reverend Rodney Lensch ministered in their midst.
Months later the gifts of the Holy Spirit were manifested at Sunday services.

Since 1972, Ferb Bahr has taught at Living Waters, in addition to being a spiritual advisor and faithful friend. His ministry is
built on a blend of love for his people, the patience to wait on the
Lord and good old common sense. I still don't know if Martin
Luther spoke in tongues but I'm sure he is proud of his protégé!

## Speakers, Bleepers and Gold Seekers

The 1970s ushered in a steady stream of seekers, speakers
and teachers of every size, shape and spiritual persuasion. Some
were one-night stands and others were suited for standup comedy. Some were sent by the Lord and others came of their own
accord.

Many we invited under the pretense of rest and relaxation
became full-blown workaholics by the time they departed! Their
R&R ended the instant they set foot on the grounds and came to
grips with the schedule Karen cooked up. Meetings, seminars,
retreats, banquets and outreaches were all part of the program.
Lulls were promptly eliminated by treks to the hospital and prisons to pray for the sick and the sad.

When vicarious vacationers arrived with only bathing suits,
sandals and sand toys, my wardrobe became community property. The sheep get nervous in the service when the shepherd
preaches in swimming gear! I lost everything from leisure suits to
longjohns during these decades. Some sly speakers preached guilt-
producing sermons on "giving to the poor" before working over
my wardrobe. I shelled out enough attire to clothe every
Milwaukee mortuary client for eternity!

In the early years the blokes from Britain invaded the colonies as if they were reclaiming them for the "Queen Mother!"
Besides Derek Prince, Arthur Burt and Harry Greenwood's gang
there was Tony Nash and Vic Dunning.

Tony Nash, a no-nonsense preacher, is best remembered for
his masterful messages on overcoming masturbation. Tony took

on topics that even angels fear to touch. Even his infamous mentor, Harry Greenwood, was silent on the subject!

Vic Dunning, our link to the Fort Lauderdale "discipleship movement," brought a more inspirational word. I asked him to deep-six any reference to "discipleship" because we were still digging ourselves free from the "deliverance debacle." Living Waters didn't need another downer!

One Sunday afternoon, while Vic and I were visiting in our family room, the pastor of the local Faith Baptist Church burst through the door with fire and brimstone in his eyes. Dispensationalized from teeth to toes, he railed about the use and abuse of "Charismatic gifts" in this age. Spouting scripture with the force of "Old Faithful" he claimed the gifts ceased upon canonization of the Bible and any dummy delving in them today was doomed by the devil's deception!

The Pastor's unprovoked attack in the privacy of our own home rendered us tongue-tied! It was God's mercy. He probably overdosed on Fiber One for breakfast which fed into his prejudices. At any rate, discerning that this gloom and doom disciple was in no mood for a "Life in the Spirit" seminar, we showed him the exit. With the message delivered, the messenger disappeared as mysteriously as he arrived. From that day forth, I always locked the doors on Sunday afternoons!

Dr. Robert Frost was the forerunner of the California contingent who ministered at Living Waters. Before Bob arrived there were reports we had resurrected the famous New England poet. Those spreading these rumors were obviously led down the wrong road. Bob's most popular talk was entitled "Abba Father." By the time he finished, people felt as if they were sitting in the Father's lap.

Robert Frost, who was baptized in the Holy Spirit in 1955, became a pioneer of Charismatic Renewal. After years of teaching biological sciences at the college level, he entered full-time ministry in 1969. His groundbreaking books, including "Aglow With the Spirit," introduced thousands of '60s and '70s Christians to the outpouring of the Holy Spirit. Bob and Ruth Frost's daughter, Alicia, and granddaughter, Melinda, lived with us for a period of time.

Reverend Dick Mills is a California evangelist who looked as if he had made his mark in Cecil B. DeMille's movies. Blessed with rugged good looks and a special gift for sharing scriptures, he feeds the sheep with individual Bible verses. Dick delivers the Word with such conviction even seasoned skeptics are convinced.

Dick Mills hit the Full Gospel Businessmen's Fellowship circuit with a vengeance—speaking at more chapters than appear in the King James Bible! One time when ministering for the Milwaukee chapter at the Ramada Sands, he publicly gave a word that Reverend Harald Bredesen should contact us. Harald had to invoke the assistance of Alexander Graham Bell to spread the word, as we were twenty miles away at the time. His call set off a wild sequence of events that have been sequestered for a sequel.

## My, My, My Ministries

Reverend Wendall Wallace, a Full Gospel circuit rider with spirit-binding oratory, gets so enthralled in his message, he often leaves little time for ministry. Once at the Sweden House in Milwaukee Wendall called the entire flock forward for prayer. When they closed their eyes, he slipped out the back door, leaving Bill Toll to take over. Bill, looking perplexed, paired people off to pray over each other. Wendall caught his plane to the Twin Cities with only five minutes to spare!

Taking a dim view of "dispensationalism" Wendall teaches that Charistmatic gifts should become a heavy part of every believer's baggage. When he gets that "glory gleam" in his eyes and shouts, "My, My, My," you know you're in for some preaching. Armed with a spontaneous recall of scripture, Wendall is ready to wage spiritual warfare on any battlefield. Anyone taking notes is doomed to develop writer's cramp as he talks faster than Niagara Falls falls. Even tape recorders are left reeling!

When Wendall pastored a church in Portland, Oregon, Willa Dorsey trained his choirs. In the middle 70's the devil beat down the back door, dividing this integrated church. Wendall and his wife of 20 years were divorced. The walls came tumbling down, when he remarried a young white woman from the flock.

Wendall's fall from grace also affected his fellowship with the Full Gospel Businessmen. His invitations to speak were as scarce as "soul food" at a Ku Klux Klan clambake!

Pushed out of Portland, Wendall and Sherrill took flight to Phoenix. Pulpitless, he worked construction. His huge hands swung into action at 4:00 a.m., before the scorching sun could sap his strength.

On our next trip to Phoenix we invited Wendall for dinner. We wanted to hear the story straight from our friend's mouth. Wendall reacted like a kid caught cracking the cookie jar open who couldn't figure out what the fuss was all about. He was more broken than blaming and more confused then contentious.

We found out facts that would never make it to "Moody Monthly"! There were no "lily white" characters in this calamity. The split was confined to two sides until other sidewinders snuck in surreptitiously to spread the story to every saint who had an itching ear to hear. It became the sizzling subject at every Christian Coffee klatch as caffeine addicts added their own ammunition. Before they left their hallowed grounds a full-scale holy war was brewing!

Wendall, feeling abandoned by most of his former backslapping brethren, mirrored the pain of public chastisement. He was reaching out in the Lord to be reinstated. Finally an earthly friend answered his plea. Joe Ninowski, from the Detroit Chapter of FGBMFI, worked on re-establishing Wendall's ministry in Motor City. Edsel couldn't make a comeback, but maybe Wendall would. Aligned to dissimilar management, Wendall looked to the Lord while Edsel relied on Ford!

Discerning that Wendall needed Christian fellowship, we took him to Tulsa to attend a Charismatic leaders' conference at Oral Roberts University. The featured speakers were Father Francis McNutt, Sister Jean Hill, Dr. Howard Ervin, Rev. Tommy Tyson and a cast of thousands.

Wendall, who was from a Church of God background, was amazed at the kaleidoscope of characters at this gathering. He confessed that he didn't know many card-carrying Catholics personally, but had shared the platform with a few.

Originally a hundred leaders had been invited to this Healing Ministry Conference but somehow it had ballooned to over a thousand. If Oral Roberts could have filled the "City of Faith" by the same ratio, it wouldn't have folded.

Tommy Tyson, a Methodist evangelist baptized in the Holy Spirit in 1952, spoke the first night. Tommy's 1967 "Camp Farthest Out" meetings in Tennessee paved the way for Father Francis McNutt's infilling of the Holy Spirit.

When you hail from the South, religion is a family affair. Tommy's daughter, angular, articulate and attractive, led the singing in a high-energy style homogeneous to high school cheerleading. It was swing and sway the spiritual way as she waved in all directions while her legs pumped to the beat of the music. Wendall smiled and muttered, "My, My, My." By the time our leader left the stage, everybody went limp from exhaustion.

Only Tommy could follow his offspring. A clone of Jonathan Winters with cleaner jokes, Tommy is as lovable as lily pads bursting forth with fresh fragrances of expression. His gift is delivering deep spiritual messages while seemingly skimming the surface. Once hooked by his soothing southern drawl, you are lifted to higher revelations.

Wendall flourished from the love lavished on him at the conference. His ears were perked towards the podium no matter what roots the speakers had sprouted from. In addition to the Catholic contingent and Tommy the Methodist, Dr. Howard Ervin, a Baptist, and Dr. Charles Farah, a Pentecostal, participated.

It came time to stop talking and start walking. Respecting Wendall's gifts, the committee asked him to assist in the healing service on the final night.

The trip home was triumph after the long battle. Wendall, languishing in the Lord's love, stayed at our home a few days to minister. People received him like a returning war veteran who lost some skirmishes but won the big one. Manifesting a spiritual freedom he hadn't known for years, Wendall confessed to denominational pride and shared what the Lord revealed at ORU about embracing His entire body.

Wendall launched his ministry in Motor City with Joe Ninowski's help. Wendall had a weekly radio program and preached in churches throughout the area.

He returned to Milwaukee three times a year and stayed with us. Sometimes his family, which had expanded to four, would join him. One time they showed up unexpectedly in a house trailer. As I greeted Wendall I exclaimed, "My, My, My, brother! What has the Lord blessed you with now?

Wendall is no weekend warrior—he's a full-time servant. In addition to teaching, preaching and praying, Mr. Personality helped us over some hurdles in our Living Waters service group. Wendall cuts through concrete controversies with a blade of grass, backed up by the "Sword of the Lord."

Wendall came within a whisker of moving in to co-labor in the Victorian's vineyard. After deliberating for days he decided to stay in Detroit for more pruning. Living Waters came close to changing its name to "My, My, My Ministries!"

## The Voice of Hope

We always were aware when Wendall Wallace was with us— he made his presence known. It wasn't pride, it was personality. He is the bubbling fountain from which the parched wet their whistles.

By contrast, Pastor Werner Honsalek is Mr. Low Profile. After Werner emigrated to the United States from Germany, he was ordained by the Assembly of God. Werner, his wife Erma, and their children moved to Pewaukee, Wisconsin in the early 1970s and attended Living Waters.

Werner was so unassuming that he sat in our meetings for two years before we discovered he was a pastor! Possessing a pleasant smile that accompanied his heavy German accent, all Werner would admit to was writing pamphlets while working on his English.

One day his friend, George Zabel, suggested we schedule Werner to speak on a Sunday night. When he told me Werner was an Assembly of God minister, I was shocked. Seeing my surprise, George quickly added, "Oh, yes, Werner preaches in the German churches throughout the state."

When I apologized to Werner for my lack of awareness, he wasn't wounded. I attempted to conscript him for speaking, but he humbly declined based on his broken English. I agreed he wasn't ready to rival King George! However, Werner's accent fit in fine in the Milwaukee area.

Months later, the same little bird buzzed about Werner's published books and local TV program. Our silent partner was preaching the gospel in German on the screen every week!

Shortly after, when Werner moved to Dallas, I was concerned that those long tall timbers would turn his tongue into a Texas twang. In Milwaukee, Texan was the foreign language!

We were well-rewarded when we wooed Werner back as a "guest speaker." His practical, profound teachings minister peace as he draws people into a deeper presence of the Prince of Peace. He returns every year to minister among us and lead Living Waters retreats.

Werner's outreach has spread worldwide under the name Voice of Hope. Europe and South America are always on his itinerary. Werner's ecumenical spirit encompasses the entire body of Christ as he ministers to a diverse range of denominations.

Unimpeded by a German accent or Texas twang, Jesus accomplished his mission in three years. Werner has time left as the "Voice of Hope" for those who haven't heard the word and for those who have, but haven't heeded. A low profile produces a humble servant.

## Crown Him With Many Crowns

Not everyone who ministered at Living Waters was invited back. Duke and Dolly Cassidy were Charismatic circuit riders who never returned. They came highly recommended by friends who shall remain anonymous. The rave reviews which preceded their coming turned into a "run them out on a rail trip!" In addition to our friend's fervor, the sign that sold us on the Cassidys was due to their popular demand, they couldn't schedule us for six months. After the Jimmy Swervert episode we were paranoid about any preacher who could pop in at a moment's notice.

Adding fuel to our fears was a recent encounter with a fiery Fond du Lac Avenue dentist promoted as a proficient painless practitioner by a Chicago protégé.

Upon arriving at Dr. Dudley's Milwaukee office, we were ushered into the chairs immediately. There was no one else there. Circumventing the traditional claustrophobic cubicles, Dr. Dudley operated out of one large room with the latest attention-diverting equipment. A high-tech multi-colored board projected waves of calming images on the wall as celestial sounds soothed the senses. Adding an earthly touch, a toothless lowland gorilla sporting a Grand-Canyon grin was plastered on the ceiling. So many relaxation techniques tingled our interiors, I suspected a setup to being sawed in half!

Dr. Dudley's most creative device was dual dentist chairs for husband and wife that looked like they belonged in the delivery room at Columbia Hospital! Spouses could hold hands and commiserate together.

Dr. Dudley was as friendly as Felix the Cat. His hair was long gone but he compensated by outsmiling his companion on the ceiling. As a walking witness to his work he exposed a set of choppers a beaver would be proud to parade! Dr. Dudley had so much gold in his mouth he must have done time at Fort Knox!

Seeking routine checkups, Dr. Dudley promptly ignored our humble pleas and promoted grandiose greenback schemes. After plastering impressions of our teeth he gleefully proposed a ten-year plan for rearranging our oral orifices. His plan for me had to be hatched in Hitler's torture chambers! As my teeth were chiseled out, they would be moved around my mouth like pawns in a chess game. Dr. Dudley was possessed with a Mt. Rushmore mentality!

When Dr. Dudley detected I wasn't swallowing his ideas, he switched to fear tactics. He barked, "Your bite is so bad you will be chewing your chin by spring!"

Undaunted, he suddenly shifted his conivings to crowns. Seeing wall-to-wall silver fillings lining my mouth, he prophesied that my entire cranium was about to crumble! As he showed me the gruesome details with his flashy mirror, I suspected his favorite hymn was "Crown Him With Many Crowns!" Not being related to royalty, I passed on the crowns, also.

Dr. Dudley finally ditched his gold and crown pitch and got down to earth. He scraped plaque off my tongue with a tungsten tongue cleaner held by a loop handle looking like it had been stolen out of Tiny Tim's tool box. The metal device attacked plaque like a painter scraping off blistered wood siding. I purchased two tongue cleaners for ten dollars apiece as part of my escape plan.

Still shaking, we played his game by placing our names in his appointment book. The pages were empty—we could come back anytime!

As we were leaving, Dr. Dudley introduced us to an older man dressed in surgery garb emerging from a back room. It was a father-and-son operation—the dad had the same grin and gold.

That back room bothered us. Could it be that the ten-year plans and tongue cleaners were just a front for an abortion clinic? Not about to test any more of Dr. Dudley's devious devices, we canceled out next appointment immediately upon arriving home.

Being more discerning, it took us two months to find a dentist who knew how to clean teeth. At least we had our ten dollar tungsten tongue cleaners to tide us over. Karen contributed hers to our car in case we needed to pry off a hubcap. They were guaranteed for the life of the product, which could be 1,000 years. Dr. Dudley didn't deal in junk!

## Duking it out with Dolly

Duke and Dolly Cassidy seemed safe after dealing with Dr. Dudley.

The Cassidys were to hold three night meetings at our house. Their method of team ministry consisted of switching back and forth many times during the evening as they integrated the masculine and feminine approach in their teachings. This was fine with us as long as there wasn't a ten-year plan!

When the worship ended, Duke started his talk low key until Dolly interrupted him. She took issue with his teaching while he sat passively puffing on his pipe. Duke regained the floor once more only to be challenged again.

Team teaching had turned into a tempest. People were fascinated more by the feistiness of the messengers than the message! I don't recall the subject matter but it must have been "submission" to provoke such an uprising!

After the scene simmered down, the team sought words of knowledge for the flock. When the Cassidys got too personal I preempted them. The Bible says, "Confess your sins one to another," not "Blab your brother's boo-boos to the entire congregation!"

The next night Duke did most of the talking. Puffing on his pipe he pursued man's relationship to the universe." Karen's smile did a sunset as she leaned towards me whispering, "He's getting metaphysical!" Karen is knowledgeable about these age-old philosophies due to her dad's encounters with the "cosmic consciousness."

Later that evening we dissected the meat of Duke's message. Duke saw no danger in mixing metaphysics with Christianity. Taking a more evangelical view, we believed the marriage was doomed to divorce—there were too many irreconcilable differences!

The following day we took the Cassidys to Waukesha Hospital to pray for our friend, Clyde Shaw, who had acute cancer. While interceding for him, Dolly saw a detailed vision of Clyde as a kid in Missouri. Playing in an old abandoned barn one night, his companion's clothes caught fire from careless use of a lantern. The boy suffered severe burns before Clyde could suffocate the flames. Despite Clyde's heroic action, he blamed himself for his friend's fate.

Clyde was astonished at the accuracy of Dolly's description. Exhibiting a quizzical smile he said, "No one could have known this."

We were in wonder also! Trusting that this was a sign from the Lord, we laid hands on Clyde, praying for the pain of the memory to be lifted. Next, we stormed heaven for his physical healing. When we left Clyde's room we had peace that he knew the Lord loved him.

By the time we reached the elevator, our halos from the spiritual high had been toppled by the onslaught of heresy! Duke and Dolly were so enamored with the biblical Jesus, everyone else was relegated to reprobate status! Only Jesus' words were worthy! Peter and Paul, who they progressively pushed off a pedestal, loaded their language with prejudices. Fallen from grace, the Cassidys fought to erase the apostles' place in Christian history.

They painted Paul as a bloke who became blinded to the truth after he hit his head. Peter was banished to the same boat—his lack of faith doomed him as a failure. Anybody who denied the Lord couldn't have any lofty leverage on future Christians. Peter and Paul's part in God's plan was kaput!

We had encountered a few "Jesus Only" people among Pentecostal ranks but their main claim to infamy was baptizing believers in the name of Jesus instead of asking the entire Trinity to contribute. The Cassidys' anti-Peter and Paul position added another plank to the platform!

We were pro-Jesus in a big way, but why wipe out all his proven apostles? Did Dolly have an innate fear of being silenced in the church? Question customs, but don't castigate the brethren by banishing them. Red-letter editions of the Bible aren't meant to be devilish dispensational dissecting kits!

We persuaded the Cassidys to pack their "Peter and Paul persecution papers" in the bottom of their bags. The Living Waters' flock didn't need any more fireworks!

The day the Cassidys were leaving a Cleveland couple came unexpectedly with their eight-year old son suffering from Muscular Dystrophy. The desperate parents drove all night. The Cassidys' ministry to this lad fostered dependency. It was as if Jesus was sent to the back of the bus to sleep during the session! We found out later that this family followed them all over the country. At some point people have to be set free to sit in the strong arms of the Great Physician!

Our spirits lifted when the Cassidys finally left. They were extremely gifted, but some gifts come with strings attached. After thanking the Lord for the lesson, we tried to convince him we learned from it. Flashing a full schedule is not a sign to turn over your house to eager beavers who will attack your very foundation!

# 25

# Willa - the Eighth Wonder of the World

Another good friend of the family is the famous Gospel singer Willa Dorsey.  Her father, a black Baptist pastor from Atlanta, gave Willa voice lessons from early childhood.  Both of her parents passed away when Willa was in her teens, but their voices weren't silenced.  Willa carried on in the family tradition singing Gospel music all over the globe.

She has nixed numerous nightclub offers, but occasionally is open to oratorio to keep her multi-octave voice vibrant.  Her many albums include a recording with the Dallas Symphony.  As a Mahalia Jackson sound-a-like, the welcome mat for Willa has been rolled out from the Lawrence Welk Show all the way to the White House, with intermediate stops at the Billy Graham Crusades.  She is seriously challenging Bob Hope for the most tours of US Army bases on foreign soil.

Willa's link with Living Waters began in the early 1970s.  The first time she ministered in our midst she hit the Baby Grand with such power I expected the keyboard to crash.  Determination deluged Willa's face as she extended her jaw with eyes closed and broke into a rousing rendition of "Joshua Fought the Battle of Jericho." Fervent fortissimo in full voice, with her head bobbing back and forth, challenged the plaster on our weathered walls.

As outstanding as Willa's vocal talents are they don't upstage her warm, tender heart for people of all socio-economic and religious persuasions.  She is personable towards publicans and plutocrats alike.

Willa mixes music with testimonies as she ministers.  Many times I saw Willa embrace troubled teens as she prayed with people afterwards.  The Lord often pours prophetic words through her to encourage the person.

Once, Karen brought Willa to St. Joan of Arc Church in Okauchee to pray for Father Joseph Konkel's back. Father Konkel, a conservative Catholic priest, who could be gruff on occasion, took to the Baptist Gospel singer like holy water! He invited Willa to give a concert at St. Joan of Arc and arranged for a reception in the rectory afterwards. When Willa returned to town, Father Joe went to hear her at Olympia Resort and the Performing Arts Center in Milwaukee.

Willa came twice a year throughout the '70s. Sometimes her son Billy, who stood six-and-one-half-feet tall, would come with. Billy and I shot buckets in the big barn for hours.

One time Billy contracted hepatitis from Army base food in West Germany. By the time he arrived in our home, his eyes were yellower than the yoke of last year's lost Easter eggs! Our entire household marched to the Wilkinson Clinic for gamma globulin shots. We must have been hit with large doses because nobody could sit down for days!

## The Four Faces

Once when I got up to introduce Willa, my mind went blank. Her name was as distant as the North Pole as I saw her smiling face waiting in the wings. With no last second lifeline forthcoming from the Lord, I was forced to settle for, "Here she is! The one and only whom we all know and adore. Let's give her a hand as she comes." The second I sat down her name popped into my brain. Willa didn't razz me verbally until later, but she sported a slap-happy smile during the entire concert!

Willa's seasoned sense of humor never let me forget the faux pas. We have laughed ourselves silly over it.

An Army Colonel in Germany suffered a similar fate. Assigned the responsibilities of introducing Willa and her three musicians at a concert, he forget their names and presented them as "The Four Faces!" This wasn't court martial material, but it did cause a stir. Willa was a belly laugh away from rolling off the piano bench as she related the story.

Willa takes "praying without ceasing" seriously. Her only diversion is singing and laughing. With a prayer list as long as Santa's Workshop ledger, she often is on her knees all night.

Once while Willa was visiting, we received a frantic phone call from a lady living on Okauchee Lake. Her neighbor's four-year old boy had been dragged from the lake, and all efforts to revive him failed as he lay lifeless inside an ambulance.

When Karen raced to Willa's room for prayer, Willa immediately dropped to her knees and commanded the Spirit of Death to leave the boy in the name of Jesus! Later that afternoon the lady called back jubilant. The lad had suddenly coughed up suffocating muck from his mouth before arriving at the emergency room! When he was declared out of danger by the doctor, we praised the Lord for setting this young captive free.

## Haute Couture on Mt. Hood

The next summer when we visited Willa in Portland, we took her to Timberline Lodge near the top of Mt. Hood. This Cascade Mountain monolith was built by FDR's WPA boys during the dark days of the Depression. Timberline's mammoth wood structure is a citadel of the surrounding villages.

Bobby Huffer from Chicago, who was eleven by now, accompanied us on this western trip. His main duty was to keep track of David, who was barely out of diapers.

One day while giving David a stroller ride resembling the roller coaster at Riverview, a front wheel got hung up on a rock. As the stroller went heels over head, seatbeltless David soared through the air with the greatest of ease! When gravity finally grounded him, Mother Nature did a number on his forehead. David, unencumbered by denial, let Her now how he felt about Her handiwork!

Following the ear-piercing screams to their source, we found Bobby fervently attempting to comfort the kid. Benefiting from Karen's TLC plus prayer, David was back to normal a few hours later. Bobby was reassigned to reading to the kids quietly in the evening.

Karen's luggage was light compared to Willa's. Glittering opera dresses stuffed into gigantic foldovers adorned the top of our station wagon. If the luggage rack hadn't been reinforced, we would all be wearing Willa's wardrobe!

Willa definitely wasn't the outdoor type. Her idea of "leisure wear" was closer to a haute couture creation the Queen Mother would don for a coronation! Upon coaxing Willa into walking with us up a short trail, she emerged in a full-length cardinal evening dress with gold sequins. Black high heels bottomed-off the ensemble. Shocked to my shorts and hiking boots, I encouraged Willa to go back and change. As she broke into her patented belly laugh, she answered, "Into what? What you see is what you get."

For the first three hundred yards Willa kept up the pace. She had that same determined look she gets when she hits a high note. However, her high heels became hazardous when we hit rougher ground. If she broke an ankle we would all be marooned—the closest CPR team was Portland!

The altitude was taking its toll on the attitude. Willa was chugging like a locomotive low on steam. After a lively debate we decided to lumber back to the lodge in the interest of self-preservation. Winded and waning, Willa yelled, "Okay, Sergeant Jack, you lead the way." She always called me "Sergeant" because I barked orders and wore green most of the time.

After dinner each night we retreated to Willa's room for a gabfest. We made so much noise I feared the night manager might join us. With midnight my maximum in this mountain air, I retreated to my adjoining quarters to sleep. The ruckus in the revelers' room penetrated the walls. Willa and Karen laughed, prattled and rolled until two o'clock every morning.

The first three nights I put up with the partying. The final night Sergeant Jack swung into action early as we had to drive hundreds of miles towards home the next day. After issuing an ominous "tone it down" edict before crashing , I was awakened at midnight by gales of laughter escaping from Willa's room. Willa and Karen were cackling so loud I thought we would have eggs for breakfast!

Spying huge spotlights moving down the mountain, Willa discerned they were flying saucers and the Martians had landed!

Karen opted for the "Bigfoot theory." Freaked, they called the manager for further enlightenment. He claimed it was a snowmobile club on night maneuvers. Liking their versions better, the two flakes fought the poor fella for five minutes. I invaded their room and bellowed big time, but it didn't do a bit of good—they were still super-charged by science fiction! It was 3:00 a.m. before the night owls stopped screeching!

We all suffered a long grueling ride the next day. After dropping Willa and her wardrobe off in Portland, we drove another 700 miles before turning in at a tiny Wyoming town. Two days later we were back in Wisconsin.

The next few days I felt I was still on the road. "Never Again," was the eternal cry from the whole crew. Plagued by an acute case of amnesia, we set out on another insane safari the next summer!

When Willa visited the following fall, I teased her about hitting the Mt. Hood trail in her regal regalia. She claimed her real physical feats were riding bicycles. Somewhat suspect, I offered her the kids' ten-speed for a spin. With her chin in first gear and her dress dangling dangerously close to the chain, Willa went whipping down our steep gravel driveway like "Wonder Woman!" Expecting a fender-bender at the bridge, I was amazed to see her bounce across unscathed. Willa wasn't ready for the Tour de France but she proved proficient on two wheels, even in high heels.

### The Worry-Free Worldwide Traveler

Bikes were as much as Willa could handle. Planes proved to be her downfall—not navigating them, just getting on the aircraft! She never allows enough time. In her thirty-year career, Willa has missed more planes then a tanked traffic controller! As an instinctive intuitor, she will never suffer from ulcers—it's her friends that reach for their nervous stomachs!

This time Willa was scheduled to catch an 11:45 a.m. flight from Milwaukee to Portland. Recalling previous panic pushes, I informed her we had to roll by 9:30 a.m.

After pulling the wagon in front for the fifty minute trip, I headed for her room. She was talking non-stop to a troubled teen, while her dresses were still dangling in the closet. When I gave her the "high sign," she smiled sweetly in return. She knew Sergeant Jack meant business because I was decked out in khaki green cords.

I disappeared downstairs to give her ten more minutes. When I returned, the teen was huddled in the hot seat being prayed over. Willa rebuked everything from "Rock 'n Roll" to reefers! Meanwhile her luggage was still in limbo. As a committed Christian I couldn't beat them, so I joined them. Our prayer session ended at 10:35 a.m.

Willa, switching into her laughing mode, exclaimed, "Sergeant Jack, don't worry, we'll make it." From then on we operated on Willa's faith—I had lost all of mine!

Ten minutes later I was summoned to sit on the bulging bags so Willa could snap them shut. We succeeded on our third attempt. Willa sounded as if she had hit the Oregon Trail again, so I made her rest while I dragged her bags down the backstairs. By the time Willa kissed all the kids good-bye and secured her seatbelt, it was 11:06 a.m.

Willa appeared relaxed as we raced out the driveway. She didn't have a watch and chances are she didn't have her tickets either. The last time I drove this fast on I-94 was the night Karen's water broke while carrying Krista. On this trip, I needed deliverance!

When the skycap wrestled her luggage into the ticket agent it was 11:52 a.m. and the aircraft was taxiing down the runway! In the stressful sport of airplane steeplechase, close doesn't count.

Willa didn't flinch an inch. Personifying perfect peace she calmly asked the agent to put her on the next plane to Portland. What was a three-hour wait and an additional change of planes in the Twin Cities to a worry-free worldwide traveler? Only sensates get shook over these things!

I offered to keep Willa company but she sensed I was anxious to split. She laughed once more about Sergeant Jack and his green pants before we parted. I'm sure she spent her waiting hours working over her prayer list.

On another occasion Willa made a plane she wished she had missed. Her agent booked her on China Airlines for a concert tour of the Orient. Chinese airplanes were constructed for Chinese passengers, not robust Gospel singers. Willa was forced to purchase two tickets and remove the armrest.

The real crunch hit when it came time to use the facilities. She backed into the washroom but couldn't wiggle out! Wedged hopelessly in this confining cubicle, Willa pushed the panic button. The entire crew, except the pilot, came running to her rescue.

Willa said, "the worst part about being pulled out was facing the passengers. Some were preparing for an emergency landing!" Willa laid low on liquids while leaping high into the everlasting arms of Jesus the remainder of the trip.

# Epilogue
## " A True Case of "Pulp Fiction"

After three hundred plus pages of progress we have only advanced to the middle 1970's. My publisher has run out of paper, Elvis is dead and I am not feeling so hot myself! In addition to tennis elbow, heel spurs, and shin splints, I have developed an acute case of writers cramp.

Having rejected any device more technical than a tennis racket, it is obvious I am still suffering from computer-phobia. With the decline and fall of almost everything in our culture, I will need a complete faith-lift to continue my career. The stories of Movie Moguls, adoption adventures, Anglican angst and the Catholic connection will have to wait until the next dispensation.

# Post Epilogue

In the interest of environmental responsibility, please recycle this paper by passing it on to the bookworm in the next bunk. This epic is entitled, *Farewell to Fences*, not *Farewell to Trees*.